# A COMMON HUMANITY

# A Common Humanity

*Ritual, Religion, and Immigrant Advocacy in Tucson, Arizona*

LANE VAN HAM

The University of Arizona Press     Tucson

The University of Arizona Press
© 2011 The Arizona Board of Regents
All rights reserved

www.uapress.arizona.edu

Library of Congress Cataloging-in-Publication Data
Van Ham, Lane Vernon, 1969–
  A common humanity : ritual, religion, and immigrant advocacy in Tucson, Arizona /
Lane Van Ham.
      p. cm.
  Includes bibliographical references and index.
  ISBN 978-0-8165-2965-0 (pbk. : alk. paper)  1. Foreign workers—Arizona.  2. Latin
Americans—Employment—Arizona.  3.  Latin Americans—Social life and customs—
Arizona.  4. Emigration and immigration—Government policy.  I. Title.
  HD8081.H7V36 2011
  305.9'0691209791776—dc23

                                                          2011034939

Publication of this book is made possible in part by the proceeds of a permanent
endowment created with the assistance of a Challenge Grant from the National
Endowment for the Humanities, a federal agency.

16   15   14   13   12   11      6   5   4   3   2   1

Portions of chapters 3 and 4 were originally published in an earlier form as "Sanctuary
Revisited: Central American Refugee Assistance in the History of Church-Based
Immigrant Advocacy" in *Political Theology* 10.4 (2009): 621–45, © Equinox Publishing
Ltd. 2009.

# Contents

# Acknowledgments

I am the son of Lee Van Ham and Laurel Johnson, who are the children of children of immigrants to the United States of America. My father's mother, Wilhelmina, was the granddaughter of Dutch immigrants who arrived in the mid-nineteenth century. The parents of Peter, my father's father, emigrated from Holland in 1911. My mother's father, Vernon, was the grandson of immigrants from northern Europe who came in the final quarter of the nineteenth century. My mother's mother, Ellen, was the daughter of ethnic Germans who lived in Riga, Russia (now Latvia) and emigrated in the early 1900s. In countless and even unknowable ways, I am indebted to the yearnings, ambulations, labor, and love of these parents, and I thank them for their presence in my life.

The early years of this project evolved under the guidance of five mentors in the academy: Barbara Babcock, Adele Barker, Malcolm Compitello, Alex Nava, and Karen Seat. Alison Goebel, Diane Wiener, Mike Mulcahy, Charlene Tuchovsky, Jeff Larson, and Sang Hea Kil provided important leads along the way.

Help in later stages came from Sarah Roberts, Kat Rodriguez, Amanda Shauger, Juanita Sundberg, Lauren Van Ham, Michelle Fealk, Brenda Burkholder, and two anonymous readers who provided feedback on the first draft. Thanks, too, to my indexer, Elizabeth Ullman.

I appreciate as well the people I have worked with at or through the University of Arizona Press: Patti Hartman, Scott De Herrera, Kristen Buckles, Robert Milks, Al Schroder, Kathryn Conrad, Leigh McDonald, Arin Cumming, and Holly Schaffer.

Finally, I would be remiss if I did not acknowledge the hard-working employees at the following coffee houses, who kept me fueled for the journey: Ike's and Bentley's in Tucson, Arizona, the Meadowlark Café in Lincoln, Nebraska, and LatteLand in Kansas City, Missouri.

In the words of the late Daniel Preston at John Fife's retirement party: *Bless 'em real good, Creator God.*

# A COMMON HUMANITY

# CHAPTER ONE

# Migrant Deaths and Immigrant Advocacy in Southern Arizona

By the time they found her body, four weeks had passed since she had been left behind, and it had already been ravaged by scavengers and the elements. Pieces of her extremities were strewn about, radiating from her decomposing torso, which had released its store of oils and left a stain where they seeped into the ground. Her name was Prudencia Martin Gomez, and she was eighteen years old.

Martin came from Guatemala, a country rich in soil but poor in social welfare, where crushing deprivations affect over half the population and a disproportionate number of women, children, and the indigenous. A World Bank study published in 2003 found that "life expectancy, infant mortality and maternal mortality" there are lower than in many of the country's similarly impoverished hemispheric peers, and further noted a grotesque level of malnutrition among children that it ranked as "among the worst in the world" (ii).

Like most of Latin America, Guatemala has a massive underclass whose members dream of a better life, but see few opportunities to realize it close to home. For many, the answer lies in exodus, severing themselves from their native land and migrating north, to seek their fortune amid the hyper-affluence of the United States. But although the United States permits legal immigration from Guatemala, the eligibility standards are very high. With rare exceptions, visa recipients must either be related to a US citizen, receive sponsorship from an employer who cannot find a US citizen for the job, or qualify for political asylum. Even those who meet these stringent requirements may wait years between application and approval. In any

1

case, official channels are not viable for people desperate to flee the death knells of hunger and disease, and many opt instead to make a dangerous but potentially lifesaving attempt to enter the United States illegally.

Prudencia Martin Gomez's husband was among them, and when Martin heard that he had found steady work in California, she decided to make the trip herself and join him. She journeyed first to northwestern Mexico, then in early June 2007 crossed into the United States with a small group intent on walking through the Sonoran Desert of Southern Arizona. For a few days, Martin and her group fared well. They avoided capture by the Border Patrol and persevered against the blazing summer sun, trekking some sixty miles north of the international boundary into Ironwood Forest National Monument. The landscape must have seemed cruelly ironic, for even as the terrain at their feet was coarse and thorny and made no accommodation to human travel, they could see to one side a series of monuments to civilization in the massive utility towers of the Trico electric cooperative (whose slogan, incidentally, is "The Power of Human Connections"). Perhaps they also took heart at the sight of empty bottles and other traces of sojourners who had preceded them.

But here, on the cusp of deliverance, the punishing heat finally took its toll. The highs on those long summer days were in the upper 90s, and prolonged exposure to such temperatures rapidly sends the body into overdrive, sweating to cool off the skin and demanding water to compensate. Without adequate rest and hydration, the brain and other vital organs begin to malfunction, and any misfortune or twist of fate can easily tilt the odds against an individual's survival. Martin, as it happened, was menstruating, and as she bled, her body lost the strength it needed to keep moving. She fell ill, and, unable to continue, lay down in the meager shade of desert scrub. Leaving her with water and electrolyte packets, the rest of her group tied a red bandana to a nearby tree and reluctantly pressed on, noting landmarks so they could report her condition and location as soon as they were able. When they got to a phone, they called her husband, who contacted Samaritans, a Tucson-based organization that provides emergency aid to immigrants traveling through the desert. Initially, the small group of Tucsonans who agreed to search for Martin sought her in area hospitals, hopeful that she had been rescued. But when she wasn't there, they reached the dire conclusion that she had not made it out of the desert alive. Using details provided by members of Martin's group, eight volunteers rose early on a July morning to comb the location on foot. They soon found the body. After the Pima County Medical Examiners removed most, but not all, of Martin's remains, the search party collected the pieces that had been left behind, dug a small hole in the ground, and buried them next to where she had fallen.

A few days after the body was found, I received a mass e-mail from one of the search party, relating Martin's story and announcing a commemorative event at the site of her death. It gave directions for people wishing to attend to "honor [her] life and courage" and suggested that participants bring stones to build a small memorial. As of that summer, I had spent three years researching Tucson-based efforts to improve the welfare of undocumented immigrants, interviewing participants, archiving publications, and attending events as a participant-observer. A major city just a ninety-minute drive from Mexico, Tucson is steeped in the politics of border control, including illegal immigration. Area residents consistently speak out about it in impassioned and often vitriolic ways, resulting in a lively debate that captivates its participants and students of society and culture as well. Though the barrage of border-related news can sometimes be overwhelming, I took great interest in this particular e-mail because of my fascination with activists working on behalf of immigrants, especially those whose efforts are inflected with religious traditions.

So when the date arrived, I joined approximately thirty people who met at Southside Presbyterian Church and carpooled west of Tucson for the memorial. We walked a quarter-mile off a dirt road and formed a circle around the spot where Martin had expired, a tiny patch of earth darkened and discolored like bruised clay. No one present had ever met her, but for half an hour, the attendees paid her extemporaneous tribute with words and objects. A member of the search party told of how her body had been found, and others added stories and observations as they saw fit. Material and oral testimonies accumulated as we improvised a kind of shrine on the burial site. We used the rocks we had brought to build a cairn. One person left flowers. Another, her shoes. Another, bottles of water. There were long periods of silence, and now and then the wind kicked up the scent of human tallow. When it seemed everyone who wanted to contribute had done so, someone began the song "Peace Is Flowing Like a River," and others joined in:

Peace is flowing like a river
Flowing out of you and me
Flowing out into the desert
Setting all the captives free

Then, without any announcement or discussion, the program concluded. People stretched, stepped away from the circle, embraced, collected their belongings, and turned back to the road to make the drive home.

Compared to congressional votes and presidential addresses, Martin's death and the desert memorial service in her honor are minor incidents. But they are poignant reminders that whatever happens on an epic political scale also happens on a human scale, and that each, in fact, is a window on the other: anecdotes can invigorate abstractions, and context can add meaning to minutiae. In the case of Prudencia Martin Gomez and her mourners, quotidian actions like walking, lying down, making a phone call, and moving a rock transcend their banality and signify, in condensed form, the divisive and seemingly perennial national conflict over immigration in the United States.

## Mythic Immigration and the US—Mexico Border

The story of immigration is one of the United States' most potent myths. I mean "myths" unpejoratively, in the value-neutral sense of a narrative that expresses the key cultural values and beliefs of the group that tells it. The sheer volume of immigrants to the United States during colonization and the Industrial Revolution suggests a nation that is quintessentially generous toward foreign newcomers and fulfills Thomas Paine's messianic cry that the country should be "an asylum for mankind." By this familiar fable, the United States welcomes and accepts all, exhibiting a peculiar genius for making diversity a badge of honor and a source of strength. But like many self-flattering narratives, this one has been heavily vetted for conflicting evidence and does little to suggest how immigrants have most often received an "ambivalent welcome" (Simon and Alexander). It is true that some groups in US history have favored opening the country to greater numbers of foreign arrivals. But these proimmigration forces, which may be called immigration expansionists, have usually been business interests more concerned with exploiting cheap labor than providing havens for the world's oppressed (Calavita, "U.S. Immigration and Policy," *U.S. Immigration Law*; Fry). The myth downplays or omits altogether the prominence of immigration restrictionists, who seek to reduce the number of immigrants in the population by curbing the arrival of newcomers or expelling nonnative residents.[1] Virulent anti-immigrant streaks course throughout US history, not among a lunatic fringe, but in the very mainstream of political thought and social respectability. The ostensibly religious-liberty-seeking Puritans hanged Quakers (Eck 36), Benjamin Franklin wrote diatribes against Germans in Pennsylvania (Perea 972–73), genteel antebellum readers made fabricated anti-Catholic "exposes" into best-sellers (Bennett 42–47), representatives on Capitol Hill described Chinese as "hordes . . . of a most degraded corruption" (Carlson and Colburn 185), and gangbusting Chicago lawman Frank Loesch attributed the scourge of organized crime to "largely unassimilable foreign immigrants from Eastern and Southeastern Europe" (Fox, *Blood and Power* 133).

Such comments are consonant with public opinion. One study, directed at polls conducted since the start of scientific surveying in the 1930s, found that although regard for particular immigrant nationalities tends to increase the longer those nationalities are present in the country, "the most consistent theme" in such surveys over the years "is the essentially negative attitudes held by a majority of the US public toward persons wishing to come to the United States" (Simon and Alexander 45). Contrary to cherished notions of the United States as a hospitable nation, public opinion has consistently favored telling those knocking at the venerable "Golden Door"[2] that whatever may have been true in the past, there is no more room for them now.

Anti-immigrant sentiment is particularly acute in the case of immigrants who are in the country without permission, known in the parlance of immigration law as "undocumented" or "out of status." Estimates vary on just how many out-of-status immigrants reside in the United States, but the average tends toward twelve million. Some enter legally and overstay their visas, while others enter illegally by sea or by land. Those who cross the 1,950-mile-long border with Mexico, though, are the most vilified. To many observers, their presence and ongoing arrival constitutes a breach of national security and even hints at a breakdown in governmental legitimacy.

Both before and since the creation of the international boundary between the United States and Mexico, people have moved back and forth across the land where that border now stretches. The land traversed by undocumented immigrants today is a pre-Columbian and arguably ancient corridor for the flow of objects, ideas, and people.[3] Those making the journey have always faced deadly environmental hazards, but since the mid-1990s, the dangers have been augmented by changes in US border enforcement strategies that some observers have dubbed "militarization" (Andreas; Dunn, "Border Enforcement," *Militarization*; Nevins). The watershed moment in this process arguably came from 1993 to 1994, when the Border Patrol deployed enough new equipment and personnel to establish an overwhelming presence in border towns and cities that were the most popular sites for illegal entry. Since the plan's implementation, the borderlands have been transformed into a martial panorama of bulwarks, stadium lighting, and underground sensors; checkpoints, drones, and helicopters; contracted security firms, National Guard troops, and government agents.

With the most-favored crossings all but sealed, the only available option for would-be entrants became the treacherous wilderness spanning southern Arizona. Policymakers, by their own admission, believed the landscape would act as a deterrent,[4] but their assumptions fatally underestimated the desperation and determination of aspiring border crossers. Instead of ending undocumented migration, the urban garrisons merely created a "funnel effect" that shifted traffic into the desert between San Diego and El Paso. As a result, the twofold trend dating to the mid-1990s is for more undocumented migrants to die in Arizona, and for more of them to die from exposure to the elements. The death toll rose in the late 1990s until it became incontrovertibly clear that the deterrence strategy had failed and the region was faced with a humanitarian crisis. Statistics kept by the Border Patrol show that over federal fiscal years 1998–2009,[5] the bodies of over fourteen hundred undocumented entrants were recovered in the Tucson Sector, which covers most of Arizona (McCombs, "Efforts"). Incidents during 2004, for example, included the following:

- In early April, a hiker found the body of a solitary migrant buried under snow in the Huachuca Mountains ("Hiker Finds Body").
- In July, a family crossing the border together made it some twenty miles into the United States and were on Tohono O'odham reservation land when one of the sons collapsed. The rest of the family sought help; en route, they found the body of another migrant under a tree, her head lying in dried blood that had run from her mouth and nose. By the time they contacted a tribal police officer who was able to investigate, the son had died as well (Marizco, "When the Deadly").
- In August, a group of eleven ran out of water in the middle of the desert and sent six members on to get help. The group of six then divided in half: one group found a home where people called the sheriff's department; all three in the other group perished ("Illegal-Entrant Death Count").

Statistics vary according to who does the counting, but conservative counting methods indicate that the total number of recovered bodies in all border sectors from 1995 to 2009 exceeds four thousand. Even then, as a report by the Binational Migration Institute at the University of Arizona pointedly argues, no one can provide an accurate number of deaths because there is no way of knowing how many bodies are never found (Rubio-Goldsmith et al. 1, 19).

## Immigrant Advocacy in Tucson: Surveying the Global Neighborhood

Across the southwestern United States, watchdog and grassroots organizations have mobilized against the border enforcement crackdown and anti-illegal-immigrant sentiment, decrying the deliberate routing of immigrants into a deadly landscape and proclaiming the need for border policy to be reformed along humanitarian lines. These efforts are recent examples of a diffuse and discontinuous social movement that may be called immigrant advocacy.[6] In contrast to immigration restrictionists and expansionists, immigrant advocates work to humanize the image of immigrants and act as sympathetic intermediaries between immigrants and society at large. They publicly assert the legal entitlements and social equality of immigrants, and often seek to empower immigrants themselves.

Immigrant advocacy in Tucson dates at least to the mid-1950s, with the first initiatives on behalf of the undocumented appearing two decades later. These efforts originated in two distinct but frequently intertwined tendencies. One was among Mexican Americans, whose principles of ethnic, transnational solidarity engendered sympathy for undocumented entrants from south of the border, Mexican or otherwise (Gutierrez). Another consisted of self-identified "faith-based" individuals and institutions, primarily, but not exclusively, Anglo Protestants. Throughout the 1980s, these groups collaborated to aid Central Americans seeking political asylum, most famously in the Sanctuary movement (Coutin; Crittenden; Cunningham, *God and Caesar*; MacEóin, *Sanctuary*; Otter and Pine).

An organization that emerged in the wake of Sanctuary, the Coalición de Derechos Humanos (Human Rights Coalition), shouldered much of Tucson's immigrant advocacy during the 1990s. But as discontent over militarization and migrant deaths spread, new efforts and strategies sprang up to address the growing crisis. By 2004, the city was host to at least four more groups critical of US border policy as too restrictive and punitive: Border Action Network, Humane Borders, Samaritans, and No More Deaths. These organizations developed at different times, with different foci, and they conduct a wide range of activities. What unifies them across their varied origins and operations is a conviction that immigrants are entitled to treatment and protection according to standards that are universal and panhuman, regardless of whether they have entered the country legally. Furthermore, though all of the groups engage in stopgap efforts intended to prevent the worsening of present conditions, they also direct a broad critique at the social structures that cause the death and denigration of immigrants in the first place. Material aid, informative workshops, and the like are intended to ameliorate suffering here and now, but they are also strategic interventions in the controversy over border enforcement, intended to name immigrant suffering as injustice, and not merely remedy the injustice, but eradicate its causes.

Work of any sort on behalf of immigrants courts unpopularity, since newly arrived foreigners may not be accepted if their lifeways and beliefs conflict with the standing norms in their new surroundings. Until they prove their loyalty, they are often treated with suspicion and scorn—sentiments that are easily extended to their advocates as well. The degree of enmity varies according to circumstance, but if acting on behalf of immigrants is already, in some cases, frowned upon, then defending the undocumented easily acquires the taint of aiding and abetting criminal activity. Such is the case with immigrant advocates in Tucson, whose opponents commonly rally around exhortations to maintain national sovereignty. They argue that eligibility for certain benefits available in the United States—social welfare, economic opportunity, and civil liberties—should be reserved for those whose presence on national territory has been approved by the state. Since national borders are sites for regulating access to state-secured benefits, any violation of them imperils the ability of the state to provide for legitimate recipients and challenges the state's claim to uphold order. Hence, illegal immigration corrodes the integrity of the country, and because immigrant advocates contribute to the corrosion, they must be opposed as much as illegal immigration itself.

Restrictionists occasionally attack Tucson immigrant advocates on legal grounds, particularly when advocates provide migrants with direct material aid. Section 274.A of the U.S. Immigration and Nationality Act, entitled "Bringing In and Harboring Certain Aliens," defines a number of crimes, which include helping someone enter the country by anything other than state-controlled ports or encouraging them to enter in such a manner, as well as transporting someone who has entered the country thus or concealing that person from detection.[7] Penalties for violation range from fines to imprisonment. Immigrant advocacy groups in Tucson have taken great care to see that they operate within the law, and though they object to certain state policies, they do not promote violating those policies as acts of civil disobedience. Nonetheless, some restrictionists have denounced the provision of material aid as illegal and called for those engaging in such actions to be prosecuted.

But behind the accusation of lawbreaking is a more subjective and highly charged insinuation that immigrant advocates are guilty of treason. Roger Barnett, an Arizona rancher active in organized restrictionism, has said of church officials doing immigrant advocacy, "It's fine and dandy to help someone, but what do (the clergy) want for this country?" (S. Carroll). Wes Bramhall, president of Arizonans for Immigration Control, goes further in saying, "We do have plenty among us—be they politicians, newspaper editors, church groups and some Hispanic organizations—who don't seem to know to which nation they owe their allegiance" (Bramhall). Barnett, Bramhall, and their cohorts foreground national citizenship as the paramount identity for moral action. Since loyalty to country and compatriots supersedes all other attachments, the livelihood of citizens takes priority over that of noncitizens, especially noncitizens who are breaching the nation's borders. Enabling an undocumented entrant to continue traveling by providing water or denouncing the deportations from a job site raid undermine law enforcement efforts that are vital to the very survival of the country. Hence, even if what immigrant advocates do is legal, the sentiments behind their actions are not consistent with the responsibilities of citizenship. On the contrary, they actively subvert the United States.

The views of immigrant advocates, in contrast, invoke what may be called universalism—"a belief in the oneness of humanity" (Waterman 48) that mandates "the extension of ethical behavior beyond ascriptive social categories and particularistic social relations" (Sharot 8–9). One of the most prominent ways immigrant advocates frame their universalism is in terms of religious—usually Christian—actors, institutions, language, and symbols. To provide just a few examples: during the years of my fieldwork, news conferences by the Coalición de Derechos Humanos likely included a Christian priest or minister on a panel of speakers; Humane Borders met and had office space in a Christian church whose minister, Reverend Robin Hoover, was also the group's most oft-cited spokesperson; and the Samaritans, who also met in a Christian church, took their name from a story told by Jesus in the Gospel of Luke (11:29–37). Religion also permeates immigrant advocates' public demonstrations. Since the deaths of migrants trying to cross the desert are the most egregious symptoms of the current policy's failure, these demonstrations often take the form of memorials for the dead. The memorials, like the gathering for Prudencia Martin Gomez, offer a service of hymns, prayers and scriptures, which is sometimes followed by a march in which participants carry small crosses inscribed with the names of the dead. Whatever the venue, immigrant advocates routinely use religion to call for people to turn from current strategies of border enforcement and embrace an egalitarian, universalist alternative.

This is not to say that the rhetoric of immigrant advocacy is wholly composed of religious elements. Indeed, the Tucson-based Border Action Network has organized and campaigned since 1999 with little to no religious rhetoric at all, and groups that do utilize religious institutions and traditions combine them with other ideas. The secular universalisms of human rights and humanitarianism, for example, are evident in the very names Derechos Humanos and Humane Borders. Membership in the groups is not contingent on church membership, nor any profession of creed, and though clergy may be supportive or directly involved, they do not direct the groups' day-to-day operations. Furthermore, in those cases where clergy members are prominently involved with the movement, the congregants of their churches are not involved en masse. It is impossible to say how many sympathetic observers don't get involved because they see the movement as either too religious or not religious enough, but it can be readily observed that the groups routinely unite both religious (again, primarily Christian) believers and those who have no formal religious affiliation at all.

Nonetheless, the religious contributions to immigrant advocacy may seem incongruous, since religion's relationship with modern nationalism has often been more synergistic than adversarial. Innumerable patriots have equated their homelands with the Almighty, as with Joan of Arc's cry that "[t]hose who wage war against the holy realm of France, wage war against King Jesus" (qtd. in Pierard and Linder 41). Others have seen fit to claim divine favor for their country's ventures, a prime illustration being the "Gott mit Uns" (God with Us) belt buckles worn by German troops in World Wars I and II. Harnessing transcendent authority results in an ethical system where piety and good citizenship become synonymous, and patriotism can become a religious obligation. As a prominent US scholar-theologian argued during World War I, "For an American to refuse to share in the present war . . . is not Christian" (qtd. in Ahlstrom 885). In manifold ways, nationalism co-opts and even supersedes the objects of religious devotion, to the point that preserving the nation through obedience to the state has been made consistent with religious fidelity.

And yet religions have continued to hold at least some autonomy from nation-states and assumed the prophetic stance that social welfare should be defined and achieved across political borders. One of the most out-spoken immigrant advocates on this count is Rick Ufford-Chase, a Sanctuary veteran, founding member of Humane Borders and Samaritans, and moderator of the Presbyterian Church (USA) from 2004 to 2006. In an essay published during his tenure as moderator, Ufford-Chase references the Gospel story in which a lawyer revisits the Old Testament injunction to "love your neighbor as yourself" (Lev. 19:18) by asking Jesus, "Who is my neighbor?" (Luke 11:29). In response, Jesus tells the story commonly known as "the Good Samaritan." The story begins with a Jewish traveler who is assaulted by robbers and left for dead by the side of the road. Two Jewish clerics pass by him in succession and refuse to aid him. But a man from Samaria, a region that had mutual antagonism with the Jews, shows him mercy by bandaging his wounds and paying for his lodging at an inn. The potency of the story is not just that the Samaritan performs a compassionate act but that he recognizes someone from another social group as a neighbor, over and against the conditioning that could have led him to disregard the traveler as undeserving.

Ufford-Chase asks people to consider the story in light of Agua Prieta, a Mexican town about 120 miles from Tucson and just across the border from Douglas, Arizona. Noting that "Agua Prieta exists on the border between the 'first world' of the developed North and the 'two-thirds world' of poverty and economic marginalization in the Global South," Ufford-Chase suggests that the US-Mexico border "is perhaps the most important place one could go in the Western Hemisphere to consider the question 'Who is my neighbor?'" (85). The salience of the border as a vantage point for this inquiry stems in part from the United States and Mexico being contiguous and therefore literally "neighbors." But it also stems from the border's ability to analogize the average US viewer's relative advantage in health, wealth, and comfort to the position of the Samaritan, who voluntarily sacrifices those things for someone on the other side of a social division. Moreover, by locating Agua Prieta on a border between the global North and South, Ufford-Chase suggests that the contrast between the United States and Mexico is especially meaningful because it is symptomatic of the much greater latitudinal divide of rich and poor that circles the entire world.

Grisele,[8] a member of Derechos Humanos, meant much the same thing when she told me that "[t]he border is where people cross and that's where everybody's dying, but it's just a symbol." Her cohort Patricia elaborated,

"The border is basically just where the physical manifestation of the problem is happening. The problem is the mass displacement of people on a global scale and a huge misdistribution of wealth and land and power. The human rights crisis of it is that people are dying because of that reality." If the "physical manifestations" of the border are seen as "a symbol" of larger geopolitical inequities, then, in Ufford-Chase's words, the mandate to overcome social divisions and care for the needy means "that relationships between neighbors cannot be limited by nation-state borders, or even by our inability to know one another personally. Our neighborhood crosses *all* borders, and our neighbor is now everyone, everywhere" (89, emphasis in original). The faithful response to migration to the United States, then, must be "to practice the kind of radical hospitality that Jesus insisted upon in the story of the Good Samaritan" (Ufford-Chase 95)—an ethic superordinate to nation-state-based patriotism, extending mercy and compassion regardless of the recipient's "documentation."

From the standpoint of Rick Ufford-Chase, Grisele, Patricia, and many other immigrant advocates, Prudencia Martin Gomez's death and memorial are more than indices of the controversy over border enforcement. They are parables of globalization. "Globalization" can refer to a vast range of phenomena including human diasporas, accelerated transportation and telecommunications, and transnational organizations such as charities, corporations, and regulatory agencies. But it can also refer to a change in human subjectivity—a globalization of consciousness based on the perception of proximity to and connectivity with other parts of the world. Just as faster travel and the Internet facilitate intimacies and loyalties across borders, government consultations with supranational entities like the United Nations and the World Bank indicate a variety of ducts and cracks in the fortress of sovereignty. These and other touchstones of a global society seem to throw down the gauntlet for nation-state-based hierarchies of allegiance.

Accordingly, much scholarship pertinent to globalization is given to heady speculation as to whether the nation-state may eventually be replaced by new social solidarities—a prospect augured by the words and deeds of immigrant advocates. Mourning for foreign nationals that others think of as "invaders," claiming them as "neighbors," and practicing Ufford-Chase's call for "radical hospitality" are a far cry from the religious nationalism of "Gott mit Uns." They jam the very premise of the accusation that immigrant advocates "don't seem to know to which nation they owe their allegiance," in fact, because they argue for an ethical code that is not a matter of this or that nationality, but of something bigger than nationality altogether.

And yet, as the following chapters reveal, I have found that most immigrant advocates do not express the viewpoint that the nation-state is obsolete. They in almost all cases embrace their US citizenship and usually have a strong conviction that the problems they are trying to address can be fixed through government action. At the same time, they have great skepticism about the government's ability to act justly on its own and feel that the government has to be prodded by the public in order to implement just practices. Furthermore, they hold that people have to draw on some paradigm of value beyond the national interest to set the nation-state on the right path. Participants often identify that higher paradigm in religious or spiritual values that are actualized in a stance of "global citizenship." In their actions, the legacies of Judeo-Christian scriptural teachings, Enlightenment philosophes, and twentieth-century human rights accords converge on the highways and street corners of southern Arizona, suggesting, at times, a new formulation for the nation-state, and at other times an attempt to transcend the idea of the nation-state altogether.

## The Goals and Limitations of This Book

I began this project to document the ideas and actions of immigrant advocates in Tucson not just for posterity but for the present. As I have already indicated, immigrant advocacy has relevance for academic inquiries into the relationship between religious and political identities and the influence of globalization on nation-statehood. More obviously, by joining the volatile, fractious controversy about border enforcement, immigrant advocacy has become a controversy in and of itself, in which the participants are pilloried as traitors or criminals and praised as ethical visionaries. My hope is that this collection of case studies and insider perspectives, combined with a modest amount of analysis and contextualization, will be useful for conversations about immigration at the scholarly and popular level alike.

One way or another, the variables that characterize present debate over immigration in the United States will eventually be resolved, at which point historians will be able to assess how action on behalf of the undocumented impacted culture and public policy. Until then, immigrant advocates merit study for all the creativity and agency that is implicit in the term *social movement*. In his account of student-worker militancy in 1970s Italy, Robert Lumley suggests that "[s]ocial movements can be seen . . . to offer an ideal vantage-point for looking at the changes being brought about in a society, and for understanding the reactions to them. At the same time, the movements are themselves often laboratories of experimentation, incubating future ideas and forms of behavior" (3). The experimental, dynamic aspect of activism is compounded, in this particular instance, by working along the US-Mexico border, which journalist Charles Bowden has described, in terms similar to Lumley's, as "the laboratory of our future" (117). Consequently, my documentation of immigrant advocacy is rife with contingency and indeterminacy, and best seen not as a still life with crisp edges, but a blurry action shot of a work—or a world—in progress.

From 2004 to 2007 I carried out interactive fieldwork and interviews among three groups, the Coalición de Derechos Humanos, Humane Borders, and Samaritans, who welcomed me as both an observer and a participant. I focused on documenting three main areas of culture and thought among them: first, the moral paradigms by which participants identify border and immigration policies as in need of redress; second, the ways in which they represent those paradigms in speech, writing, material, symbol, and physical action; and third, how immigrant advocates understand their identities as citizens, Christians, human rights activists, and so forth in a political cosmology that unifies earthly responsibilities with ultimate reality. The most routine part of my research involved participating in meetings, public events, and various kinds of business in order to gather concrete examples of how group members reveal shared assumptions and knowledge while talking with each other. I was never excluded from an event, and members often invited me to join them for more informal occasions. The impressions I gathered from these experiences provided a general picture of group operations and suggested areas for follow-through in personal interviews. During the interviews I asked participants to discuss their personal involvement and their own sense of what movement symbols represent, tying together life experiences, beliefs, and group action. This kaleidoscope of individual perspectives alongside collective projections shows the groups' heterogeneity and mitigates the tendency of a composite portrait to falsely unify members' perspectives.

In what follows, I emphasize my informants' beliefs more than the veracity of those beliefs and what their prescriptions for action reveal about their worldview more than whether such prescriptions are feasible. Yet it will be obvious that I approached them with sympathy for their views and activities, and the task of honoring that sympathy while producing work that is scholarly in content and presentation has caused me some anxiety. The imperious gaze of the researcher, no matter how well intentioned, tends to objectify its human subjects disagreeably and produce distorted portraits. I fear the people I worked with will not recognize themselves in what I have rendered and believe they have been turned into specimens—trivialized and intellectualized, immobilized and silenced. All I can do is disavow any claim to omniscience or to have represented things in their totality, to submit my observations with humility, flagged with the disclaimer that they are provisional assessments subject to amendment.

The blurry snapshot I am offering, then, shows just one angle and has been cropped for wider consumption. But I would not bother showing it if I did not think it could still be useful. Our lives confront us at every turn with the need to decide between right and wrong, and the debate over illegal immigration taps into some of the most vexing and consequential decisions that we ever have to make. What are our responsibilities as human beings to other human beings? Do these responsibilities apply to all humans, or only particular ones? What specific social identities are best for carrying out those actions? To what social collectivity are we bound and accountable? And what standards do we use to decide the answers to these questions? In a grander sense, of course, trying to reconcile the truth of human pluralism at the individual and group level with the truth of human unity at the species level is a dilemma that abides in the human condition. It is a recurring theme in art, philosophy, and religion throughout the ages; immigrant advocates merely deal with it in a contemporary form.

My intention is for this book to provide insight into how some people are approaching these quandaries and assessing the implications of their strategies for both local and global human activity. Immersion in their views involves and invests us (albeit vicariously) in vital questions about the world we want to live in, for the borderland of displaced people, barricades, legal limbos, and cheapened lives is not just the Southwest, it is everywhere. It is in small-town Georgia, where a commercial property owner boasts he will not rent to Latinos (Swarns); it is in the Canary Islands, where Africans make perilous trips by boat to enter the European Union (Vogt); and it is in Yemen, where Somalis flee in search of $50-a-month jobs and refuge from war (Lacey). Immigrant advocates working in these and other borderlands are creating social structures and subjectivities consistent with what they believe is ethical and essential. I hope that exposure to the many ways in which the Tucsonans in this study are thinking about the conundrums of ethics and identity in a global society will provide a springboard for readers to do the same.

INTERSTICE

*"I'm just convinced that history is whoever tells the best story the longest."*

— ANNIE, DURING A SAMARITAN PATROL, APRIL 2005

# CHAPTER TWO

# Political Imagination in the United States

Toward the end of his life, Founding Father John Adams reflected on the formation of the United States and advised that despite appearances to the contrary, the American Revolution should not be confused with the War for Independence. "The Revolution," he wrote, "was effected before the war commenced. The Revolution was in the minds and hearts of the people; a change in their religious sentiments[,] of their duties and obligations." Although "[t]he people of America had been educated in an habitual affection for England, as their mother country" and "thought of her as a kind and tender parent," when their petitions for equality revealed England "willing like Lady Macbeth to 'dash their brains out' . . . their filial affections ceased and were changed into indignation and horror. This radical change in the principles, opinions, sentiments and affections of the people was the real American Revolution" (qtd. in Ahlstrom 262).

Adams supported armed struggle when it came, and went on to serve as a diplomat, vice president, and president for the newly independent United States. But his characterization of the real Revolution highlights the need to think of politics existing not only in legislative assemblies and bureaucratic chambers but in the more mysterious, subjective realm of what he calls "minds and hearts," where people tie their everyday sympathies to what they consider ultimately good, beautiful, and true.

In all places and at all times, the eminent pragmatism of politics is accompanied by what seems to be superfluous decoration: where there is budgeting, there will be bunting. The reason for this lies in the contrived and somewhat arbitrary basis of society. Language, holidays, and so forth have no natural validity, nor is any human being genetically programmed to recognize them. What fills concepts like religions and nations with ontological force is that their constituents believe themselves to share certain traits that both bind them together and distinguish them from others. But since cultural practices are invented, the bedlam of infinite innovation forever encroaches on the domain of order. Therefore, in order to endure, every way of life must seem more appealing or necessary than the endless number of alternatives. Cultures obscure their inventedness so as to appear natural and even sacred, which hinders the development of alternatives and ensures some measure of consensus and day-to-day continuity.

Since collective identity is based on culture, not chromosomes, Benedict Anderson has argued that any societies larger than face-to-face relations should be understood as "imagined communities" because even though the members may never know each other, "in the minds of each lives the image of their communion" (6). Though the standard covers philanthropies, alumni associations, trade unions, and many other groups, Anderson is primarily concerned with nationalism, which he calls "the most universally legitimate value in the political life of our time" (3). That is, one may belong to many imagined communities at a given moment, but around the world, nationalism, in the form of the modern nation-state, is the imagined community that trumps all others. Anderson means no insult by the word "imagined," and he is not trying to pejoratively separate communities that are false from communities that are genuine. Rather, his aim is to open investigation into "the style in which they are imagined" (6). Once we think of communities as imagined, we can consider how the imagining is done, and how this cultural work produces hierarchies of loyalty and commitment that interlock with actual forms of statecraft.

Furthermore, what is imagined can be reimagined and transformed. Throughout US history, social actors have quarreled over where the lines of imagined community should be drawn, variously using secular and religious rhetorical appeals to justify their efforts. Some call for the boundaries to be widened, others for them to be narrowed, others for them to be maintained as is; regardless, the disputes reveal that membership in the nation-state is not a given. Neither, for that matter, is the nation-state itself a given. Just because one form of political community reigns at a given moment does not mean it always will, and if nationalism has become the key to sovereign power in modern times, its supremacy over attachments born of other forms of imagination is not definitive. The rise of institutions and networks that are not just international but arguably global has prompted speculation that the credibility of the nation-state may be in decline, and indeed, social processes of globalization have been accompanied by cultural practices that question the national basis of identity, territorial sovereignty, and citizenship. In the United States, controversy over undocumented immigration provides a case in point. Against considerable animus toward immigrants, religious mandates and secular notions of panhuman equality have begun to assert the need to practice an ethic that exceeds borders, promoting a consciousness in which nationalism may be superseded by some reimagination of solidarity and governance.

## Deaths in the Family: The Symbolic World of Collective Identity

John Adams's account of the American Revolution fulfills one of the expectations for any strong collective identity, which is to have a cosmogonic narrative, that is, a creation myth. In the classic explication of religion scholar Mircea Eliade, cosmogonies begin with a time that is formless and disorderly until the heroes of creation triumph by bringing forth the present world and its inhabitants.[1] Order, however, has a price. In the archetypal cosmogony, the life of the group begins only through the suffering and sometimes the death of the culture hero or heroes. The group attributes its deepest values and sense of itself to this primal sacrifice, and thus the creation myth also establishes the basis for those who share the myth to see each other in terms of allegorical kinship. That is, in the heroic shedding of blood, they come to understand themselves as descended from a common ancestry, united for mutual aid in the present, but also connected to their past (their progenitors) and the promise of a future (their progeny).

Return, for a moment, to Adams's remarks on the meaning of the Revolution, which Eliade helps us understand as a succinct, archetypal cosmogonic myth. First, Adams offers the metaphor of the normal state of society as a family. When Adams calls England a "mother" to the colonists, he means nothing biological. If the colonists "thought of her as a kind and tender parent," this was purely a mental, imagined construct. Nonetheless, the metaphor attempts to give the relationship between the colonies and England the legitimacy of something that is natural. Their bond is not described as a "friendship," which must be formed through effort, but as paternity, which cannot be chosen or undone. A child has parents as surely as the sun rises and the seasons change. But as Adams describes, this union with the unquestionable order of things was destroyed by the violence of the parent toward its children. The mother attacked them, seeking "to dash their brains out," and the world plunged into chaos. In the wake of murder and persecution, the colonists had no choice. Following the bloody sacrifice of their comrades, "their filial affections ceased" and their part of the proverbial family formed its own, separate lineage based on different "principles, opinions, sentiments and affections."

A "family" as such endures as long as the members continue to imagine themselves as kin and as descendants of heroic, self-sacrificing progenitors. Because these perceptions are not inborn, the formless chaos that preceded creation forever threatens to return, overwhelming the boundaries that give the group stability and coherence. Facing the prospect of dissolution, the group strives to imitate the culture heroes, for if the existence of the group is proof that disorder was vanquished in the past, upholding the practices and attitudes that brought the world into being can preserve order in the present. Group survival depends, therefore, on the group's knowledge of itself over time, which is often called "social" or "collective memory," even though none of the rememberers may have directly experienced what is being recalled.

To promote collective memory—or, more accurately, the simulation of it—groups develop cultural expressions that serve as mnemonic devices for making the sacred past palpable. The most stereotypic mnemonic in this regard is ritual, but any cultural creation can serve the same purpose. Words, sounds, images, places, bodily gestures, and so on can all contribute to storytelling about group identity and how the group figures into the whole of reality. Whether in the context of special occasions or embedded in everyday routines, they provide reminders about the group's defining, fundamental values, without which the group would cease to exist.

Some of the most important rituals and symbols of collective life connect people to their ancestors, biological or cultural. Jon Davies makes a strong argument that "the life of a community is comprehensible, subjectively and objectively, only when it is understood as grounded in a covenant of mutual loyalty between the living and the dead" (12–13). Societies create mourning rites to laud as heroes those who established the boundaries of the group, but also those who subsequently defended them. To mourn says that the living are indebted to the dead in ways that compel them to give time, energy, and wealth in tribute. The honorific grieving called "memorial" is based, of course, on the word "memory" and through such acts, collectives praise the preceding generations and position themselves as worthy inheritors. Memorials often recall times when hostile forces threatened (or appeared to threaten) group boundaries, but were defeated through sacrifice by culture heroes. Rites offer a gateway to the primal creation myth, the group's symbolic home, in which the community "reactualizes the event" (Eliade 81) and revisits the principles and bloodshed that enabled its birth. Ritualized memory of ancestral sacrifice bolsters not only every individual's sense of belonging to the group but also the group's sense of being a group, keeping the blood circulating and suturing wounds so the blood will coagulate.

The symbolic expressions of collective identity may seem inherently conservative, and to a point that is true. They are intended to reinforce, not undermine, the sacred basis of the standing order. Yet any dissension from the standing order will, sooner rather than later, also take up ritual and symbol as means of expressing opposition. Symbolic practices are the wellspring of all imagined community—status quo or insurgent, ancient or novel; they are integral to the reproduction of social life as it is, and to all contest over what it might be.

## Imagining Nation and Community in the United States

Consider, in this respect, Adams's argument that the Revolution should be thought of as the shift in sentiments that preceded and enabled independence. One concrete expression of the colonists' change in attitude was the Sons of Liberty, an underground organization that sparked incipient resistance to British rule in the 1760s. Their very name bypassed any "filial affection" to England by proclaiming a new ancestral line in which they were the offspring of no finite political entity, but the abstract principle of freedom. Likewise, their regalia included medallions that featured a Liberty Tree, which traced the genealogy of their core principle to the earth itself. The metaphor eventually took literal form when anti-British activists in diverse locales used large trees as gathering places for public protest and the commemoration of martyrs. Though the Liberty Tree was not connected to any denominational religious tradition, British Loyalists perceived it as a cultic, transcendent force, describing it as a "deity" (qtd. in Albanese 63) and noting its capacity to stimulate "more enthusiastic frenzy than what is expressed by the frantic infidel at the tomb of Mecca, or the bigoted pilgrim at the chapel of Loretto" (qtd. in Albanese 64)— both candid conceptualizations of sedition in terms of heretic idolatry.

These expressions of dissent were cultural, taking everyday things like a word or a tree and investing them with meanings capable of mobilizing the colonists' resentment of English rule and their desire to create a better society. John Adams's reflections describe the Revolution, but it may be more accurate to say they describe two revolutions. One was the creation of the United States as a sovereign entity, separate from Great Britain. More significant, though, was the second, which rode a trend of century-old philosophical developments in Europe that eventually transformed the entire globe. This second revolution was of a more general sort, having less to do with the formation of specific sovereign countries than with the very concept of sovereignty and the distribution of power within it. For generations, the model of the polity in Europe had a top-down, pyramid structure with a monarch at the pinnacle, followed by a miscellany of aristocrats, and the great mass of people at the bottom. Sovereignty, in this system, rested solely with the monarch. Granted, this arrangement had undergone some modification here and there — the grievances of the Sons of Liberty, John Adams and their peers, after all, were directed both at King George and the English Parliament. But the change in thinking that propelled revolution in the United States and became the cornerstone of political modernity was that government and the sum of sovereign power associated with it resides in a popular base, that is, "the people," and not in a singular office.

The idea gained traction, eventually becoming so powerful that the existing cultural systems could no longer command people's loyalties. The result was the modern nation-state, which, like any imagined community, had to be invented. In the United States and elsewhere, nation-statist identities gradually cohered by borrowing from available traditions to articulate a new history of ancestral sacrifice (Alonso; Anderson; García-Canclini; Zelinsky). The ritual mourning of nationalism focused on war casualties, venerating the dead in order to rally the living. "Remember the Alamo" — or "the Maine" or "Pearl Harbor," and so on — are at once eulogies and battle cries, by the syllogism that if people remember the event, they will find themselves moved by the sacrifice of their kin, and if they are moved by the sacrifice of their kin, they will be moved to sacrifice themselves in kind. Like any other imagined community, political nationalism promoted its heroic past through all manner of media and asserted a figurative kinship among community members. Its distinctive style, however, created a new collective identity by redefining government, citizen-subjects, territorial boundaries, and the relationship between them in distinctive ways.

Law scholar Linda Bosniak has succinctly identified the basic terms of the new consciousness in what she calls the "national imagination," which "treats the national society . . . as the predominant community of normative concern and presumes the legitimacy, if not the inevitability, of its borders" (596). Nationalism was thus a new dispensation in which a person's dignity required citizenship rights as it had, in a prior age, required the sacraments, and exclusion from those rights was as dire a condition as excommunication. Self-interest was monopolized by national interest, and national interest depended on clear and absolute distinctions between the nation and the outside. Members of the "national society" were favored, and excluded people made less important. But how was membership in that society determined?

One way of marking inclusion was spatial, along the lines of Bosniak's point that nation-states regarded borders as integral, defining features of their existence. Whereas premodern states tended to be defined by their political centers of command and were delimited by geographical barriers or vague "frontiers," European statehood from the 1600s on began to coalesce around the idea of a population tied to a specific, quantifiable territory (Nevins; Sorensen), determining membership in the nation through immigration and citizenship policies. The second means of determining membership was to imagine the nation as a set of idealized biological and cultural traits, with people who did not match that idealized norm ruled ineligible for full protections and privileges.

Blocked from the fruits of citizenship despite foundational rhetoric about "the people," subjugated groups and their allies began to reimagine the nation in wider terms. Thinkers, artists, and social movement organizations reinterpreted familiar rhetoric and developed new symbolic repertoires to argue that the polity could be expanded to include a greater percentage of the population.

Religion played an important role in these struggles, aiding both conservative and dynamic forces in their contests over how the national community would be defined. In the colonial period, British colonists widely held that Christianity monopolized truth and that Protestantism was the most authentic form of Christianity. Because their nation had broken from papal authority, the colonists propounded an analogy between their situation and the biblical Exodus, in which they, as "chosen people," were delivered from tyranny and divinely appointed to do God's work in the "new Israel" of the American colonies (Curti 67–68; Longley; A. Smith; Wood). Such religious nationalism combined with perceptions of "race" to justify the external warfare and internal oppression that defined England's empire in the Americas. The superior truth of Christianity elevated colonists over the "darkness and miserable ignorance"[2] of indigenous belief and justified the conquest of indigenous land. Meanwhile, scriptural justifications for slavery made it possible for free whites to positively differentiate their political community from unfree African slaves, living under the same British jurisdiction (Wood).

After independence, religious tenets and practices remained relevant to public life even though the First Amendment of the Constitution precluded government endorsement of specific sects. They continued, for one, to contribute to political legitimacy in that many people saw religious convictions and participation (or the appearance thereof) as essential to the healthy functioning of the country. R. Laurence Moore observes that "American politicians learned early to trot out conceptions of American nationhood that blended the claim of popular origins with the claim of divine origins" (70), and many listeners doubtless agreed with a mid-nineteenth-century orator that the Bible was "a . . . manual for the Patriot as well as for the Christian" (qtd. in Curti 78). A practice from the camp meetings during the Second Great Awakening reconciled patriotic and religious identities with impressive efficiency: "Laypeople acted out figurative revolutionary battlefield scenes, where their wounds, physical and spiritual, could be transcended in salvation and independence simultaneously. . . . By 1805 backcountry Carolina Baptists had developed even more richly evocative replications of the revolutionary army experience to stimulate revivals among second-generation Americans, who had never undergone battlefield experience" (Butler 241).

Nothing could be more ritually archetypal than this narrative of expiration and renewal, and nothing could better symbolize the era's commonplace that being a good US citizen meant being a good Christian. Indeed, the upshot of the new republic's self-confidence was a collective self-apotheosis that maintained the social hierarchy of British colonialism (with white, Anglophone Protestants at the top) but adjusted the rhetoric so that divine blessings favored the new country instead of its former master.

Skeptics, though, were at pains to argue that the self-congratulatory mood was ill founded and that the chimes of liberty, ringing prematurely, were drowning out the cries of the oppressed. They organized social movements that aimed, in effect, at democratizing democracy by extending citizenship to the ranks of people who were relegated to second-class subjecthood. The struggles, manifest in part through such means as votes, dollars, and violence, were also waged through symbolic reconfigurations of the style in which the nation imagined itself. The most startling example may well be African American Christianity's radical reclamation of the Chosen People myth, which reversed the notion of European colonists being delivered from Old World bondage for an American Promised Land. In the hermeneutics of black theologians, dominant white society became a new Egypt, and subjugated blacks the righteous elect, suffering in the present but destined for liberation. By turning the oppressor's religion into a cosmology that gave them a sense of self-worth, African Americans transformed the derogatory into the emancipatory (Glaude; Raboteau).

Similar efforts could be found among citizens at more privileged economic strata who were frustrated that their lives of relative comfort came at the expense of a principle as sacred as the dignity of other human beings. For instance, abolitionist "benevolent societies" used the premise that the United States was a chosen or covenanted country to make the whole society accountable to God. To be part of a body politic that included slavery, they argued, was to be implicated in its evils and hence compelled to undo them. The movements organized thus as a kind of "public confession against the special sins of the nation" (M. Young 666) while pointing to the redemptive potential of concrete political reforms.

The imagined community of the United States, like imagined communities in general, includes symbolic practices intended to give the appearance of having some organic or divine origin, and to establish, by facilitating the sense of shared, sacrificial ancestry in the mind of its members, a "community of normative concern." Though subnational groups continuously quarrel over which norms and laws should guide the United States, they do not question the more foundational assumptions that ancestral sacrifices should receive proper commemoration, and that membership in the nation accords with the ultimate order of reality, whether natural or supernatural.

## Globalization as the Reimagining of Political Community

The proliferation of nation-states since 1945 appears to confirm the unrivaled appeal of nationalism as a style of political imagining. So standard has the nation-state become as the form of particular sovereignties that it has also become standardized as the form of sovereignty-in-general. That is to say, any community aspiring to legitimacy in the world order must acquire nation-state status, because that is the approved-of vehicle for people to better themselves and humanity overall. In Stephen Tipton's words, "the goal of progress," rationalized, regards nation-states as "the boundaries within which progress is to occur" (57).

Yet at the very same time that the nation-state has attained comprehensive planetary dominance, it has been presented with a gamut of destabilizing pressures that fall under the rubric of "globalization." On a personalized scale, globalization is most evident in technologies that compress space and time and enhance the ability of users to maintain a sense of connection with miscellaneous elsewheres. Improvements in the speed of communication, especially through the Internet and cellular telephones, have enabled people to exchange information and share experiences simultaneously across vast, even antipodal distances. International transportation, though more cost prohibitive, provides travelers with opportunities to build a sense of self associated with sites external to their home country. Globalization can also be seen in a range of transnational institutions, some of which have no inherent geographical base. These include multilateral associations such as the European Union (EU), North Atlantic Treaty Organization, and the United Nations (UN); businesses that have highly mobile operations and owe their allegiance more to worldwide stockholders than to any sense of *patria*; and nongovernmental organizations (NGOs) from charities to political pressure groups that operate around the globe according to need.

All of these developments impact—sometimes subtly, sometimes enormously—the way in which people define community, the good of community, and how to achieve that good. Though not expressly hostile to individual nation-states or the nation-state as a general concept, they complicate the national imagination by creating routines and interpersonal connections that cross over compatriots and territorial boundaries. Personal investments in transnational culture at least potentially weaken the coherence and sentimental hold of the nation as a commanding political identity. By the same token, greater interconnectedness among nation-states discredits the idea that any country can define or pursue self-interest on terms wholly of its own choosing. Of course, the situation can be presented (or taken) too hyperbolically, as if the very idea of being "Norwegian" or "Argentinean" were in imminent danger of vaporizing. But if nation-states are tenacious, they are not impervious, and where the forces of globalization erode their viability, people will create new forms of community to replace them.

If we follow the lead of anthropologist Arjun Appadurai, cultural activity of this sort may be thought of as a "postnational imagination" that hypothesizes alternatives to the assumptions of modern sovereignty. Just as outrage over England's abuse of the thirteen colonies would have been inchoate without some belief that independence was possible, postnational thought hinges on the formation of ethical identities that are disentangled from the nation-state. More in the form of a tendency than a clearly defined charter or project, postnationalism works to demystify the reification of nation-states as natural, inevitable containers of human feeling.

Some of the most important voices regarding the flexibility of national boundaries come from border dwellers and border crossers, who are intimately familiar with the sensation of being pulled between two nation-states and the experience of being, somehow, both and neither. Paradoxically, borders gratify concern that the nation must be separated from the foreign, yet also provide places of contact and exchange with the foreign. By combining elements of "here" and "there" in what the postcolonial literary critic Homi Bhabha has called "third spaces" or "interstices," borderlands spur identities that are based on familiarity with the to-and-fro of various kinds of "crossings," whether geographical or cultural, and since the last quarter of the twentieth century, many interstitial familiars have sought to legitimize these identities through artistic, especially literary, production. Writer Luis Alberto Urrea, for instance, reflecting on his childhood in the US-Mexico borderlands with one parent from each side, concludes: "America is home. It's the only home I have. Both Americas. All three Americas, from the Arctic circle to Tierra del Fuego. . . . I am nobody's son. But I am everyone's brother. So come here to me. Walk me home" (*Nobody's Son* 58–59). Urrea subverts the narrative of the national fatherland or motherland by describing himself as having no clear parentage or inheritance. He does, however, claim a sibling relationship with his readers and even invites them to visit his "home," which is no nation-state but an entire hemisphere. His testimony is less a yearning for postnationalism than a claim to incarnate it, as if to prove, by his very existence, that the world is not made up of fundamental and irreconcilable national differences.

Religion has provided another base for postnational imaginings in the form of commandments to extend love and generosity to people regardless of birthplace, skin color, and other socially ascribed status markers. Such an ethos is clearly incompatible with the national imagination's hierarchy of citizens and noncitizens, and religious institutions that might purvey it have often been content to act as denominational units of the nation-state instead. But if modernity caused the doctrines of universalism to be downplayed, they were not altogether eliminated, and their adherents have persisted in articulating alternative visions of social solidarity. They have denounced, as discussed in the previous section, the cultural nationalism that treats some co-nationals as unequal. They have also critiqued the state for enforcing those inequalities through discriminatory laws. Moreover, they have critiqued the legitimacy of nation-states and nation-state chauvinism overall, sometimes to argue that "'the common good' can increasingly be defined only in global, universal, human terms and that, consequently, the public sphere of modern civil societies cannot have national or state boundaries" (Casanova 229).

A secular counterpart to religious universalism may be found embedded in modernity and the conceptual root of popular sovereignty. Popular sovereignty argued for the existence of rights that were inalienable and based in nature, not the jurisdictions of states. Ironically, the premise of a dignity innate in humanity overall actually resulted in nation-states with finite populations. "Nationalism," to wit, "was the legatee of a failed universalism" (Navari 36). But the ideal of inviolable liberty as the birthright of all people persevered in the rhetoric of human rights, which proclaimed that justice had to reach beyond borders and was not to be reserved solely for one's compatriots. Human rights by definition precede the privileges granted by governments, implying the existence of person-to-person bonds that are prior to any citizenship. More restrained than religious universalism in that it does not include imperatives to assist those in need, the logic of human rights still imposes limits on the pursuit of self-interest. It demands, by virtue of human rights being antecedent to any social authority, that nation-states recognize and obey principles higher than those of their own making.

Whether shaped by interstitial testimony, holy dictates seasoned by centuries, or precepts of natural law, postnational imaginings offer the prospect of personhood independent of nation-states—or, at least, nation-states as they are presently understood. Politically, they are far from programs for the seizure of sovereignty. Nonetheless, their cultural influence surely gestures toward the global, authorizing modes of consciousness for solving problems that are bigger than any one country.

## Immigration and Imagined Community

Immigration debates are conspicuously heavy with postnational implications for the obvious reason that immigrants raise questions about identity, rights, and community across nation-state lines. The basis of political nationalism is the imagination of co-nationals as peers, with all foreigners consigned to some measure of inferiority, and territorial limits serving to define and reinforce that distinction. Yet these boundaries, in all their

manifestations, are permeable, and states may devote considerable attention to procedures that modulate the value of certain foreigners, even to
the point of transforming them into citizens. (This bit of bureaucratic nec-
romancy is commonly known as "naturalization," for it imitates, through a
cultural process, the natural means by which membership in the faux family of the nation is normally gained, i.e., childbirth.) The state, as sovereign,
claims definitive power to set all manner of policies regarding the value of
foreigners, such as who will be admitted into the country, who will be eligible to pursue citizenship, what strategies will enforce the regulations, and
so on. The emigrant's plea for a visa thereby pulls the conundrum of "who
counts as 'the people'?" into the global arena, where foreigners are classified
as desirable or undesirable, welcome or unwelcome, included or excluded.

By directing citizens to extend sympathy to some immigrants and with-
hold it from others, the state attempts to manage the boundaries of the
imagined community. But alternative definitions of those boundaries
constantly vie to achieve primacy in both law and public opinion, each
differing on who should be regarded as imaginary kin. Standing on the
more expansive side, immigrant advocates in the United States commonly
run programs that assist immigrant populations by providing educational
services (English and citizenship classes), legal assistance, cultural events,
mediation across linguistic and cultural barriers, and material aid. Many
times they also interface with officeholders and society at large, calling
for change when practices harm immigrants or impose unfair barriers to
immigration. Immigrant advocacy in the United States includes religious
and secular influences, but the religious presence has been particularly
strong in efforts on behalf of undocumented immigrants in the US-Mexico
borderlands. The premier sociological observer of this trend, Pierrette
Hondagneu-Sotelo (21–22), notes that one way Christian participants
and institutions have shaped the movement has been by providing ritual
means of expression. In San Diego, for instance, activists have put a new
spin on the Posada, an Advent ritual in some Mexican American neighborhoods during which an ensemble of local residents walk from door to
door, reenacting Mary and Joseph's struggle to find haven in Bethlehem
(Hondagneu-Sotelo 133–69; Hondagneu-Sotelo, Gaudinez, and Lara).
Performed in a space adjacent to the international border and set against
a fortified wall designed to make the boundary impassable, this "Posada
Sin Fronteras" (Posada without Borders) challenges viewers to apply biblical teachings of hospitality to the contemporary immigration debate. As
a clergyman emceeing the event one year proposed, "there's a spirit that
transcends the border" (qtd. in Hondagneu-Sotelo 135).

The more constrained version of community and mutual care is exemplified by the Federation for American Immigration Reform (FAIR), one of the largest anti-immigration groups in the United States. In 2007, FAIR members mounted a massive lobbying campaign when the US Senate began deliberations on a bipartisan immigration reform bill that would have enabled some undocumented residents in the United States to apply for citizenship. Though the route to naturalization involved stringent requirements, a convoluted process, and considerable expense, restrictionists adamantly opposed it as an amnesty for criminals. One grassroots opponent said, "This hit home with me because I knew it was taking away from our people," and added, "What happened to taking care of our own people first?" (qtd. in Preston 24). Another was puzzled that President George Bush was supporting the bill, since Bush, he said, "has always been a person who stood for some basic human values, and now he's going to give away the country?" (qtd. in Preston 24). These comments clearly indicate how postnational perspectives based on solidarities across borders patently conflict with restrictionism's emphasis on the nation-state as the basis for ethics and identity. For FAIR supporters, "basic human values" mean looking after "our own people," which is to say "citizens" (and possibly authorized visitors). To do otherwise is tantamount to miscalculating the worth of—"[giving] away"—a prize of supreme value.

Unpacking the premises of restrictionist and advocate frames makes it clear that the argument over immigration is something of a proxy for the much larger question of whether national sovereignty is an adequate moral compass for individuals and collectives. Philosophies of justice routinely address how members of the same polity treat each other or how states treat their own citizens. But if there is a universal standard against which human action should be measured, then the scale for weighing justice must also sustain questions of how states and state subjects treat noncitizens. The premise that there is such a standard raises some vexing correlated questions. For example, does a state have to take into account how efforts to maintain its borders affect foreign nationals? And if government at the nation-state level can't uphold human rights that are supposedly universal, who will?

In the United States, as around the world, nationalism has become the dominant political imagined community. But transnational migration and other forms of globalization readily summon a conflict between the national imagination's regard for borders as indispensable and the postnational imagination's regard for borders as negotiable. Nation-statists have deep attachments to the peculiarities of the nation-state and wish it to be the sole, ultimate arbiter of right and wrong in whether the collective prospers or falters. Those engaged in postnationalist imaginings greatly threaten those who see nation-states (particularly their own nation-state) as singular reserves of virtue and uniquely qualified agents for promoting the good. Insofar as participants in the immigration debate articulate their positions as sacred imperatives for a political collectivity, their work can be characterized as a struggle to reimagine the meaning and function of borders in global society.

INTERSTICE

*A highly individualistic society that tries to eradicate a sense of coop-
eration and "we're all in this together" re: meeting basic human needs
will tend to commodify rights. That is, rights are formally guaranteed,
but practically employed only with backing of large sums of resources.*

*Is the American Dream universal? Can it be universalized?*

*Is the American Dream a means to an end, or an end? If an end,
and the end is material wealth, then the current standard cannot be
universalized. If a means, then it is supposed that there is some ethical
standard for development. What is it? (What is the ethical means and
what is the desired end?)*

*Is it assumed that the American Dream comes at the expense of
others? Or can it happen without detriment to other people? Is it based
in scarcity? If so, who is modeled as "fit" (or having certain traits that
bring success)? Or who is modeled as deserving?*

—AN UNDATED MEMO DURING FIELDWORK

# US-Mexico Border Enforcement and the Emergence of Immigrant Advocacy in Tucson

As Interstate 10 works across the greater Southwest; it bisects Tucson with a jagged line and sprouts Interstate 19 southbound to Nogales. I-19's main distinction is being the quickest route from Tucson to Mexico, but it is also notable for its signage, which provides distances using the metric system. The signs present a perplexing novelty. Why change the style of measurement, especially for such a short segment of road? Why should this stretch of asphalt in particular warrant references to meters and kilometers, especially since the metric system is rarely used in the United States?

The international preference for the metric system, it turns out, is precisely the point. According to a representative from the Arizona Transportation Department, the road was signed that way because planners recognized it would primarily serve traffic to and from Mexico (McDivitt). Not that this necessarily explains anything, since it's hard to imagine how indicating distances in miles would pose an inconvenience or hazard. Yet it speaks a certain truth about Southern Arizona and the transitional, liminal qualities of the borderlands. The closer you get to the border, the more the surroundings tend to take on characteristics of life on the other side, sometimes juxtaposing elements of "here" and "there," "us" and "them." A sign marking an exit in "2 km" is, in a sense, wholly appropriate to the setting—not just as a place where the United States joins Mexico, but as a place where the United States joins the rest of the world.

Southern Arizona is an obvious seedbed for postnational imaginings. As a region that was once part of Mexico, where the former Mexican population was folded into the United States through conquest, and human activities continuously cross an international boundary, it complicates the idea of national cultures as essences hermetically sealed by territorial boundaries. Portentously, the US-Mexico border is also a meeting place for global haves and have-nots: nowhere else does contiguity of two countries reveal such drastic differences between the First and Third Worlds. To use Bhabha's term, southern Arizona is an interstice, reverberating with past and present conflicts over the inclusion and exclusion of people within communities of mutual concern.

Over the twentieth century, economic disparities between the Southern and Northern Hemispheres of the Americas made immigration at the US-Mexican border an increasingly controversial issue. The "push" factors of poverty and political upheaval in the South, combined with the "pull" factors of wealth and relative stability in the North, have encouraged millions to leave their homes and enter the United States from Mexico. US citizens using what in chapter 2 I described as the "national imagination" have interpreted the influx of undocumented immigrants in particular as a threat, and responded with efforts to give borders stronger definition and prohibitive power. The response of immigrant advocates, in contrast, has been to receive undocumented arrivals as part of one or more kinds of postnational community in which borders are more permeable.

Though Tucson immigrant advocacy bears the imprint of personalities and networks that are all its own, it has been influenced by regional, national, and global events and influenced them in turn. A scattered and sporadic phenomenon until the mid-twentieth century, immigrant advocacy in the United States eventually increased in influence through faith-based and secular organizations that coalesced around the plight of European refugees after World War II. Tucson played a minor role in nationwide efforts to resettle these and other refugees in the postwar era, but as the locus of immigration quarrels shifted from coastal ports to the border with Mexico, the city assumed greater prominence in the movement. By the 1980s, when Tucson achieved notoriety as a center of work on behalf of undocumented Central American refugees, immigrant advocacy had undergone a major philosophical makeover. After two postwar decades in which immigrant advocacy groups tacitly accepted state-mediated systems for identifying border crossers worthy of assistance, they began in theory and practice to relativize the nation-state vis-à-vis a superordinate ethos that combined theology with the language of human rights, claiming a degree of autonomy from the state and extending their efforts to populations outside of federal sanction.

## Federal Immigration Policy and Transnational Labor in the Southwest through 1924

For half a century after independence, immigration to the United States was slight, scarcely rousing passion or bile in anyone. But that changed when a surge of mostly Irish and German arrivals in the late 1820s inaugurated nationwide controversy over whether immigration should be expanded or restricted. Businesses generally took an expansionist stance and argued that immigrants contributed to the national interest because they provided a source of cheap labor. With labor costs down, businesses made more profit, resulting in economic growth that benefited the national population as a whole. Restrictionists countered from two perspectives. The first shared the expansionists' disposition to make the economy the standard of national interest, but argued that immigration threatened the national interest when it undercut the efforts of native-born workers seeking to maximize wages. The second kind of restrictionism, separately or in combination with the first, framed national interest in terms of social cohesion, not material prosperity. To wit, it was nativism, arguing that immigrants were dangerous because they introduced foreign elements (whether biological or cultural) that undermined a homogeneity thought to be essential for harmonious collective life. More precisely, immigrants destabilized an ethnoracial and ideological composition deemed consistent with the health of the United States. Though both expansionists and restrictionists made their claims in terms of national interest and maximizing the welfare of the United States, their disagreement on how that welfare was to be measured proved intractable. The lines of disagreement persisted during the unprecedented immigration levels of 1880–1920 and, in fact, have largely held true to the present day (Calavita, *U.S. Immigration Law*).

But while the vast majority of industrial-era immigrants were Asians and Europeans who made their journeys by sea, another sort of immigration was happening by land, at the southern border. Following the US-Mexican War of 1846–48, the United States had annexed the northern half of Mexico, creating a nearly 2,000-mile-long international boundary.[1] As there were no limits on immigration numbers at the time and very little border regulation, people readily crossed from one side to the other in either direction. Immigrants from Mexico, though, maintained a greater degree of cultural continuity with their native land than immigrants who came from overseas. First, they were migrating to a place that was not only contiguous with their country, but even used to be part of it. When they crossed the border, they came to a familiar landscape, populated by many people with whom they held a common language and culture. Though foreign in name, life in the United States was in some respects just an extension of home—particularly for those whose families spanned the line. In addition, because travel by land was less expensive and less time consuming than steamship voyages, it was easy to come and go, crossing both ways in migratory cycles according to need. Consequently, the barrios in border states and territories enjoyed a kind of binational dialogue with Mexico that would have been unachievable between the residents of Illinois and Italy. Barrio life brought Mexican nationals and Mexican Americans together in a continuous exchange between citizen and noncitizen, native born and immigrant.

What tensions may have existed among them were eased by the strong sense of ethnic solidarity manifest in various mutual aid societies or *mutualistas*. Like ethnic mutual aid societies elsewhere, Mexican mutualistas sponsored cultural events, provided life insurance and other services for dues-paying members, and served as an organizational base when the interests of the ethnicity as a whole had to be defended. In Tucson, for instance, the Alianza Hispano-Americana formed in 1894 partly to counter the establishment of nativist organizations in town that same year (Sheridan 108–11). Another mutualista, the Liga Protectora Latina, was founded in Phoenix in 1914 and began a Tucson branch in 1916 (Sheridan 170). When the Arizona legislature considered a ban on the employment of non-English-speakers in hazardous occupations, the Liga recognized it as a cloaked attempt to prevent Mexicans from getting mining jobs, and contributed to its defeat. After the United States entered World War I, the Liga simultaneously urged Mexican Americans to enlist and offered legal assistance to protect Mexican nationals from illegal conscription (Sheridan 170–72). The Alianza, the Liga, and other mutualistas were not specifically devoted to immigrants as such, but their programs for coethnics regardless of citizenship status mark early stirrings of immigrant advocacy in Tucson's barrios.

Meanwhile, changes were underway on Capitol Hill that would eventually shift more attention and controversy to the border. At the end of World War I, momentum built for imposing numerical limits on immigration for the first time in US history. As a result, Congress approved temporary caps in 1921, and then extended them indefinitely through the Johnson-Reed Immigration Act of 1924. Limits on immigration were, to be sure, a major victory for restrictionists. But they were likewise a major victory for nativists, whose goal was not just to reduce immigration, but specific kinds of it. Nativists held that only Protestant Anglo-Saxons had sufficient intelligence and moral fortitude to run the United States, and noted with great concern the rise in immigration among Catholics, Jews, and various European nationalities they thought unintelligent, unassimilable, or politically subversive. More than merely an irritant, the arrival of these despised populations posed a threat to survival in which, as one of the Johnson-Reed bill's cosponsors put it, "our capacity to maintain our cherished institutions stands diluted by a stream of alien blood" (qtd. in Daniels 283). As a prophylactic measure, then, Johnson-Reed based quotas on national origin, which were contrived so as to minimize admissions from countries in eastern and southeastern Europe, where many of the objectionable immigrants came from.

Yet this sweeping legislation, carefully calculated to exclude presumed inferiors, did not apply to Mexicans, even though nativists had long defamed Mexico for its Catholicism and history of European-indigenous miscegenation. By the 1920s, periodic worker migrations from Mexico had become so routine that western and southwestern business interests, particularly in agriculture, argued they were integral to the economic survival of the region. Growers therefore pushed for a bill that would preserve transborder employment fixes, believing that the seasonal nature of the work was a disincentive for workers to move with their families and put down roots (Ngai 50, 95). Congressional action in Johnson-Reed, though shaped by multiple factors, eventually delivered what the grower lobby wanted by making the Western Hemisphere exempt from the admissions quotas.

The subtext and practical consequence of Johnson-Reed, then, was a major reconstruction of the relationships between immigration, labor, and citizenship in the national imagination. By capping admissions from Europe and elsewhere, the bill greatly reduced the number of immigrants who naturalized. Meanwhile, the exemption of the Western Hemisphere from numerical limits was partly legitimized by the enticing prospect of tapping foreigners who would toil for low wages without seeking to become part of the national community. The position had been candidly staked out as early as 1911, in a Senate commission report that declared, "the Mexican . . . is less desirable as a citizen than as a laborer" (qtd. in Calavita, "U.S. Immigration" 58). In short, as of 1924, US border policy was explicitly based on utilizing people in the Americas as workers without offending the hegemonic bias toward a white-dominated citizenry (Calavita *U.S. Immigration Law*; Ngai)—a poetic condensation of the country's Janus-faced take on the value of immigrants. By the time Congress placed limits on immigration from the Western Hemisphere through the 1965 Hart-Cellar

Act, the Southwest had completed its transformation from a dangerous, sparsely inhabited frontier to a center of commerce, industry, and tourism. Much of that transformation had been enabled by transnational Mexican labor. If, by the familiar phrase, the United States may be thought of as a nation of immigrants, the Greater Southwest, from Texas cotton fields to California fruit orchards, should be thought of as a region of migrants.

Federal enforcement of the border remained thin through the first decade of the twentieth century, but gradually increased, reflecting a shift from treating immigration as an economic issue to treating it as one of law enforcement. Congress first endeavored to make immigration policy more coherent and comprehensive by establishing the Bureau of Immigration in 1891 (United States. U.S. Immigration and Naturalization Service 5). The bureau spent a total of nearly fifty years in first the Department of the Treasury and then the Department of Commerce and Labor, and was renamed the Immigration and Naturalization Service (INS) before being moved to the Department of Justice in 1940 (United States. Office of Policy and Planning, U.S. Immigration and Naturalization Service 7).[2] Two days after granting a gateway function to the southern border with the passage of Johnson-Reed, Congress created the Border Patrol under the Bureau of Immigration to police that gateway. Even during the period when immigration from Mexico was unaffected by quotas, border crossings were regulated with miscellaneous requirements which, if bypassed, could make one an "illegal alien" (Nevins 27; Ngai 65–71), and part of the new agency's mission was to detain and deport people unlawfully present in the United States (Nevins 28–31). Whatever appearance of order may have resulted, however, did not end the phenomenon of undocumented people, "whose inclusion within the nation was simultaneously a social reality and a legal impossibility" (Ngai 4) that increasingly inflamed immigration debate in the decades ahead.

## The Postwar Surge of Immigrant Advocacy

Although immigrant advocates pushed against the restrictionist surge that triumphed with Johnson-Reed,[3] only after World War II did the movement successfully assert itself on the national stage, finding prominent institutional champions and rolling back some of the anti-immigrant sentiment of a decade before.

Following the war, popular and official resolve to create a more cooperative world faced an immediate test in the form of European refugees.

The peace that came to Europe in 1945 found thousands of "displaced persons" or "DPs" in camps maintained by Allied forces and an array of international relief agencies (Genizi 19–22; Loescher and Scanlan 3–9). Prevailing trends offered little reason to think that the DPs' plight would inspire much sympathy in the United States, but an undaunted coalition of secular and religious groups quickly set themselves to the task of enacting federal legislation that would bring a portion of Europe's refugees to US shores. Spearheading the efforts was the Citizens Committee on Displaced Persons (CCDP), which formed in 1947 and included among its endorsers the Federal Council of Churches, the National Catholic Welfare Conference, the governing bodies of many mainline denominations, and dozens of labor, civic, and immigrant advocacy organizations (Newman 746–49).[4]

DP advocates noted the need for the United States to be an exemplar for other countries in a changed and changing geopolitical scene. The nation's size and wealth, they said, required it to participate in global reconstruction by admitting its "fair share" of displaced persons.[5] Faith-based advocates regularly made this argument in terms of religious duty, pleading their case on scriptural grounds. One of the most widely used passages employed in support of welcoming refugees was Leviticus 19:33–34: "When an alien resides with you in your land, you shall not oppress the alien. The alien who resides with you shall be to you as the citizen among you; you shall love the alien as yourself, for you were aliens in the land of Egypt: I am the Lord your God" (RSV). Christians supplemented passages from the Pentateuch with the parable of the Good Samaritan (discussed in chapter 1) and Matthew 25:35–40:

> "For I was hungry and you gave me food, I was thirsty and you gave me something to drink, I was a stranger and you welcomed me, I was naked and you gave me clothing, I was sick and you took care of me, I was in prison and you visited me." Then the righteous will answer him, "Lord, when was it that we saw you hungry and gave you food, or thirsty and gave you something to drink? And when was it that we saw you a stranger and welcomed you, or naked and gave you clothing? And when was it that we saw you sick or in prison and visited you?" And the king will answer them, "Truly I tell you, just as you did it to one of the least of these who are members of my family, you did it to me." (RSV)

DP advocates used these scriptural injunctions to love the alien and welcome the stranger, respectively, to define their work as providing hospitality to outsiders in need.[6]

Assuming a vanguard role on DPs also had strategic value for the United States in light of the perceived ambitions of the USSR. Many DPs feared repatriation to Soviet or Soviet-influenced lands, and historian Haim Genizi has argued that casting the refugees as political and religious martyrs in the struggle against communism proved to be the tipping point for organizations otherwise reluctant to modify immigration policy (Genizi 74–75).

What began as an uphill battle ended in success when Congress passed legislation permitting the arrival of select DPs in 1948, and then again, in revised form, two years later. The logistics of refugee resettlement involved a division of labor between the government and the private sector. While the State Department screened and approved refugees, churches and other organizations known as "voluntary agencies" sought out sponsors who could guarantee new arrivals adequate housing and employment. Once sponsors had been found, the government awarded DPs passage overseas to their new homes in the United States (Genizi 114–20; Loescher and Scanlan 58–59).

The arrangement soon became standard, as the precedent of displaced Europeans prompted the government to act in ensuing refugee crises around the world. Though Congress and the executive branch quibbled for three decades over the legal mechanism for approving refugee admissions, the State Department evaluated applicants according to steadfast but slanted criteria. Over the first half of the twentieth century, refugees had become a distinct class of immigrants, and in 1951 the United Nations' Convention Relating to the Status of Refugees formally defined them as people who had moved outside the jurisdiction of their home country and had "well-founded fear" of persecution if they returned (Gorman and Mihalkanin 174). The convention defined refugees as political victims and distinguished them from emigrants who were motivated only by the pursuit of economic gain. The United States applied these generalities in ways that made refugee policy a propaganda tool in the Cold War, welcoming anyone fleeing a communist country, regardless of motive, under the principle that life under communism was inherently persecutory. These refugees, sometimes referred to as "escapees," were said to be "voting with their feet" by leaving countries that didn't have democratic elections (Loescher and Scanlan). Those fleeing putative allies, on the other hand, were branded "economic" in their motives and refused admission (Genizi 114–20; Loescher and Scanlan 58–59). Hence, the most important waves of refugee admission over the next thirty years involved people leaving countries with communist governments, from Hungarians after 1956 through Cubans and Vietnamese in the 1960s and '70s (Loescher and Scanlan).

Like their cohorts across the country, several Tucson churches took up voluntary agency work in the decades after World War II. Cardinal among them was St. Mark's Presbyterian, which moved into voluntary agency activity through the guidance of its minister, Dave Sholin. Sholin had acquired a sense of the refugee experience in the 1930s, when he and his missionary parents were evacuated from Spain during the country's civil war, and he chose to work in the Southwest specifically because he spoke Spanish and wanted to work in a place where different cultures intersected. St. Mark's resettled Hungarians in 1956, and in 1962 it joined eleven other churches in an ecumenical project to resettle seventy-three Cubans (Kirby).[7]

Flush with success, many groups who rallied for refugee admissions began to tackle other transnational migration issues as well. They weighed in on two major immigration policy reforms, opposing the McCarren-Walter Immigration and Nationality Act Congress passed in 1952 (Genizi 208) and supporting the Hart-Cellar Immigration and Nationality Act approved in 1965 (Ngai 250; Reimers 68). The reign of old-line restrictionism thereby unraveled, replaced by a new framework that used two dichotomies to evaluate the merit of foreigners crossing US borders: immigrants who came in legally and refugees fleeing political repression were worthy, immigrants who came in illegally and refugees seeking financial gain were not.[8] The most telling illustration of the postwar consensus was that many interest groups that supported DP admissions united against the presence of Mexican migrant workers over the same time span. During World War II, Congress had turned to Mexico to relieve the national labor shortage by admitting guest workers through a bilateral accord known as the Bracero Program (a name derived from *brazo*, the Spanish word for arm). But when the program continued beyond the war and into the 1950s, a host of pressure groups rose up in opposition, arguing that the braceros were being grossly mistreated and that their presence impeded efforts to improve conditions for farmworkers who were US citizens (J. Garcia 49, 140–41; Garcia y Griego; Gutierrez 135). Foes of the Bracero Program argued even more vociferously against the use of undocumented workers, who compounded the problem by being even more exploited than Mexicans with papers. They gave partial or complete support when a Border Patrol roundup brazenly called "Operation Wetback" deported thousands of undocumented workers in 1954 (J. Garcia; Gutiérrez 165), and applauded when Congress canceled the Bracero Program ten years later (Gutiérrez 182).

That organizations backing DP resettlement would categorically reject guest workers illustrates that they predicated their advocacy on a high regard for national sovereignty. Yet the rhetoric of proponents with a faith base sometimes hinted at an underlying tension between the moral demands of religion and the juridical logics of the state. In congressional testimony during the debate over DP admissions, for instance, one clergyman argued, "the final decision" on immigration policy "must be made [on] not what a man thinks but what the Almighty God thinks who has proclaimed that all Christians should love their neighbors as themselves. No earthly law can, in the final reckoning, be higher than this law of God, legislating once [and] forever the social and economical relationship of all human beings" (United States. House 538).[9] In the postwar era, then, many religious and secular organizations endorsed a series of selective immigration increases on the premise that the United States was part of a greater community of nation-states and that local action could help tip the global scales of justice. Eventually, however, they began to reflect more expansively on the meaning of justice in that community.

## Questions and Protests: Transnational Migrant Advocacy from 1965 to 1980

By the end of the 1960s, a sequence of tumultuous changes in national life was causing immigrant advocacy to chafe against the terms that had sparked its postwar efflorescence. For fifteen years, civil rights activists had forced the country to address how personal and institutional racism denied equality to large sections of the population. But as movement veterans developed an analysis of race as a basis of domestic oppression, they also saw it in the way the United States perpetuated a neocolonial world through sham elections, repression of civil liberties, and military action so that resources could flow from the Third World to the First without interruption.[10] Where dissatisfaction with US policy at home and abroad grew, many came to question the integrity of the country's cultural mainstream overall and sought alternative schools of thought. Together, these trends discredited and even reversed the normative assumption of Euro-American superiority. For dissenters seeking new models of society, the colonized people that Franz Fanon called "the wretched of the earth" merited sympathy for enduring centuries of exploitation, but they were also people with valuable knowledge and admirable character who should be teaching the imperial core instead of being taught by it. Two expressions of this greater regard for the Third World had especially catalytic value for immigrant advocacy. First, Mexican Americans adopted more sympathetic positions toward Mexican nationals in the United States. Second, religious groups working with refugees became disillusioned with government policy and began to denounce it as inconsistent with biblical principles.[11]

For generations, Mexican American activists tended to view Mexican immigrants and some aspects of Mexican culture as drags on the upward mobility of their community. But from the mid-1960s to the mid-1970s, Mexican American social movement activity was invigorated by a wave of new organizations, leaders, strategies, and analyses that called these habitual thought patterns into question. The first of these focused on improving wages and conditions for agricultural workers in the vales of California, a struggle sometimes simply referred to as *la causa* (the cause). Mexican Americans predominated among the farmworkers, and the most famous farmworker leader, César Chávez, determined that the struggle could be successful only if it used political and religious reference points of Mexican culture. But despite foregrounding Mexican ethnicity in their efforts to win a fair share of the nation's prosperity, farmworker organizers, including Chávez, opposed the presence of foreign labor on the grounds that documented and undocumented migrants alike provided growers with a ready pool of strikebreakers (I. Garcia 30–32).

Even as la causa gained ground, some Mexican American activists began to argue that the labor movement had to adopt an international perspective that would include citizen and immigrant workers side by side. The most prominent among these voices was Bert Corona, a giant in Chicano history who had been involved in a succession of Mexican American civil rights and labor campaigns dating back to the 1930s. Drawing undocumented workers into the labor movement was a fairly new and controversial idea, but Corona found a model in the San Diego–based La Hermandad Mexicana Nacional (the Mexican National Brotherhood or HMN), which had been trying to organize Mexican workers regardless of documentation status since the 1950s. In 1968, Corona and HMN cofounder Soledad "Chole" Alatorre (A. Garcia 72) opened an office to provide legal services and political education for undocumented people in Los Angeles. Known as the Centro de Acción Social Autónomo (the Center for Autonomous Social Action, or CASA), the program spawned multiple chapters in Southern California, the Southwest, and elsewhere (A. Garcia; M. Garcia).[12]

An outlier position in the late 1960s, arguing on behalf of undocumented workers increased in popularity among Mexican American civic groups within just a few years. One reason for this was the Chicano movement, a Mexican American baby-boomer insurgency that rejected assimilation-ism as a means to social equality and sought to reclaim Mexican heritage as a source of pride and strength. The other was that starting in the early 1970s, media outlets and politicians began to sound alarms that rampant illegal immigration was to blame for sundry social ills. Bristling at the re-alization that anti-immigrant sentiment would inflame prejudice against native-born and naturalized citizens who appeared Mexican or had Span-ish names, veteran and upstart Mexican American groups began to fight anti-immigrant attitudes and legislation (Gutiérrez 152–205).

In Tucson, immigration law and border enforcement became new spheres of political struggle at a social service agency called the Manzo Area Council, which dated to the creation of the Office of Economic Op-portunity (OEO) in 1964 as part of the War on Poverty. The OEO imple-mented a program of community centers overseen by boards composed in part of area residents and empowered to establish their own programs so as to maximize responsiveness to local needs. Tucson had several centers in the OEO program, but Manzo, serving the overwhelmingly poor and Hispanic west-side barrios of El Rio and Hollywood, became the most famous.

In 1972, Manzo hired a new director, Margo Cowan. A native Tucso-nan, Cowan had just returned from Southern California, where she had spent the last three years, first with VISTA and then as an organizer for the United Farm Workers (Monroe).

As control of the border with Mexico became a more potent political issue and the legality of one's residence and employment became more salient characteristics of one's identity, Manzo's charge to be responsive to the needs of its population meant confronting the consequences of tight-ened immigration restrictions. People started coming to Manzo for help filling out visa applications, or answering questions about eligibility for citizenship and legal residency, and by 1975, Manzo had begun providing these forms of assistance. Cowan and other Manzo workers believed they were simply filling a need in the neighborhood that they were supposed to serve, but immigration authorities thought otherwise. On April 9, 1976, federal agents raided the Manzo Area Council office and confiscated ten boxes of case files pertaining to immigration counseling.[13] US attorneys said the objective of the raid was to acquire evidence for a grand jury inves-tigation as to whether Manzo employees were providing illegal forms of as-sistance to undocumented immigrants (Rawlinson), but the Border Patrol also used the files to locate and deport Manzo clients who were seeking to legalize their status (Donovan, "Agents Using"). That fall, four Manzo employees, including Cowan, were indicted on twenty-five charges of violating immigration law. However, in an ironic twist, the charges were dismissed the following year ("All Manzo Counts"), and Manzo soon won a federal contract to perform the very services that had brought them under criminal charges (Donovan, "Once Indicted").

Meanwhile, voluntary agencies working with refugees were beginning to push for policies based on human rights standards over Cold War propaganda value. The first flash point in this regard involved civilian populations displaced within South Vietnam. The US government had been at least partially funding a variety of religion-based relief efforts in the country since the late 1950s, but as the war escalated, many agency volunteers were moved to speak on behalf of a humanitarianism that was not beholden to the state. By the end of the 1960s, members of refugee assistance groups were openly criticizing US conduct, particularly the absurdity of offering aid to people who had been ejected from their homes by US forces so that vast areas of the countryside could be carpet bombed (Nichols 101–107).[14]

Shortly thereafter, a second flare-up arose at home over contrasts in the reception given to Haitian and Cuban émigrés. During the 1960s and early '70s, US officials regularly bent or ignored immigration law to accommodate Cubans, but took an altogether different stance toward people leaving Haiti. Despite widespread human rights abuses by the Haitian government, Haiti's strategic value as a US ally made official recognition of such persecution a political embarrassment. Therefore, the State Department and INS pronounced most Haitians economic refugees and ineligible for asylum status. The United States established no special admissions or resettlement programs for them and in many cases simply had them deported. The double standard confounded and outraged those who worked with Haitians, including church groups in southeast Florida who criticized the fairness and even legality of the policies at congressional hearings in 1975 and 1976 (Loescher and Scanlan 68–84). In 1968, they observed, the US Senate had ratified the 1967 United Nations Protocol Relating to the Status of Refugees, which obliged the United States not to repatriate any refugee whose "life or freedom would be threatened on account of his race, religion, nationality, membership in a particular group or political opinion" (qtd. in Loescher and Scanlan 84). Deporting Haitians, therefore, violated US and international law.

Though separated by half the globe, US citizens confronting dislocated populations from Vietnam and Haiti were upending the assumptions that had framed immigrant advocacy work since World War II. As one scholar puts it, voluntary agencies "came to see their function as compensating for government policies rather than complementing them. The most important new idea underlying this shift was that the United States *created* refugee flows" (Nichols 105, emphasis in original). Refugee advocates thereupon started petitioning the government to adopt policies based on human rights criteria alone, regardless of whether they caused embarrassment or conflicted with other geopolitical objectives.

The drive for a more evenhanded admissions procedure also put a new spin on a familiar form of immigrant advocacy in Tucson—refugee sponsorship at St. Mark's Presbyterian Church. In 1973, Chile's president, Salvador Allende, was overthrown in a US-backed military coup and replaced by a military junta. In the days and months that followed, Allende supporters around the country were arrested and detained; thousands were tortured and hundreds were killed. International organizations negotiated with the dictatorship and arranged to resettle some of the regime's political prisoners as refugees, but US officials were unsympathetic to Allende backers and lent only lukewarm support to the effort. St. Mark's pastor Dave Sholin and his friend Gary MacEóin, a Catholic Latin Americanist, had both visited Chile during the Allende presidency and took a keen interest in the unfolding situation.[15] When the United States bowed to pressure and began to accept a small number of Chileans in October 1975, they quickly enlisted St. Mark's in the resettlement program. "We were trying to help people who were really in trouble on both sides of the aisle," says Sholin, "but primarily our church has always been a pretty progressive one. And consequently we took on jobs that some other churches wouldn't." In doing so, the church demonstrated a commitment to working with refugees regardless of where they stood in relation to Cold War binarisms.

Despite obvious differences between resettling political refugees and providing legal services for undocumented immigrants, Tucsonans in both of these projects interfaced and collaborated throughout the 1970s. Clergy in Tucson's barrios, most notably Redemptorist priest Richard "Ricardo" Elford and Reverend John Fife of Southside Presbyterian Church, lent their support to the epoch's proliferation of Mexican American activism (Crittenden 9–10; Otter and Pine 15, 23). The Presbytery de Cristo, a Presbyterian Church administrative subdivision that included Southside and St. Mark's, donated money to a Manzo defense fund after the 1976 raid ("Parish News"), and when Manzo lost its federal funding in 1978 (Donovan, "Board Cuts"), local supporters, including various churches, took up the slack. The relationships between la causa, Chicanismo, barrio activism, and church-based refugee resettlement projects were beneficial in their own right, but also built the nucleus for a social movement that eventually put Tucson immigrant advocacy in the spotlight of national media as well as the crosshairs of an undercover government operation.

## Central American Refugee Advocacy

In 1978 and 1979, Manzo began to see a new group of people among their clients: refugees from Central America seeking political asylum. Armed conflicts in Central America had become a focal point for US policies carried out under the rhetorical banner of anticommunism, and the escalation of violence in following years uprooted a multitude of refugees—first Salvadorans, then Guatemalans as well—seeking relief anywhere they could find it. They fled, at the very least, from the ravages of civil war, but also from the threat of persecution ranging from imprisonment and torture to assassination. Yet they were different from the range of refugees sanctioned by US authorities in two crucial respects. First, most Central Americans, like the Chileans admitted a few years earlier, were seeking haven in the United States even as the United States politically and militarily supported the regimes that they were trying to escape from. In line with the State Department's conventional bias of evaluating eligibility for political asylum through the lens of anticommunism, witnesses to the realities of death squads and torture were liabilities, not assets, for US foreign policy. This meant that Salvadorans and Guatemalans could not leave their countries by applying for asylum through the US embassy in their respective countries. Therefore, they were further differentiated from other refugee groups in that they chose to enter the United States illegally, crossing the border more or less by the same routes as immigrants who were looking for work.

The influx of Central Americans did not initially generate much attention or public interest, but it entered national consciousness in horrifying fashion in 1980, when a haggard group of Salvadorans was discovered on the Fourth of July in the parched and rugged landscape of Arizona's Organ Pipe Cactus National Monument. They were members of a larger group of Salvadorans who had entered the United States illegally with the help of Mexican smugglers.[16] Quickly worn down by heat exhaustion and thirst, they were then abandoned by smugglers; of the original, twenty-some cohort, half perished. The survivors were hospitalized, placed under arrest, and slated for deportation upon recovery.

When it became apparent that the Salvadorans were political refugees with every reason to fear forcible return to their homeland, Sholin and MacEóin at St. Mark's recruited churches and other donors to secure the survivors at least a temporary reprieve by bailing them out.[17] The next year, however, Manzo immigration counselors discovered hundreds of Salvadorans being kept at the INS detention center in El Centro, California. Clearly, the problem was much bigger than the incident in Organ Pipe. At El Centro, Salvadorans seeking political asylum were processed just like other illegal crossers and encouraged to participate in "voluntary departure," a procedure in which detainees waive their right to a legal hearing and consent to deportation. Unaware that they had any other options, Salvadorans were signing off and ending up back in the country where their lives were endangered. Manzo representatives Margo Cowan and Lupe Castillo took the news about El Centro to the Tucson Ecumenical Council (TEC), an organization of mainline churches that included several friends of Manzo, and formed a loose alliance for Central American refugee advocacy.

Convinced that the refugees had unimpeachable claims to asylum, Manzo-TEC participants initially devoted themselves to the single strategy of getting those claims a judicial hearing.[18] But the second half of 1981 saw the emergence of a parallel strategy called the Sanctuary movement that became the most famous of all endeavors on behalf of Central American refugees.[19] The philosophical architect of Sanctuary was Jim Corbett, a Harvard-educated Quaker who had spent several years herding goats and writing on a small property just outside of Tucson. In May, Corbett had tried to help a Salvadoran migrant and discovered on his own that the INS detention system permitted an untold number of refugees to be apprehended and deported before anyone could file an asylum claim on their behalf. Convinced that refugees stood a better chance of survival if they could be kept out of the legal system entirely, he began sheltering them on his land that summer. When he became acquainted with the Manzo-TEC members in Tucson, his one-man operation set off discussion about the merits of providing refugees with "sanctuaries" that would shield them from detection. Beneficiaries would get cover for more long-term settlement, and could also help counter the government's misinformation on Central America by sharing their personal stories with communities across the country.

The TEC endorsed the plan, as did several religious institutions, including Southside Presbyterian Church, where John Fife was in his twelfth year as head pastor. Fife had played a relatively minor role in the

Organ Pipe bailout,[20] but as he deepened his consciousness about the situation in Central America, he felt moved to make a greater commitment to refugee relief efforts. He took his concerns to Southside's governing board of elders, and in October 1981, the church voted to begin sheltering undocumented Central Americans—literally inside the sanctuary. And so, through a cross-country system of conductors and way stations that some described as the new Underground Railroad,[21] volunteers in Tucson assisted Salvadorans and, later, Guatemalans, to enter the country illegally and find safety farther north.

In sync with allies elsewhere,[22] Tucson Sanctuary went public via a news conference that was, if not quite ritual, at least theater. Scheduled to coincide with the second anniversary of the assassination of the Salvadoran archbishop Oscar Romero on March 24, 1982, the conference was held at a long table set up beneath a large Celtic cross hanging over Southside's front doors. Behind the table were two banners in Spanish; one read, *Este es el sanctuario de dios para los oprimidos de Centro America* (This is the sanctuary of God for the oppressed of Central America), the other, *La Migra no Profana el Sanctuario* ([INS], Don't Profane the Sanctuary). Fife sat at the center of the table, with Gary MacEóin and Jim Corbett to his left. Ricardo Elford was two seats to his right, and between them sat Alfredo, a Salvadoran refugee, who wore a cowboy hat and bandana to conceal his identity. A row of people behind them included two other refugees and Dave Sholin (Crittenden 72; Otter and Pine 49).

To begin, Fife read aloud a letter that had been sent the day before to the US attorney general, William French Smith.[23] The letter's opening paragraph declared an intention to "publicly violate" US immigration statutes, but it also argued that the government itself was engaging in illegal activity by deporting asylum seekers.[24] If, as Sanctuary backers argued, the State Department was still using an anticommunist ideology to filter admissions, then refugee advocates were upholding the law and the government was breaking it.

The justification of Sanctuary on secular, legalistic grounds was only a preamble to the more audacious claim that participants had a "God-given right" to aid those in need and that doing so was "obedience to God." That is, in addition to holding the high ground juridically, Sanctuary claimed the high ground morally as well. Like the Declaration of Independence, with its reference to a "Creator" who endows us with "inalienable rights," the authors located the source of their legitimacy in something more eternal than federal codes and cast themselves not as rebels, but as faithful servants of transcendent wisdom.

The legitimation of Sanctuary eventually had its fullest and most formal elaboration in Jim Corbett's concept of "civil initiative." Though deeply concerned with the human propensity for selfishness, Corbett also regarded humans as capable of establishing concordant relations with each other, the natural world, and the divine. He thus had a profound respect for the principle of law, the primal form of which he located in "society-forming right," not "government-made statutes" (100). While codified governance serves to approximate the will for good, Corbett argued that "'[l]aws' . . . are chronically in need of interpretation, testing, and adjudication." Hence "*a* law is not *the* law" (100), and state policies sometimes violate principles intrinsic to the civil bond, driving a wedge between the conscientious subject's desire to share the benefits of social order while conforming to the desiderata of human mutuality. Detecting the potential for chaos and unbridled individualism in the term "civil disobedience," which framed the subject's response in terms of transgression, Corbett offered instead the idea of civil initiative, which would be carried out by subsocietal groups covenanted to each other and committed to discerning the primal sense of right. By so covenanting, consistent with the original collective bond from which earthly authority springs, it was possible to "disobey the government from within the enforced social order in a way that supports the rule of law" (101). By Corbett's reckoning, Sanctuary as civil initiative actually perpetuated the proper functioning of society, whereas the US government ruptured it.

What made civil initiative especially provocative in the case of Central American refugees was that by challenging the validity of immigration procedures, it also challenged the state's prerogative to regulate its territorial boundaries in any way that it wished. Sanctuary backers had weighed their understanding of scripture against the onus of enforcing border policy, and found the latter wanting. At a 1985 Sanctuary symposium, biblical scholar Davie Napier observed that God gave instructions to welcome strangers without any evaluation as to the legality of their arrival: "The Hebrew term for the alien, the sojourner . . . is *ger*. . . . There is no suggestion of concern about how and why the ger is among us, no interest in differentiation by preresidence background. There is nowhere any suggestion of propriety of presence, that is, 'documentation'" (36). Corbett, in particular, pursued these implications until they resounded with millennial prophecy. At this stage in human history, he wrote, there is a pressing challenge to institute "an international society based on human rights" (108), and, reminding his readers that a root of "religion" is the Latin *religio*—"to bind together"—declared that local covenanted communities represented a new paradigm for global order that could "bring Leviathan to maturity" (111). The "transnational *religio*," as he dubbed it, would be interfaith, "united by no creed or ritual but by a shared covenant to honor and protect basic human rights" (113). Because it would practice hospitality regardless of whether a person has entered a territory legally, such a "church"—Corbett himself used the term with scare quotes—"decisively rejects the sovereignty of the nation-state" (114).

The declaration of Sanctuary at Southside was only the first of many efforts to enact through collective representation what Corbett later put into words. Anthropologist Susan Bibler Coutin, who did fieldwork among Sanctuary groups in Tucson and the San Francisco Bay Area, found that movement rituals usually involved modifying the "slots" of existing religious liturgies with material tailored to the context (204). That is, the participants adapted time-honored practices to new circumstances, bridging past and present within traditions, but also bridging differences across traditions. Three features of the political imagination of Sanctuary are especially notable in these rites. First, since participants came from different religious backgrounds, the gatherings resembled ecumenical collages, combining and affirming practices across the spectrum of Jewish and Christian worship. Second, participants acknowledged the transnational character of the work and their location in the borderlands by conducting portions of the liturgies in Spanish and incorporating references to social movement activity in Guatemala and El Salvador. The most ubiquitous of these was a call-and-response sequence borrowed from Central American protests in which a speaker recites the names of martyrs and the crowd cries, "¡Presente!" meaning that the dead are still "present" in the movement's work.

As acts of remembrance, the "¡Presente!" cries also contributed to the third marker of Sanctuary's political imagination, which was the creation of a sacred, sacrificial history. The liturgies, for instance, included readings from and in honor of such figures as Archbishop Romero, Anne Frank, and Martin Luther King, Jr. Though apparently a mishmash of times and places, the international pantheon implied an underlying thematic unity among people who faced political oppression, refused violence, and lived and died for their faith. At other times, Sanctuary participants used public displays of burial markers and coffins to symbolize the many thousands of people killed in Central America (Coutin 201–13). Crucially, these evocations of suffering and martyrdom did not single out any institution as a problem, nor elevate any existing one as an answer. They did, however, encourage their audiences to spare some measure of affect for the victims, and create, in doing so, an imagined sacrificial history that exceeded nation-state boundaries.

A few years into Sanctuary, Tucsonans augmented their repertoire of symbolic rhetoric by publicly transporting refugees in caravans. The caravans began as part of a Freedom Seder in which participants gathered at Southside, then drove in a two-mile long procession to Temple Emmanu-El, a Reformed synagogue whose rabbi, Joseph Weizenbaum, had supported Sanctuary from the start. At the temple, they partook in a version of the Jewish Passover meal that involved refugees from El Salvador, Guatemala, Eastern Europe, and the Soviet Union. Together, the caravan and the Freedom Seder reenacted the mythic archetype of the Exodus, the flight from Egypt, which had also figured prominently in the history of national independence and African American liberation. A second version performed the caravan over a longer distance, when a fleet of vehicles decorated with Sanctuary signs and Statue of Liberty imagery delivered a Guatemalan family from Tucson to Seattle (Cunningham, *God and Caesar* 232; Otter and Pine 103–104).

Though slow to react, in May 1984, the INS commenced an undercover operation that infiltrated the Tucson Sanctuary for the purposes of prosecuting and convicting participants. In January the following year, the investigation brought down indictments on a handful of people in Nogales and Tucson, including Fife. Given the breadth of Sanctuary activities, the indictments were necessarily selective, but officials hoped to make an example of the few to intimidate the many, and thereby crush the movement. In May 1986, after a seven-month trial in which the defense was prohibited from introducing arguments based on religion or refugee law, the jury delivered several convictions on charges of smuggling immigrants. Six of the defendants, including Fife, were sentenced to five years' probation. Two received three years' probation (Crittenden 336–38). Instead of cowing the Sanctuary movement, however, the trial actually spurred its growth. From the initial arrests of Tucson Sanctuary participants in 1985 through the conviction of several defendants in 1986, the number of religious institutions affiliated with the movement doubled (Cunningham, *God and Caesar* 62–64; MacEóin, "A Brief History" 25–28) and the network continued to function across the country until the end of the decade, when a decline in refugee arrivals and changes in US asylum law brought its reason for being to a close.[25]

# Conclusion

Immigrant advocacy took shape in Tucson following World War II, generally along the same lines of operation and philosophy as peer efforts across the country. Still, the notoriety of Sanctuary calls attention to Tucson as a site that exemplifies a crucial transformation in the way that some immigrant advocates thought about sovereignty and the state. At the time of the DP admission campaign in the late 1940s, if a population of worthy refugees was excluded from emigrating to the United States per US law, advocates waited to take action until policy reforms made that population eligible. In the 1970s, though, advocates began to argue that unauthorized entry by refugees could be legitimate and that working with such entrants was legitimate as well. Holding out that the government could make amends and do the right thing, activists simultaneously pressed for change within the system,[26] but churches and other religious institutions were not going to wait for permission to do justice. In short, they became more skeptical about the benevolence of government agencies, more willing to criticize immigration policy as a whole, and more committed to work on behalf of people regardless of the "legality" of their arrival.

On the surface, Sanctuary conservatively left intact the distinction between worthy political refugees and unworthy economic refugees and merely asserted that the rule be applied more evenly. But Sanctuary work also destabilized that dichotomy by spurring many participants to link human rights violations to disparities in wealth. Though some undocumented Central Americans were simply fleeing the indiscriminate havoc of war, others had been marked for death because of their involvement in unionization, peasant organizing, and other activities aimed at improving the lives of the poor. Even if few Sanctuary volunteers ever carried out movement work in El Salvador and Guatemala, the logistics of transporting newly arrived refugees familiarized many supporters and sympathizers with the US-Mexico border, which Gloria Anzaldúa famously described as "where the Third World grates against the First World and bleeds" (3). Northern Mexico metonymically suggested the poverty of Latin America as a whole, and elevated volunteers' consciousness about being at the top of a hemispheric hierarchy in which the United States dominated its southern neighbors militarily and financially (Coutin 61–62; Cunningham, "Transnational Social Movements" 187). Consequently, they began to critique the attitudes and assumptions tied to standards of living in the United States and diagnosed the root cause of migration in terms of economics, not violence. At the 1985 symposium, Episcopal priest Philip Wheaton ventured that the real crisis underlying Sanctuary was "not refugees and not dictators and not democracies but the maintenance of an economic order in which we Americans consume most of the wealth and the resources of this planet" (47). The terror of Central America revealed what that "maintenance" consisted of. Human rights are nothing if not means by which people may seek to improve their lives. But when the improvement of the disadvantaged threatens the luxury of the privileged, the violation of *political* human rights can serve to crush the realization of *economic* human rights.

Sanctuary furthered the idea that hospitality could and should extend to people who had entered the country illegally. Even if the movement was procedurally restricted to fugitives from politically motivated violence, the premise that there were moral obligations above and beyond regulation of national boundaries also opened up space to question the axiomatic exclusion of migrants motivated by economic necessity. Many participants began to see migrants as having been displaced by the violence and economic policies used to maintain a geopolitical order favorable to the enrichment of the United States. These issues lingered beyond the wars in Central America and became integral to the next stage of transnational migrant activity. For those who came out of Sanctuary with a political consciousness that encompassed the Americas as a whole, the movement's demise brought not a stop but a segue to related points of concern.

INTERSTICE

*All the action is early on. Three busloads before 9:00. After that, noth-ing, really. One arrives, but only three people get off. Three that are actually being deported for the second time that morning.*

*"Being deported twice in the same day and it's not even noon," says an NMD volunteer. "You gotta respect that."*

*"Or not," I say.*

*"I think you do. There's something admirable about persistence."*

—FIELD NOTES FROM THE NMD MARICOPA STATION, 2006

# CHAPTER FOUR

# Immigrant Advocacy in Tucson Responds to the Gatekeeper Complex

Assisting Central American refugees evade torturers and assassins in their homelands, the diverse strains of immigrant advocacy in Tucson built one of the most impactful campaigns for social change of the 1980s. What were originally fledgling and improvised responses to a crisis cohered and grew into a movement characterized by inspiring leadership, a committed rank and file, and a set of beliefs, terms, and actions flexible enough to accommodate both religious and secular constituents. Moreover, the movement was effective, for it transformed the lives of refugees and government policy.

The movement also transformed the worldviews of the participants, not so much by grand design as by the need to understand the logic and practice of border enforcement. As activists applied their values to this somewhat arcane realm, they developed and sharpened a robust contrarian critique of two assumptions at the foundation of US immigration policy. First and foremost, the inability of Central Americans to win asylum through official channels undid the principle that illegal entry and illegal entrants were inherently bad. Less obviously, but just as importantly, recognizing that poverty was at the root of the wars in Central America challenged the easy distinction between "political" and "economic" refugees. By proposing that human rights and biblical mandates of hospitality trumped state decrees, they were reimagining community in postnational terms.

This critique primed advocates for Central American refugees to lift their work outside a paradigm of political asylum and attempt a more comprehensive reckoning with immigration policy that would address undocumented workers. Such a reconfiguration did in fact occur, though not immediately. Rather, the metamorphosis came in reaction to a series of precipitous changes during the interim, in which border enforcement became better funded, more militarized, and reoriented to a deterrence-based strategy. By the late 1990s, these measures were squeezing migrant traffic into southern Arizona, bringing dozens and then hundreds of deaths to a swath of land between Tucson and Mexico.

Tucson immigrant advocates have responded to these developments by creating organizations whose practices are at once new and deeply rooted in local and national precedents. These organizations differ in their approaches, which include documentation of human rights abuses, legislative lobbying, public education, and the provision of direct material aid to migrants in the course of their journey. But they share the conviction that migrant casualties in the desert condemn US border policy as a catastrophic failure and that there must be an extensive campaign to promote the dignity and legal standing of migrants in public consciousness as a step toward ending the death toll. In the ongoing dynamic of Tucson immigrant advocacy at the turn of the twenty-first century, participants put values into action, changing and being changed by the greater world as they reimagine and practice the community that Jim Corbett called a transnational *religio*.

## Responding to IRCA

In the spring of 1986, as the convicted Tucson Sanctuary defendants awaited sentencing, Congress was debating the Immigration Reform and Control Act (IRCA). IRCA was the biggest federal immigration reform package in a generation, and the first to specifically target illegal immigration from Mexico. Among IRCA's noteworthy components was an amnesty under which undocumented people in the United States could obtain citizenship,[1] but the political price of the amnesty provision was a budget hike for the INS and Border Patrol to please ardent restrictionists (Massey, Durand, and Malone 49). The infusion of monies enabled the agencies to amplify trends in place since the Carter administration by militarizing their operations with high-tech equipment and collaborative ties with the armed forces (Dunn, *Militarization*). As funding for border enforcement crept upward at the decade's end, persistent references by many media outlets and public figures to "illegals" carrying out an "invasion" were joined by the rhetoric of an international "War on Drugs." Amid such martial metaphors, restrictionists began to describe border enforcement as a test of collective will in which illegal immigration from Mexico was not just a matter of job loss, declining wages, or undesirable cultural elements but of national survival.

Prescient observers quickly recognized that the demonization of illegal entrants could lead to abuses of power by government agencies,[2] and the need for checks on state power in the borderlands resulted in a new network of immigrant advocacy that included Tucson. Around the time of IRCA's passage, the prime movers of the Manzo Area Council decided to dissolve the organization and carry out their work under another rubric. One reason for doing this was to alleviate the psychic toll and exhaustion resulting from years of work on political asylum cases.[3] Another, though, was that Manzo stalwarts felt compelled to stop thinking in terms of direct service provision and shift their energy to education and policy advocacy capable of addressing long-term, systemic change. Their starting point was to join a project the American Friends Service Committee (AFSC) had initiated to document human rights violations by US law enforcement in border communities.[4] Through the AFSC project's Tucson chapter, known as Arizona Border Rights Coalition (ABRC), Manzo veterans and others began to advance the goal of making human rights an integral part of immigration policy. In 1992, ABRC began documenting claims of human and civil rights abuse along the border; in 1993 it opened an office and hired a director. It soon became autonomous from AFSC, and the following year it assumed the name Coalición de Derechos Humanos. (In English, the name is "Human Rights Coalition"; the group is more colloquially known as Derechos Humanos or simply Derechos.)

The name indicated not just a new group but also a new, postnational perspective on immigration. Isabel Garcia, a Tucsonan who became involved with Manzo after the 1976 INS raid, recalls,

> We took the name Derechos Humanos because we wanted to be real up front. I don't know if we would need to do that again today, but back then we needed to put it up front as the name—"Derechos Humanos"—so we would all begin to think in terms of a human rights framework, versus civil rights. Civil rights are whatever they decide to give you in the legislature. And we believe that human rights are just what they say they are: every human has certain rights.

Derechos put philosophy into practice by continuing to document human rights violations by law enforcement agencies and by conducting "Know

Your Rights" workshops that educated people about what they could do to protect themselves.

But they also directed themselves to raising public consciousness about the root causes of immigration, particularly the "push" factors that compelled people south of the border to leave their homes. In doing so, Derechos assumed a position at the leading edge of social movements in the global North who were beginning to focus on the ways that their governments were recolonizing the Third World through economic policy.[5] Economic imperialism was not new, but the radical form it assumed beginning in the late 1970s marked the ascendance of a particular socioeconomic ideology known as neoliberalism. Based on the premise that human welfare is best served by giving over as much social activity as possible to markets, neoliberalism prescribed easing or eliminating state involvement in all manner of economic activity, whether regulating business, providing social amenities, or inhibiting imports that undercut domestic production. Neoliberal thought penetrated the Third World through two primary vectors. The first vector was loans from the World Bank and the International Monetary Fund (IMF), two institutions established to promote economic development after World War II. In the early 1980s, the World Bank and the IMF began loaning money to developing countries on the condition that those countries apply neoliberal principles like eviscerating government spending on social welfare and selling off public services to corporate interests (Bello 27–28). The other neoliberal battering ram was a variety of multilateral negotiations premised on integrating national economies through "free trade." The most far-reaching of these was the General Agreement on Tariffs and Trade (GATT), which began among a handful of countries in 1947 but steadily drew in more participants and eventually morphed into the World Trade Organization in 1995. In effect, the loans and accords transferred power from nation-states to multilateral institutions, which meant that the more places they impacted, the more they shaped the world order according to a peculiarly neoliberal form of "globalization."[6]

One of neoliberalism's most high-profile staging grounds was Mexico. The process began in the 1980s, when Mexico accepted IMF and World Bank terms in order to receive the loans it wanted in order to pay off its ballooning debt. Then, in 1986, Mexico joined GATT. But the country's neoliberalization accelerated full throttle under Carlos Salinas de Gotari, who was elected president in 1988 in a vote reasonably suspected of being fraudulent. Salinas continued the practice of making concessions to international lenders, even to the point of securing a 1991 World Bank loan by dismantling provisions in the Mexican constitution that ensured land-ownership and livelihood for Mexican farmers. His most audacious move, though, was entering negotiations for a free trade pact with the United States and Canada. Known in English as the North American Free Trade Agreement (NAFTA), the pact required Mexico to eliminate tariffs that protected domestic enterprises—a move that internal studies predicted would result in significant unemployment, hunger, and homelessness. Undeterred, Salinas inked NAFTA in 1992 and saw it take effect on January 1, 1994. By then, the neoliberal globalization of Mexico had been underway for over a decade, with highly unequal results that included a drastic slide in the purchasing power of the minimum wage alongside the creation of twenty-two new Mexican billionaires during Salinas's six-year term alone (Ross 194).

Derechos Humanos took note of these developments and decided they portended a veritable perfect storm on the border, with grievous consequences for the quality of life in both the United States and Mexico. Lupe Castillo, a Manzo veteran and Derechos cofounder, recalls the group deciding that policy change would have to be "a three-way effort: militarization, globalization and immigration reform–that we could not talk about either separate from the other, and that we had to have a holistic approach to these issues, otherwise they would not work."[7] The "holistic approach" marked a concerted effort to challenge the premise that immigrants fleeing poverty were categorically distinct from and less worthy of sympathy than those fleeing political repression. If, in the words of one critic, neocolonialism meant that "direct military force was replaced by the structural force of finance" (Duchrow 35), then the plight of the impoverished was no less unjust than that of people fleeing war.

Shortly after Derechos Humanos began, the already-volatile fray over immigration and border policy was further agitated by events in the United States and Mexico. One touchstone of rising hostility toward undocumented immigrants was Proposition 187, a California ballot initiative aimed at preventing undocumented residents from accessing public benefits like health care and education. The proposition was approved in 1994 by nearly 59 percent of voters, though a federal judge ruled most of it unconstitutional in 1998 and the state declined to appeal. Meanwhile, NAFTA's implementation in Mexico uprooted rural residents and displaced urban workers, and the national economy crashed in December 1995 with a massive devaluation of the peso. To borrow from a remark by refugee policy scholars Gil Loescher and John Scanlan,[8] however, the reception given the deracinated of Mexico and Central America was a stark contrast to that given migrants from Eastern Europe and Cuba in decades past. They were not warmly received as "escapees" from neoliberalism, nor were they praised for "voting with their feet" against privatization and Faustian debt relief deals. With immigration and antagonism toward immigrants both on the rise, the United States began to apply ever more extreme, more punishing border enforcement measures.

## Responding to the Gatekeeper Complex

Budgets for the Immigration and Naturalization Service and Border Patrol doubled from 1986 to 1992 in the wake of IRCA, but the buildup was measly compared to the massive spike that followed (Andreas; Dunn, "Border Enforcement," *Militarization*; Nevins): "by 1998 the INS budget was nearly eight times its 1986 level, and the Border Patrol budget was almost six times its former level" (Massey, Durand, and Malone 97). Amid this financial windfall, the Border Patrol enacted a series of momentous, interrelated changes in enforcement strategy. Since the agency's inception, its efforts had largely been reactive, focusing on the apprehension and deportation of people who had already entered the United States. But after a successful 1993 experiment in El Paso called Operation Blockade (Dunn, *Blockading*), the Border Patrol adopted a new approach based on using deterrence to discourage illegal entry in the first place (Massey, Durand, and Malone 93–95). The first part of the deterrence strategy, "forward deployment," involved massing the agency's new bounty of equipment and personnel in urban areas, which were the preferred sites for most illegal entry because they offered immediate access to infrastructure. When Operation Blockade (later renamed Hold-the-Line) significantly reduced the amount of illegal immigration coming through El Paso (Andreas 92–93), it was duplicated on a larger scale and with more fanfare the following year with Operation Gatekeeper in San Diego and San Ysidro. Next came Operation Safeguard, in Arizona border towns Nogales (1995), Douglas (1999), and Naco (1999). Because the San Diego version of forward deployment and militarization received the most media attention, researchers at the University of Houston's Center for Immigration Research have dubbed the overall strategy "the Gatekeeper Complex" (Eschbach, Hagan, and Rodriguez).

The second component of prevention through deterrence was strategists' calculation that reducing the feasibility of urban crossings would leave long, overland journeys through the wilderness of southern Arizona as the only alternative. Few, they reasoned, would hazard such a risky trip. The terrain is often rocky, which means that one false step can inflict a debilitating sprain or broken limb, and unlucky travelers can also be incapacitated by rattlesnakes or scorpions. But the biggest dangers are climatological—mountain ranges where the temperatures are freezing cold in the winter, and deserts where summer temperatures of 110 degrees can become 170 degrees on the ground itself (Marizco, "When the Deadly"). Within months, though, greater numbers of people seeking to enter the United States outside of legal channels began to venture into the treacherous pale. The fatal consequences are evident in Border Patrol statistics. The Border Patrol recorded twenty-nine deaths in the Tucson Sector for fiscal year 1999, when it began to compile such figures. In 2000, the number climbed to seventy-four, and this only hinted at the extent to which the desert floor would be stricken with fallen migrants in the years to come. There is no way of producing an exact count of the number of people who have died crossing the border. Different groups and agencies have different methods of counting fatalities, and even still, these numbers merely represent the number of bodies found. In all likelihood, there are many decedents who are simply consumed by the desert and never discovered. Estimates based on recovered bodies alone suggest that from 1995 to 2009, over four thousand migrants died making unauthorized entries into the United States.[9] The actual total is undoubtedly higher, but will never be known.

By the end of the decade, as it became clear that migrant traffic was being funneled into southern Arizona, Derechos Humanos began to call attention to the deaths and denounce US border policy as the cause of them. By utilizing the lethal environment of the desert as a deterrent, they argued, the Gatekeeper Complex amounted to a premeditated humanitarian crisis. In June 2000, Derechos organized a mass candlelight vigil as a show of public concern about human rights on the border. Though prompted in part by recent episodes of armed vigilante activity, the event also served as the first large-scale public memorial over migrant deaths—a phenomenon that had been cast in especially stark terms by a newspaper story that appeared the day before the vigil. Entitled "Teen Mom Dies to Save Tot" (Alaimo and Barrios), it told of a group of ten migrants from Oaxaca that included a nineteen-year old woman, Yolanda Gonzalez, and her eighteen-month old daughter, Elizama.[10] Walking through the desert in hundred-degree heat, Gonzalez gave most or all of her water to her daughter instead of drinking it herself. After four days of walking, Gonzalez fell ill and stopped to rest while the rest of the group went on. By the time the others returned with help the next day, Gonzalez was dead. Her daughter was there, too, badly sunburned, but alive due to the sacrifice of her mother.

Derechos called a similar vigil a year later, where the invited speakers included Sanctuary veteran John Fife. Despite (or perhaps because of) his felony conviction for Sanctuary work, Fife had been elected moderator of the Presbyterian Church (USA) for 1992–93, and in 2001 he was marking his thirty-second year pastoring at Southside Presbyterian. As vigil attendees looked on, Fife declared that the United States had "gone from waging a war on poverty to waging a global war on the poor" and that migrant deaths indicated it was past time for people who had been involved in the Sanctuary movement to recognize the current crisis and formulate a response. Indeed, the institutional and interpersonal connections that provided Sanctuary's base had just launched a new "faith-based" organization directed at ameliorating migrant suffering in southern Arizona, and another would shortly follow.

## Humane Borders

As the summer of 2000 approached, several Sanctuary veterans and other interested parties began to contemplate how they could build an organized, sustained way of stemming the rise in migrant deaths. Using Sanctuary churches and participants as an outreach base, organizers called a meeting on Pentecost Sunday, June 11, at the Pima County Friends (i.e., Quaker) Meeting House to discuss what could be done. Though attendees drew inspiration from the erstwhile movement to shelter Central American refugees, they felt its methods weren't suited to address the present crisis. Instead, they turned to an older, ad-hoc tradition in which many southern Arizonans, including some clergy, had provided material aid to migrants en route (S. Carroll). The practice had recently seen more systematic application in Southern California in a private initiative that eventually became known as Water Station. A resident of San Diego, John Hunter, began Water Station when federal fiscal year 1999 saw over sixty migrant deaths in the Border Patrol's El Centro sector. In response, Hunter began placing one-gallon jugs of water in the desert, marking each location with a blue flag so it could be seen from a distance (B. Fox). Participants at the Friends Meeting House gathering decided they would follow in kind, and appointed a steering committee to develop a plan for making water available in the desert.

At the forefront of the steering committee was Robin Hoover, the minister at Tucson's First Christian Church (Disciples of Christ).

Institutionally, First Christian was no stranger to transnational migrant work, for it had been a part of the multichurch sponsorship of Cuban refugees in 1962 and a charter member of Tucson Sanctuary as well. Its history dovetailed with that of Hoover, who, though only recently installed as pastor, brought a wealth of experience from years of immigrant and borderlands work in Texas. As with so many others, Hoover's gateway to border issues had been the situation of Central American refugees, and from successive positions as a pastor in Fort Worth and Lubbock he had galvanized parishioners and ecumenical allies to support refugee shelters in the Lower Rio Grande Valley.[11] First Christian became the center of Humane Borders, providing offices, meeting space, and Hoover as a leading spokesperson in-house.

Humane Borders attracted a great deal of attention from the very start. The group's activities were a hot topic in the local media and beyond, as people discussed their legality and appropriateness and speculated over likely consequences of the operation. Much of the early interest drew comparisons between Humane Borders and Sanctuary (e.g., Goodstein), and certainly there were similarities. Some of the same people were involved, both efforts had aided undocumented entrants, and participants claimed their controversial actions were fully legal. Significantly, though, whereas Sanctuary bypassed the state, Humane Borders engaged with it (Cunningham, "Transnational Social Movements"). Most of the land migrants traveled was public, so Humane Borders built relationships with government agencies to obtain the permits and rights-of-way necessary to deploy the water stations, which modified Hunter's model by utilizing large, refillable barrels that could hold on average fifty-eight gallons. In this way, Humane Borders struck a careful balance between being political insiders and outsiders, cooperating with the government where possible but criticizing it when necessary. The first stations went up in March 2001, with two sites each in Organ Pipe National Monument and Buenos Aires National Wildlife Refuge just south of Tucson. Before summer was over, there were twelve, filled and maintained on a regular basis to offer what Hoover described as "passive assistance."

In the enormousness of the desert, these makeshift oases provided only limited relief, but the need for them was reiterated in May 2001 by the grisly fate of a group of twenty-six Mexican migrants traveling through the Cabeza Prieta National Wildlife Refuge. After one day's journey, the *coyote*[12] guiding the group got lost and said he was going for help, but abandoned them instead. The migrants wandered without water for three days, becoming progressively more disoriented, and fourteen of them died.[13] It was the highest single-day death toll for migrants in Arizona—a dire distinction previously held by the Salvadoran group whose deaths in 1980 sparked the Central American refugee advocacy movement. The fourteen deaths were made all the more agonizing by the fact that Humane Borders had approached the US Fish and Wildlife Service a month before the deaths for permission to put water stations in Cabeza Prieta. The request was denied.[14]

In subsequent years, Humane Borders saw considerable growth, most of it funded by private donations. By summer of 2005 the group had installed over seventy stations, including a dozen in Mexico. Of these, two-thirds on the US side were on private land, and the remaining third were on public land variously administered by the US Fish and Wildlife Service, the Bureau of Land Management, Pima County, and the City of Tucson. The group also spawned a Phoenix chapter, which assumed maintenance of the stations in Organ Pipe. Some water tanks are maintained year-round; others are activated only during the summer months, when need is greatest. The organization also carries out other activities, such as lobbying on immigration policy,[15] sponsoring a trash pickup once a month in locations heavily traveled by migrants, donating materials to migrant shelters on the Mexican side of the border, and distributing maps in Mexico that show where water stations can be found. Its primary and defining mission, however, has continued to be putting water in the desert.

The group's mission statement reads as follows:

> Hundreds of thousands of men, women and children face economic disaster in their homelands and migrate to the United States every year. Many of them come across the US-Mexico border illegally in Arizona. Increasing numbers of them die every year making the attempt. The death toll is the direct result of US border control policy, which ignores the economic forces on both sides of the border driving human beings to make such choices.
>
> Humane Borders, motivated by faith, offers humanitarian assistance to those in need through more than 50 emergency water stations on and near the border. Deployment of water saves lives and invites public discourse: we want to legalize the undocumented migrants now working and living in the United States; create a responsible guest worker program; increase the number of visas for Mexican nationals; demilitarize the border; support economic development in Mexico; provide more federal aid for local medical service providers, law enforcement and adjudication, land owners and managers. Humane Borders invites

federal, state, tribal and county organizations and agencies, as well as individuals, churches and humanitarian groups, to join in and support our life-saving efforts. We welcome all persons of good faith.

As the organization is responsible for upkeep of most stations on public land,[16] the primary hands-on activity for Humane Borders volunteers is water station maintenance. A typical maintenance trip leaves the First Christian Church parking lot at 6:00 a.m. in one of the organization's trucks. [17] The trucks are formidable, specially outfitted for the job with water tanks, electric pumps, a hose capable of stretching from the road to the stations, and a tool kit for minor maintenance jobs. The number of volunteers on a trip varies, but the minimum is a driver who knows the route and has been specifically trained in the technical aspects of checking and refilling the stations. On the outskirts of Tucson, the sights gradually change from strip malls and traffic lights to a sparsely inhabited landscape of desert scrub and saguaro cacti that sometimes bears discarded water jugs and other traces of migrant traffic. The interstate leads to a two-lane highway and then, eventually, a rough, dirt road. In the late summer monsoon season, these roads are broken up from time to time by dirty pools of indeterminate depth, and the driver must take care not to end up getting the vehicle trapped in a muddy slough. Each route has its unique features. "Ironwood," for instance, is so called because it passes through Ironwood National Forest, northwest of Tucson. Not far from one of the five stations on the route is a small shrine in the brush that commemorates a migrant death; it is tended to on a regular basis, but no one knows by whom. Another trip, "Border Road," runs along the US-Mexico border in a segment marked by barbed-wire fence and, in at least one spot, one of the stone obelisks that were for many years the only designations of the international boundary.

Experienced volunteers know where the stations are from memory, but newcomers can try to spot them from a distance by looking for the telltale blue flag that marks every site. On arrival, volunteers inspect the condition of the station. Usually this simply requires checking the water volume and refilling as necessary, along with measuring and adjusting the level of chlorine that is mixed with the water as a safeguard against bacteria. They also pick up trash around the station. Another kind of maintenance involves repairing damage inflicted by the elements or vandals. Flags, for instance, can be knocked down, taken, or simply worn away over time. The trucks are stocked with extra flags, so volunteers can replace one on the spot or note that it should be replaced on a future trip. Sometimes the tank itself has been shot or knifed so thoroughly that it cannot be refilled, in which case the volunteers take the tank back with them and install a new one on the next run.

Unless volunteers ride together on maintenance trips or simply cross paths in the office, their main venue for face-to-face interaction is the organization's weekly meeting at First Christian. The agenda begins with a report on the trips for the week, as participants indicate how much water they pumped at what stations, and whether anything of note happened along the way. After these reports there are announcements, reviews of recent media coverage of the group, and an itemization of work that needs to be done, ranging from equipment repairs to filing paperwork. The meetings are almost exclusively devoted to logistics and procedural questions. In a meeting one December, for instance, the group reviewed its policies over what to do upon encountering migrants who need reprieve from freezing temperatures. Would it be all right, under the circumstances, to put the person inside a vehicle and run the motor so they could warm up? "I'd do it," said one member. "If there's people out there and I've got a warm truck, they're coming in." The organization has no rule against doing so, but Hoover advised the speaker that a federal agent could view the situation differently. "You might end up in the Border Patrol office for eight hours" while the matter was sorted out, he said, to which the member shrugged and said, "Fine." For several years, meetings concluded with a call for final questions or points of business, but by 2007 the last item for every agenda was a "Ritual minute of silence."

Humane Borders members and supporters also gather for two special events on the group's yearly calendar, both of which are held at First Christian. The first of these, an anniversary celebration, happens every summer and features displays, a dinner, and a guest speaker. The second, the Memorial March for Migrants, consists of an afternoon service in the church sanctuary, followed by a procession of walkers or vehicles to a second location for prayer. (The Memorial March is discussed in greater detail in chapter 8.)

Humane Borders interacted with the general public largely by cultivating an extraordinary amount of media coverage. A random selection of media attention over four weeks in November and December 2004 included coverage by a Los Angeles television station, the *Arizona Republic* and *Tucson Citizen* newspapers, the Associated Press, Salt Lake City public television, and the BBC. In most cases, the stories either cover the group's water stations or solicit Hoover's analysis of current border enforcement situations and policy proposals.

*Samaritans*

By spring of 2002, Humane Borders had established several water stations in the desert and was steadily adding more. Yet the number of migrant fatalities continued to rise as well, and some participants and sympathizers were wondering what more could be done to prevent the loss of life in the desert. Once again, people came to the Pima County Friends Meeting House, where they confronted the grim statistic that seventy-eight bodies had been recovered in the Tucson Sector during fiscal year 2001, up from twenty-nine in 2000 (LoMonaco, "No Drop"). With Humane Borders on solid footing, they decided to push the water stations' "passive assistance" to a more proactive exercise of humanitarianism in which volunteers would seek direct, person-to-person contact with migrants en route and provide them with material and medical aid as needed. Though the Border Patrol had begun to conduct search and rescue operations, some immigrant advocates felt it was a capitulation to cede that responsibility entirely to the state. John Fife, who had contributed to the founding of Humane Borders, recalls:

> Our assertion was [that] civilian institutions needed to be out there in terms of the size of this crisis and human tragedy. We couldn't just leave it to the Border Patrol. The Border Patrol by this time had created a real climate of fear in the borderlands, saying, "Leave it to us, call us, we'll take care of migrants in the desert." And what we kept saying was, "No, there is a right to provide humanitarian aid, and the only way to save a significant number of lives is if everyone in the borderlands gets involved in that."

The group would work, then, on at least two levels. One would be the direct provision of lifesaving assistance. The other, more implicit, was that in doing so they would be defending a social opening, demonstrating by example what others could and should do as well. In effect they sought to challenge the government's efforts to monopolize all legitimate interface with migrants in transit and establish the largest possible domain in which humanitarian responsibilities could be legally exercised.

The group called itself the Samaritans, after Jesus's parable (discussed in chapter 1), and extended the legacy of Sanctuary by basing its philosophy and practices on civil initiative. Planners recognized that impromptu interactions with illegal entrants would require all participants to have a clear understanding of what was allowed under the auspices of the organization, so attorneys from the Sanctuary days were called in to help determine with reasonable clarity what kinds of action were permitted by law. Based on this counsel the group devised a code of operations that spelled out what could and could not be done.

After recruiting endorsements from local churches—drawing, again, from those who had been Sanctuary backers[18]—Samaritans sent a letter to the Border Patrol's Tucson Sector chief, David Aguilar. The letter, dated June 27, 2002, declared the group's existence and intention to begin patrols on July 1. Samaritan trips have gone out regularly ever since, sometimes twice daily during the summer months when migrant deaths are more numerous, and fluctuating in accord with volunteer energy over the rest of the year. Efforts originating in Tucson are complemented by an affiliate in Green Valley, a town about twenty miles to the south.

The volunteers formally explain their organization in their mission statement: "Samaritans are people of faith and conscience who want to respond directly, practically, and intimately to the crisis at the US-Mexico border. We come in many ages and sizes and bring diverse faiths, ethnicity [sic], economic strata, political biases, and educational levels to the work. We are united in our desire to relieve suffering among our brothers and sisters and honor human dignity."

Volunteers typically sign up for trips by e-mail or on a calendar that is passed around at meetings, indicating whether they will serve as "M" (medical personnel), "S" (Spanish speaker), or "O" (other assistance). On the day of a patrol, people who signed up meet in the Southside Church parking lot at 6:00 a.m. and load the vehicle with material that is stored in a shed on church property. The supplies and provisions include several cases of bottled water, food packs, new socks, medical supplies for treating blisters, and a satellite phone.

Patrols usually take a series of routes just southwest of Tucson on any public lands along and between Highway 286 to the west and Interstate 19 to the east. Periodically the patrol stops, usually near one of the washes that channel seasonal rains. Participants unload handfuls of food and water from the vehicle, then push back a few branches or edge down a rocky incline and set out on foot. The desert terrain is not lush, but neither is it barren, and the foliage is often dense enough to restrict one's unobstructed vision to just a few yards. Stop at the right places, though, and after a short time of wandering one can easily merge with any number of foot-worn paths that articulate with a trail system not found on any recreational hiking map. Some of them are of recent origin; others may be much older. As they walk into the wilderness, volunteers call out, announcing themselves in Spanish to anyone who might be able to hear.

"¿Necesita agua?" (Do you need water?)
"¿Necesita ayuda?" (Do you need help?)
"¡Somos amigos!" (We are friends!)
"¡Tenemos agua y comida!" (We have water and food!)
"¡No somos la migra!" (We are not *la migra!*) [slang for Border Patrol agents.]

It might seem like finding a needle in a haystack, and usually, in fact, there is no answer to these calls except the sound of bugs, wind, birds, and distant traffic. Many patrols return without any contact with migrants, but contact happens more than one might expect. The difference between an uneventful navigation through the bramble and an encounter with migrants may be just a matter of walking a few more paces or waiting long enough for listeners to work up the nerve to come into the open. One moment a place can feel empty and uninhabited, and the next a group of twenty or more men and women may appear only yards away, dirty, exhausted, and afraid.[19]

In the field, countless variables affect Samaritan and migrant interactions. One is balancing humanitarian need with legal obligations. Per the counsel of its attorneys, the organization reads federal law as permitting the provision of food, water, and medical aid. When a patrol encounters migrants, its first priority is to find out whether any of them is sick or otherwise in need of medical attention. Volunteers always distribute bottles of water, working under the assumption that anyone they encounter is probably dehydrated. The protocol also requires volunteers to make judgment calls about what medical needs can be addressed in the field. There are cases, for instance, where someone who has gone without water for too long needs extensive rehydration. In other cases, a person may have cramps, broken bones, sprains, or blisters so severe that his or her feet are raw and can no longer be walked on. If the situation is severe or life threatening, the procedure is to call 911 and request an emergency vehicle so that people can receive medical treatment.

Another variable Samaritans have to consider is the Border Patrol. The group does not see its relationship with the Border Patrol as antagonistic, but there is an underlying tension between the two in that the Samaritans disavow any role in enforcing immigration law. Acting as an arm of the state, they argue, would compromise the ability to provide humanitarian assistance, for if it became known among migrants that civilians offering aid were also turning them in for arrest, those in need would be less likely to seek help. By the Samaritans protocol, volunteers defer to the wishes of the migrants about contacting the Border Patrol. Often migrants have decided to stop avoiding detection and make their presence known to others in order to bring their journey to an end. Some have become too sick or disabled to continue; some may be attracting help for other travelers who were left farther back. If any migrant wants to turn himself or herself in, the Samaritans are to contact the Border Patrol and make those arrangements. But many migrants simply accept the aid they are offered and continue. Samaritans also try to provide food and water to people in custody, though access to them depends on the agents.

Samaritans furthered their connections with Sanctuary by basing themselves out of Southside Church. Southside's street address appeared on the letterhead of the declaration to the Border Patrol and while they initially used the First Christian parking lot to load vehicles and leave for trips, in 2004 these activities shifted to Southside as well. The group meets in the Southside sanctuary, which is commonly known as the Kiva and bears the circular design of the Pueblo structures that are its namesake. Facilitation duties rotate on a volunteer basis. When meetings open, the facilitator calls for a moment of silence that lasts perhaps half a minute. After a round of introductions, the facilitator solicits patrol reports from those in attendance who have gone out since the last meeting. Patrol reports cover anything that might be of interest to other Samaritans, such as encounters with anyone in need and the kind of aid provided, tracks and trash that indicate migrants' presence, and the volume and quality of interaction with the Border Patrol. Following the reports there is a period of general announcements, which usually involves upcoming events of interest. From there, the group discusses various business such as fund-raising, supply inventory, and vehicle repairs. The meeting ends, as it began, with a moment of silence initiated and concluded by the facilitator.

The Samaritans operate much more loosely than Humane Borders. Whereas Humane Borders owns several trucks specially outfitted for water tank maintenance and pays for the gas used on trips, Samaritans have had at most two donated four-wheel-drive vehicles, and though there is a small fund to reimburse volunteers for fuel costs, most either pay out of pocket to refill the tank or take their own vehicle to start with. Another point of contrast between the two groups is Samaritans' diffusion of authority. As Samaritans member Rhonda says, "There's no leadership and there's no infrastructure, which means it doesn't have any institutional things that would take active steps to keep it going or raise money, so it's vulnerable to the extent that every single thing that's done in Samaritans has to be pretty much done by the person who suggested it. That's what happens at meetings. People sit around and decide if something's bothering them, and volunteer to do something." Trash days, like the ones sponsored by Humane Borders, are one such example. Instead of a standing schedule of trash pickups, Samaritans rely on individual members' initiative to choose a date, find a deserving location, and recruit participants. Likewise, the food packs that volunteers carry into the field are assembled by pooling money, donated items, and volunteer labor on an as-needed basis.

The organization's centripetal character was demonstrated during a weekly meeting when a member rose to announce that another group in town had asked the group to endorse a particular cause. When she said, "This letter is supposed to be signed by the board of directors and the president, none of which we have," attendees laughed in appreciation of the discrepancy between how groups are assumed to be organized and how the Samaritans organization actually works.

## Derechos Humanos

Throughout the evolution of Humane Borders and Samaritans, Derechos Humanos has continued to educate and organize on a wide range of issues pertinent to immigration and civil and human rights. The group's promotional pamphlet describes its work thus: "Coalición de Derechos Humanos is a grassroots organization that promotes respect for human/ civil rights [and] fights the militarization of the southern Border region, discrimination and human rights abuses by law enforcement officials, businesses, institutions, and individuals, which affect U.S. and non–U.S. citizens alike."

The most direct way that Derechos tries to counter the militarized border policy is by stimulating and directing grassroots action. Members encourage constituents to write to their congressional representatives about pending bills, and work with local environmentalists in a coalition called Bring Down the Walls to halt or delay Border Patrol construction in ecologically sensitive areas. Mostly, though, Derechos focuses on informational outreach, whether one-off occasions or more regular events. Among the most prominent of these are periodic potluck dinners that feature a speaker or series of speakers addressing any issue relevant to the group's mission. Delegates from the organization also visit community groups upon request to present the "Know Your Rights" workshops, which, as the name implies, provide instructions on one's legal options when interacting with law enforcement officers. The workshops are also carried out in a mobile, highly abbreviated form by a Derechos-sponsored youth contingent, CopWatch. For CopWatch outreach, members choose a place to visit, typically a municipal bus shelter or a grocery store in Tucson's barrios, and distribute cards that summarize the important points of "Know Your Rights" at a glance. Another program within Derechos is the Promotoras—the Promoters (i.e., of human rights)—a group of immigrant women who carry out educational work in their neighborhoods, through one-on-one discussion and engagements at venues like churches and schools. Derechos's educational campaigns are so regularized that they receive little, if any, media attention, though the coalition periodically courts publicity through news conferences dedicated to special announcements or moments of great urgency. These conferences take the form of panels, in which clergy are frequent participants.

Derechos meetings are held weekly in a room at the Sam Lena library in South Tucson, a small, incorporated municipality within Tucson overall where approximately 83 percent of the population is of Mexican heritage and 10 percent is Native American.[20] Beforehand, people settle in by arranging the chairs and tables, looking over the new issue of *Tucson Weekly*, and casually chatting, perhaps joking about the tendency of the meetings to start fifteen or twenty minutes late. Business is always conducted in English, but bilingual members often use Spanish in informal conversations before the meeting, and sometimes to expedite a brief exchange during the meeting if at least one person involved is more comfortable with it.

The meetings evoke a rich sense of history, for they are permeated by the experiences core members have shared over many years of collaboration. Discussion of a current agenda item frequently prompts someone in attendance to refer back to antiapartheid work, a vigilante trial, or the days of the Manzo Area Council, revealing the group's roots amid the people and places of Tucson. At the same time, Derechos situates its local efforts as an expression of broader national and international movements. Meetings regularly give attention to pending state and federal legislation, and members often travel to conferences with like-minded organizations and report back on their experiences.

Day to day, the bulk of Derechos Humanos's work is done in an office by a small number of paid staff members. Though aided by private contributions, the bulk of the operating budget comes from foundation grants. The group carries out its mission in ways that do not offer volunteer opportunities on the scale of water station trips or Samaritan patrols, and supporters are more likely to show their allegiance by showing up at the group's public events, whether educational, like the potlucks, or acts of protest and remembrance, like vigils and marches.

## Other Tucson Immigrant Advocacy Responses to the Gatekeeper Complex

### The Border Action Network

In 1998, local environmental and human rights activists formed the Southwest Alliance to Resist Militarization (SWARM), the first post-Gatekeeper immigrant advocacy organization in Tucson. SWARM initially focused on raising awareness and concern in Tucson about border militarization, particularly a collaboration between armed forces personnel, the Border Patrol, and state and local law enforcement known as Joint TaskForce Six (Dunn, *Militarizing* 133–38). Within a few years, though, members changed the group's name to Border Action Network (BAN) and redirected their efforts to organizing neighborhood-based committees in Tucson and smaller towns in southern Arizona. BAN sponsors workshops aimed at training its membership in documentation of human rights abuse, public speaking, and interacting with the media. It sometimes collaborates with other Tucson immigrant advocacy groups, but BAN members stand apart from their peers in that they incorporate few religious references in their work and are the only group not to have roots in Central American refugee advocacy.

### No More Deaths

No More Deaths (NMD) began in 2004 as a collaboration that included the four Tucson-based immigrant advocacy groups and a handful of regional allies. Though it became an independent organization in 2007, it maintains bonds with other immigrant advocates in Tucson and a separate No More Deaths chapter in Phoenix by sharing members and cosponsoring events. As the name implies, No More Deaths' primary focus has been on finding ever more effective ways of preventing migrant fatalities. The group's most defining activity toward that end is maintaining one or more desert encampments in southern Arizona during the summer. The camps ensure a twenty-four-hour presence in areas traveled by migrants and serve as a base for ongoing motorized and foot patrols based on the Samaritans model and using the same protocol. A second NMD innovation emerged based on information indicating that many migrants were trying to cross the border immediately after being apprehended and deported, even though their previous journey or journeys had left them weaker than they were when they began. Guessing that at least some deaths could be attributed to migrants' inability to recuperate after deportation, in 2006, NMD worked with Mexican NGOs and the state of Sonora to establish a relief station at the Mariposa port of entry in Nogales where the Border Patrol releases deportees. From the station, volunteers provide food, water, and information to migrants upon their arrival, enabling them to rebuild some of their strength. In addition, volunteers at Mariposa conduct abuse documentation, interviewing migrants about their treatment during apprehension and detention.[21]

Unlike other Tucson immigrant advocate groups in the Gatekeeper era, No More Deaths has also been subject to federal efforts to criminalize its activities. In 2005, No More Deaths volunteers Shanti Sellz and Daniel Strauss encountered two critically ill migrants and began to drive them to Tucson for medical treatment. Sellz and Strauss were stopped, arrested by the Border Patrol, and indicted for conspiracy to transport and the transportation of illegal aliens—charges that could have resulted in ten years imprisonment. Immigrant advocates in Tucson immediately mounted a campaign to drop the charges under the slogan "Humanitarian Aid Is Not a Crime," which included a series of weekly news conferences held at Southside shortly after the arrests. Sellz and Strauss, meanwhile, refused the prosecution's offer of a plea bargain and insisted they had broken no laws. The defendants soon attracted international attention and support; they and the broader movement were vindicated in September 2006, when a US district judge threw out the case.[22] Then in separate cases in 2008, two No More Deaths volunteers were charged with littering after they left one-gallon jugs filled with water near migrant pathways on the Buenos Aires National Wildlife Refuge (Vanderpool).

## The Migrant Trail

Every summer since 2004, immigrant advocates from Tucson and elsewhere have participated in a seventy-five mile, binational walk known as the Migrant Trail. Subtitled "We Walk for Life," the event begins in Sasabe, Sonora, on Memorial Day and concludes six days later in Tucson. Though not an organization per se, the Migrant Trail is planned each year by an ad-hoc committee that garners sponsorships from a variety of national and regional immigrant advocacy groups.[23] The most consistent sponsors have been Derechos Humanos and No More Deaths, though Humane Borders and Samaritans have also cosponsored at various times.

## Comparing the Cultures of Tucson Immigrant Advocacy

Many similarities exist among Derechos Humanos, Humane Borders, and Samaritans. One especially important commonality, given their focus on immigration, is that the participants are overwhelmingly not themselves immigrants, but native-born US citizens. (A very few are naturalized citizens, and fewer still are noncitizens.) They also tend to have similarly favorable orientations to the region's Mexican influences. This is by no means a given. As borderlands scholar Oscar J. Martinez puts it, the ideological orientations of US residents to the Mexican presence in border culture include "at one extreme . . . individuals who live on the border but who are largely unaffected by it." They "are monolingual and monocultural, and their ties to foreigners or to countrymen who are racially, ethnically, or culturally different from themselves are slight or nonexistent" (62). At the other extreme "are persons whose very lives personify the borderlands milieu" in that they "are bilingual and bicultural, and . . . have a high degree of contact with the opposite side of the border" (62). Most people in the borderlands lie "between these two poles, and their position varies in accordance with their orientation toward or away from transnational or transcultural interaction" (62). Where one stands between the two extremes is often influenced by ethnicity. For bicultural Mexican Americans, "cross-border ties spring from their status as a minority group in an area physically adjacent to their traditional homeland" (138). "In contrast," Martinez observes, "transnational interaction is not inherently a part of the experience of most Anglo borderlanders" (138), which means that most Anglos tend to be "uniculturalists." Many immigrant advocates, however, fit Martinez's description of "Anglo biculturalists," who "have a broad vision of the world and a keen appreciation of cultural differences. Consequently they see the internationalism of the borderlands in a positive way" (132). Immigrant advocates of all racial and ethnic backgrounds tend toward a bicultural perspective and exhibit an attitude of interest in or enthusiasm for the cultures of Mexico and Latin America as a whole.

The organizations also share a broad consensus that US border policy is overly restrictive and that the deaths of migrants are a sign of its dysfunction. They agree that the deaths themselves are tragic, that the migrants are worthy of sympathy, and that there is a need to create more hospitable conditions by educating citizens, providing migrants with information and material aid, changing laws, and so forth. They do not engage in civil disobedience. They also seek a public presence and court the attention of media and the general population. All three affirm that religion has a place to play in immigrant advocates' private motivations and public rhetoric. They are heavily Christian, but not restricted to particular denominations. Each organization's style of advocacy includes religious features like declarations of "faith," scriptural references, and sacralized spaces, as well as institutional religious resources such as church staff and facilities.

Owing to variations in the impetus for each group's formation, however, there are slight differences in how those viewpoints get inflected. Humane Borders and Samaritans came into being specifically to stop the deaths attributable to the Gatekeeper Complex, and their daily operations are focused accordingly on humanitarian assistance. Since Derechos Humanos coalesced prior to the implementation of Gatekeeper, the group's response to migrant deaths should be seen as part of a larger critique arguing that restrictive immigration law and border militarization threaten the human rights of the very citizens such measures ostensibly protect.

Some of the most notable contrasts between the groups arguably reflect differences dating back to the 1960s and '70s. Humane Borders and Samaritans resemble voluntary agency and Sanctuary efforts by self-identifying as faith-based organizations and drawing much of their membership from mainline Protestant churches with predominantly white congregations. Spokespeople in the two groups are usually men, though women form a majority of those in attendance at most meetings. Also, since volunteers need to have flexible daytime hours to carry out tasks that are done in the morning, many members are retirees. Derechos Humanos, on the other hand, bears the imprint of the Manzo Area Council through direct carry-overs in membership as well as maintaining a commitment to addressing immigration concerns in Tucson's Spanish-speaking neighborhoods. Derechos Humanos does not identify as faith based and does not operate within a religious institution. Locally, the organization seeks faith-based groups and institutions as coalition partners, but its networking outside of Tucson is usually done with human rights and Mexican American organizations. Derechos is also distinguished in terms of membership. First, Derechos manifests a somewhat wider spectrum of ages among attendees at weekly meetings. Second, women more frequently appear in spokesperson roles. Third, the ethnicity of group stalwarts tends to be Mexican American. These tendencies can be traced back to the mid-1970s, when the Manzo Area Council was primarily Mexican American, female directed, and secular in orientation, and worked parallel to or in collaboration with organizations that were primarily white, male directed, and based in religious institutions.

The bicultural dimension of immigrant advocates is evident in the occasional use of Spanish at meetings. Among Derechos members, many of whom are bilingual, the occasional Spanish used at meetings is likely to be proficient and sustained over several sentences by the speakers. More subtly, some Mexican American members use Spanish pronunciation or vocabulary on a selective basis while speaking English. This includes people and places with Spanish names, including "Mexico" and "Mexican," which become *"Mejico"* and *"Mejicano"* or *"Mejicana."* When I asked one Derechos member, Carla, why this happens, she paused and responded, "Well, gosh. I don't know. I don't know what is happening in my mind that I feel that I need to change. I couldn't explain it to you. Maybe the word 'Mexicans'—this is what I would suggest—maybe the word 'Mexican' is not intimate enough for us, and so we say 'Mejicanos' as a more intimate way of saying the word." She added with a hypothetical air that maybe "'Mexican' seems a little foreign-sounding to us?" In contrast, Spanish is rare at Samaritans and Humane Borders meetings and is used by most members with self-conscious and self-deprecatory novelty. During one Humane Borders meeting, for instance, Hoover read a statement in Spanish and an Anglo woman in attendance responded, "I understand *your* Spanish"—meaning his accent was as bad as hers and therefore intelligible. Hoover, catching the joke, muttered back "Bwenuz diuz" with exaggerated English vowels. Spanish ineptitude among Samaritans, meanwhile, has caused members of the group to wonder what it might be like to be a migrant hiding behind a bush who hears approaching voices announce, "Tenemos amigos" (We have friends) and "Somos comida" (We are food).

Most immigrant advocates sympathize with liberal and left-wing politics, albeit through the activities of nongovernmental organizations and social movements, not officeholders or party platforms. However, this correlation is by no means absolute. Humane Borders held a weekly meeting the day after national elections in 2004, and as cupcakes were passed around for members to eat, Hoover described them as meaning "either congratulations or condolences," depending on how respective members had voted. The following week, as the group lamented public credulity over unsubstantiated allegations that terrorists are crossing into the United States from Mexico, one member said, "That's why Bush got reelected." Amid nervous laughter, Hoover interjected, "God bless our diversity; we're just out to save some lives"—preempting either the eruption of an argument or further comments that might leave the minority of Bush voters feeling unwelcome.

## Conclusion

Above and beyond impacting migrants, transnational migrant advocacy in Tucson marks a substantive engagement with interlocking social conflicts over race, citizenship, border enforcement, the meaning of the United States, and the boundaries of moral communities. Immigrant advocacy since IRCA and particularly since the Gatekeeper Complex has adapted older forms to new circumstances, and the process of adaptation continues. Immigrant advocates have had to factor in manifold new conditions and challenges since the first concerted efforts to prevent deaths in the desert in 2000, many of which have aggravated existing hostility to migrants and migrant advocates. The September 11, 2001, terrorist attacks spurred a new wave of concern over immigrants as threats to national security, and though activists were heartened by the enormous proimmigrant marches that grabbed national headlines in the spring of 2006 and squelched an egregiously repressive bill in Congress, the tenor of national debate has continued to favor stricter border enforcement and harsher penalties. Voters and legislators across the country have approved a cascade of restrictionist ballot initiatives and laws, and vigilantes have appointed themselves civilian adjuncts to the Border Patrol by carrying out surveillance, armed patrols, and detentions along the border.[24] All the while, migration from Mexico and deaths in the desert have continued.

Antagonisms exist between immigrant advocacy groups and are familiar to long-standing members, but rarely get aired outside of private conversations.[25] Even then, the tendency is to disregard intergroup conflict and stress instead the benefits of multiple approaches. As Derechos Humanos member Monte says of Humane Borders and Samaritans, "They've reached a whole lot of people that we could never have reached, so it's all positive. We all share the same goal: we have to change policy. They just have a different way of going about it."[26] Viewed up close, it is easy to see where the assumptions and approaches of these organizations are at odds. But despite little overlap in membership and the lack of a coordinated planning structure, the groups have complementary purposes and constitute a cohort of immigrant advocacy wherein religious elements are brought to bear on public consciousness and state policy.

INTERSTICE

*A group member reports that NBC came out to the Migrant Trail.*

*"He asked me, 'Do you think people don't know, or that they don't care?' And I said, 'I like to think that people don't know, and that if they knew, they would be outraged.'"*

—NOTES FROM A DERECHOS HUMANOS MEETING, 2005

# CHAPTER FIVE

# Individual Worldviews

## Humanity, Nationality, and Ultimacy

During an informal conversation in the course of my fieldwork, a Humane Borders member named Charli alluded to the time before she joined the group and said of herself, "I was one of the blind people in this city." Charli's remark compresses a personal narrative into a metaphor based on two kinds of "seeing." Most obviously, she once was "blind" because she did not perceive a situation that demanded her attention. But she also implies that when she "saw" the crisis, she "saw" the need to do something about it. In my interview with Fenton, another Humane Borders member, he related a similar account: "When I moved to Tucson about ten years ago I started reading about [migrant deaths] and I thought, 'this is really crazy.' You know, people dying just because they can't feed their families. It just seemed like the logical thing to do was to get involved." Though the words are different, the schemas of the stories are the same: the speaker moves from ignorance to awareness, and this change in consciousness requires a change in behavior.

Charli and Fenton's comments underscore a problem with describing social movement organizations, which is that although the organizations would not exist without the personal beliefs of their supporters, movement activity by its nature levels differences among members. Mission statements and the like are useful in suggesting points of general agreement among constituents, but they cannot intimate each person's perspective on how the world operates. Behind the apparent uniformity of group practices are myriad individual viewpoints or emotional investments, and these "convictions of the soul"[1] are important factors in trying to understand how movements are formed and perpetuated. Since individuals can provide more nuance and personality than collective representatives can, taking stock of their perspectives enables a richer account of the modes of consciousness that propel movement activity.

Charli and Fenton, for instance, describe how a new understanding of the objective conditions of the world led to joining Humane Borders. Their stories hint at dozens of similar experiences among other immigrant advocates in which the acquisition of knowledge led to taking actions consistent with that knowledge. One way of thinking about these transformations is to consider them as expressions of a person's self-concept. In the words of philosopher Charles Taylor, "To know who I am is a species of knowing where I stand. My identity is defined by the commitments and identifications which provide the frame or horizon within which I can try to determine from case to case what is good, or valuable, or what ought to be done, or what I endorse or oppose" (27). That is, much of who we are (or want to be) involves what we like or dislike and what we approve or disapprove of. We project those evaluations through our behavior, through performances that may be called "acts of identification" (McRobbie 723). Hence, in the case of Charli and Fenton, once the "blindness" had been overcome, once the insight had registered, some new act of identification was necessary in order for them to be, as is sometimes said, "true to themselves."

Moreover, as Taylor argues, "one cannot be a self on one's own. I am a self only in relation to certain interlocutors" (36), which is to say, socially. Therefore, a "full definition of someone's identity . . . usually involves not only his stand on moral and spiritual matters, but also some reference to a defining community" (36). Acts of identification, then, are also acts of relation, because they postulate similarities and differences between the actor and a larger group of human beings. An actor's approval or disapproval of any set of circumstances depends on how the actor perceives those who are affected, and how the actor stands in relation to them. To take sides in a social conflict, participants have to answer—to some extent unconsciously—the questions, "Who am I, who are the people affected by this situation, and what is our connection to each other?" The answers, in turn, imply certain ethical imperatives. Fenton models this thought process quite explicitly, explaining that once he decided migrants were "dying just because they can't feed their families," joining Humane Borders was "the logical thing to do." To enter into thought and action about a political controversy is thus to simultaneously diagnose what one perceives as the problem, claim one or more identities for oneself, and imagine one or more relationships with pertinent others.

This chapter draws on interviews with members of Derechos Humanos, Humane Borders, and Samaritans to describe the various ways in which the members engage in these acts of identification and relation. Sometimes immigrant advocates claim identities on an abstract plane that I have been describing as "universal": *All humans are valuable; these humans are dying; thus I do this work*. Other identities are "proximal" in that they are based on situated, circumstantial difference: *Migrants are valuable as particular kinds of social beings; I am likewise a social being in a particular relation with them; thus I do this work*. That is, immigrant advocates simultaneously take standpoints at universal and proximal levels, and discuss them with equal facility and readiness. They sometimes describe their subject of concern as a matter of life and death so primal that it seems to transcend politics, invoking values that elevate the needs of an undifferentiated body of humanity above any particular collective. But they are just as likely to speak in more concrete terms about specific historical and social conditions, including their roles as citizens of the United States, Christians, consumers, borderlands residents, medical professionals, and so on. They thereby situate themselves in political cosmologies that link individuals, collective institutions, and transcendent truths.

However, immigrant advocates, like other social actors, are bound to the obligations of many roles and collective identities at once. The ethical demands of multiple identities often conflict, which forces people to negotiate which code of action has greater authority and takes precedence, essentially ratifying one or another ethical code as best approximating "ultimacy" or what Taylor calls "the incomparably higher" (47). This prioritizing process is at the heart of controversy over advocacy on behalf of undocumented people. As discussed in chapter 2, political communities are always in a sense imagined, creating the sentiment among people who may never meet that they should reserve their highest loyalties for each other. In modern times, the reigning mode of political identity has been national citizenship, which requires that one's greatest allegiance be given to co-nationals and the territorial boundaries of the state. To the chagrin of some observers, undocumented advocates seem to be violating both of these. Recall the rhetorical question, quoted in chapter 1, from the critic who asked of immigrant advocates, "what do they want for this country?" The critic implies, at least, that if immigrant advocates had the best interests of the United States at heart, they would not do what they do.

Yet as this chapter reveals, the tendency among immigrant advocates is to argue both that migrants' lives are valuable and that it is possible to implement policies through the nation-state that will preserve those lives.

Far and away, in most cases they do not repudiate the legitimacy of nation-states, though they suggest that citizenship and patriotism are start points, not end points, for navigating moral quandaries.

To demonstrate how ideologies among immigrant advocates get expressed in various permutations, I will offer three case studies based on interviews with individual group members. These interviews were structured around questions that solicited discussion on how and why the members got involved in their respective group or groups, what problems the group or groups are trying to address, and how they respond to nationalist critiques. The case studies feature one member each from Derechos Humanos, Samaritans, and Humane Borders and are followed by an analysis that incorporates information from additional interviews.

## Case Studies

### Patricia (Derechos Humanos)

Patricia has been a member of Derechos Humanos for several years, and explained her involvement by saying, "I think that people are called to organizations by feeling connected to the way the organization works, or the people communicate. That's why I feel connected to Derechos Humanos. But if I'm honest about why I do what I do, it's my faith." For Patricia, who grew up Catholic, that faith includes going to mass on a regular basis and seeking interaction with other Catholics involved in grassroots activism.

She feels the issue driving her work is much bigger than migrants dying along the border:

> I wouldn't call it a border crisis. I'd call it a human rights crisis. I think the problem goes beyond what we see here at the border, and the border is basically just where the physical manifestation of the problem is happening, and that would be the mass displacement of people on a global scale and a huge misdistribution of wealth and land and power. The human rights crisis of it is that people are dying because of that reality.

*On the border.*

On the border, but there's lots of ways to die. I mean, globalization kills people in a lot of ways. It kills them in sweatshops, it kills them in fields, it kills them slowly. There was a migrant, he was found a couple years ago or last year, I think. He was like 34 years old, 35 maybe, and the coroner said that he had the spine of a 68-year-old man. I mean, there's a lot of ways of being killed. Slow ways, long ways. Either way, it strips you of your dignity, it strips you of your power, it strips you of your voice, and to me that's the crisis—the deaths in the desert, but the slow deaths are just as traumatic to me.

A migrant who dies of heat exhaustion or in a vehicle rollover is not an isolated casualty, then, but an expression of greater socioeconomic dysfunctions. The deaths are symptomatic of large-scale processes tied to "globalization" that destroy humans' physical and psychological well-being.

Part of the basis for her sympathies is a sense that social stations of affluence and destitution are matters of chance:

You know that saying "there but for the grace of God go I?" Have you heard that? That's how I feel. It's pure luck that I was born north of the line and not south, and if it weren't for the Treaty of Guadalupe Hidalgo, which changed the border, we would still be in Mexico. So I think that I didn't do anything for my privilege. I was born into it, in the same way people didn't do anything to deserve their poverty where they were born. So I think that if you're born rich, the way the US is, we owe the system. There's just something in the universe. You owe to all the people who did nothing to not be born with anything you had.

People in positions of relative power need to act on behalf of those with less, and this is true not just of individuals, but also of collectives, like the United States. Moreover, this warrant originates beyond human decree. It is "something in the universe."

She rejects the idea that Derechos Humanos' activities are treasonous, placing them on solid legal ground:

I used to get mad [at critics] and be like, "Screw you, how dare you question my Americanness?" That's my first reaction, because we are protesting peacefully: educational forums, peaceful marches, letter-writing campaigns, advocating, endorsing, trying to change the government through congressional representatives, through legislation. We aren't going out there armed, we aren't going out there confronting, we don't have racist rhetoric, our meetings and events are open to the public. And we're the un-American ones? We're doing this the civil, normal way. It's not about pledging allegiance.

For Patricia, then, national loyalty is performed in part through obedience to the law. Yet she also acknowledges that law is an imperfect instrument, and that citizenship is not an adequate moral framework for action in the world:

> At one point in this country, you were a good citizen if you turned in a runaway slave. I think it's all relative. I think it's more important to ask yourself what kind of a human being you are. That's a better check-in for you than whether you can say the Pledge of Allegiance or run the flag up on Memorial Day. A good citizen challenges and takes their government to task when they're not being the country they claim to be. So am I being a good citizen when I criticize the government that our policy shouldn't cause over three thousand deaths? Hell, yeah, I'm a good citizen. I'm a bad citizen if I sit by and let it happen and don't question it. No government is perfect. It's ever changing and it has to change with the world.

Here, Patricia describes her moral center as something that transcends legal conformity, but locates it in two very different places. One is recognizing one's universal status as a "human being." The second, more parochial devotion has to do with a putatively honorable national heritage. When the government is out of line with the values it claims to uphold, it is the duty of citizens to take it to task for that hypocrisy. She folds the two together somewhat similarly when she says, "Our responsibility is to make the nation what it should be, what we think it should be, what we thought we were told it was supposed to be."

She holds fast to the idea, though, of doing immigrant advocacy within the boundaries of the law, saying with a mixture of pride and self-deprecation, "I have this maybe silly faith in government and faith in the system and a lot of my friends are like, 'Oh, that's so cute. She believes it will work.'"

## Annie (Samaritans)

Annie, a native Tucsonan, is self-employed and had been participating in Samaritan patrols for about a year when I interviewed her. She does not identify herself as religious, but had recently attended worship a number of times at Southside Church. Her involvement in Samaritans came in part because of reflections that followed a stay with friends in Mexico: "I came back here and was reading all this stuff about the border buildup with the Border Patrol, so I realized it was really bad. And I thought, what if my friends [in Mexico tried to cross and] died? It would be like they died on my front porch. So I decided to go look for them or anyone like them."

As it happens, Annie had a strong reason to identify with their hypothetical plight. While in Mexico, she had gone on a three-day journey through the desert with a native guide at the peak of summer. They ran out of water on the first day, temperatures were over a hundred, and the reservoirs ahead that they planned to refill from were all dry. Only a serendipitous rainfall on the third day saved them.

Her primary orientation to Samaritans work is based on an ethic that values the lives of individual persons: "If there is a human being flopping around in the desert, how can you watch that? You can't emotionally, physically, spiritually—in no way—watch a person groaning and moaning and flopping around, dying. So I would give water to anybody. It doesn't matter who it is." She argues, though, that it shouldn't take a personal experience of near death by dehydration to foster compassion for migrants crossing the desert. "One of the huge things" driving calls for more punitive border enforcement, she says,

> is that people don't have much imagination to realize that these [migrants] are just like them, that they have lives in another country and they're valuable, valuable people. I think a lot of the people that are against this are not able to get out of the context of their lives and see that there are other lives that are equally valuable. They might see that there are other lives in need of help, like the poor Mexicans need Americans to go help them live. But they don't have enough imagination to realize that a person could be sitting in their house doing exactly what they are doing.

Annie's use of the word "imagination" here offers a vernacular corroboration of Benedict Anderson's "imagined community," though the imagination she invokes encompasses humans as a species, not as compartmentalized nationalities.

At the same time, Annie articulates a rationale for the Samaritans' work based in terms of a national economy: "Everybody in the United States is dependent—you've heard this fifty thousand times—we're all dependent on these guys coming across the border to fill jobs that we need done that nobody else will do. So they're enormously valuable in the economy of the United States. They put in thousands, millions, billions of dollars a year into the US economy, into Social Security and all that stuff."

But even as she identifies herself as a beneficiary of these contributions, the importance of universal identity returns to the forefront when she says, "My allegiance is not only to the United States of America. My allegiance is to human beings." Annie bases her sympathy for migrants on a perception of them as people in general, not people who play particular roles in bolstering the wealth of the nation-state she is a part of. She says citizenship is not part of what motivates her, and that patriotism is an impediment to figuring out "how people can get on in the world":

> It's such a little, tiny place where we live. It's really little. The only thing I remember my ex-husband said that I would ever quote him on would be, "Nothing matters, but everything counts." And that's what I think about people in politics and all that sort of thing, that every little thing counts in human interaction and it has nothing to do with politics and countries. It has to do with human beings and things that further people's lives in a healthy way. "Nothing matters," because I haven't seen anybody come back from the dead, or any indication that [the afterlife] matters. So as far as my life goes, I'm just going to do it, full force, and when it's done, it's done. But along the way, everything that we do counts.

Annie quickly segues from the proximal to the universal here, joining her attitude toward patriotism to beliefs about human mortality. Contrary to what one might expect, she says helping others "counts" even if there is no promise of life after death in return. Patriotism, though, can prevent people from doing what counts. She guesses that the world is moving toward a global community—"very soon, probably not in my lifetime, but soon, the way we know borders will not be borders that we've ever known before." Yet she is skeptical that any single set of ideas can be used to organize society: "Maybe democracy's a nice idea. Maybe communism's a nice idea. I don't know any ideology that's a good ideology." Systems are only as good as the people living in them, and for Annie, part of living in any system requires the well off to help those who are less well off. As Annie sees it, growing up amid the wealth of the United States was just a matter of chance. "I just happen to be a lucky creature that was born into a country that has running water and that the necessities of my life are taken care of," she says. "But in some countries, in most countries on Earth, the number one priority is to continue living. You know, food, water, and taking care that you have enough shelter. So I'm fortunate to be randomly born into this thing where I don't have to do that."

Given this luxury, Annie says, she can spend time on things that aren't essential to her own survival. These include leisure activities—she named gardening and painting in particular—but also volunteering for Samaritans.

## Allen (Humane Borders)

Allen, a Presbyterian, is younger than most Humane Borders volunteers, but has been involved with all aspects of group operations from office work to water station maintenance. He attributes the root cause of migrant deaths to a seemingly irreconcilable debate within the United States over immigration from Mexico:

> There's this conflict in American society between, one, our safety and our security, and, on the other side, our economy. In the economic sense, we're asking migrants to cross into the United States to fill certain positions in our economy. But the security side of our nation is saying we're going to close down the border and we're not going to provide a way for these people to come into the US. That has created illegal immigration because the economy is asking people to come over, and yet the security side of the US is saying, "No, don't come."

Using the first person plural, Allen speaks as a member of "American society," naming "our" safety, security, and economy as factors in the debate over immigration. He also personifies the latter two as social actors, with economic interests "asking" for more immigration while security concerns try to prevent it.

In a democratic society, he says, citizens have "the responsibility to participate, but also to change it if they so feel," and he says that responsibility includes religious believers and nonbelievers. "Society as a whole needs to look at issues surrounding injustices, such as what's happening on the border. It can't be just a 'Christian' or a 'religious' kind of crisis. It has to be something that's addressed by the entire country because it's affecting the entire country. I think that it needs to be addressed on a societal scale, because the laws that affect it are created nationwide, on a national scale."

In Allen's particular case, though, Christianity is the standpoint from which he participates in political life: "In terms of being a good Christian, first and foremost is living out the example of Christ and those ideals that the Bible sets forth. . . . That doesn't mean I just lose all sense of citizenship. I still participate in society, but my primary motivation is from a Christian viewpoint rather than an 'American' viewpoint."

Allen distinguishes citizenship, though, from patriotism, a sentiment he associates with much more specific acts, none of which appear in Humane Borders' work. "I always think of being patriotic as waving the flag or celebrating Fourth of July. Maybe patriotism could be broader than that. I haven't really thought of it. I don't feel like my work is patriotic. I don't really feel like it's unpatriotic, either." His perspective is a simple equation: patriotism consists of an inventory of specific acts, but since Humane Borders neither performs these acts nor impedes them, the standard is irrelevant.

The economic role migrants play, he says, is critical in determining whether what Humane Borders does is harmful to the United States, either in intent or outcome. "The people who are the backbone of our economy are migrant populations. Without such, our economy would fall apart. So I don't see it [Humane Borders' work] as anti-American." In making this argument, Allen equates the present economic order with "America," and argues that immigrant advocates are not "anti-American" because they are cooperating with greater social forces that support the perpetuation of that order.

But Allen lends nuance to this statement when he acknowledges that border policy could be changed through government action, and that this would produce wrenching "sacrifices that have to be made in terms of the status quo." For example, if migrants who are currently paid under the table were given permits to work legally, their pay would rise in accord with minimum wage laws and create higher costs that would be passed on to consumers. "I think there will definitely be resistance to [reforms that raise producer costs]. But I guess that's where the whole issue comes in. Is it okay to pay someone two dollars and fifty cents an hour for processing meat, even though the minimum wage is five-fifteen, just so you can have a cheap dinner? It's a moral issue." In these remarks, Allen indicates some ambiguity vis-à-vis his previous suggestion that the current economic order is worth perpetuating. Undocumented immigrants may produce economic benefits, but if those benefits are achieved through exploitation, then the economy itself is immoral. Secondly, he suggests "the economy" is not an autonomous social agent, but something that can be affected by personal choices of participants. If people, not implacable forces, are "inviting" undocumented migration, then it is possible for them to withdraw the "invitation" by changing their behavior patterns. And if Christian thought can motivate those changes in behavior, then Christianity has a role in the social conversation about what the personified economy should "do" and "say."

## Acts of Identification and Relation among Immigrant Advocates

Though the views of Patricia, Annie, and Allen are not necessarily those of the groups each person represents, they offer a cross section of the differences and similarities in how immigrant advocates understand themselves and their work. To further delineate the beliefs that guide individual movement participants, the following section analyzes recurring features of the case studies in conjunction with remarks from other immigrant advocates. The material is organized according to three issues: how immigrant advocates name the problem that they are trying to redress, the terms in which they establish affinity with migrants, and how they prioritize the identity or identities that provide ethical codes for action.

### Naming the Problem

Most immigrant advocates in Tucson identify migrant fatalities as at least one of the issues central to their work. Polly (Samaritans) said up front, "I think the number one problem is people are dying. When you have young people in the prime of their life, in the twenties, dying because they're trying to get a job, that's a problem." Raleigh (Humane Borders and Samaritans) was particularly moved by circumstances of migrant deaths: "The thought of people dying that way really bothers me. Not that any death is easy, but that's a really hard death, to die of heat exhaustion." Similar comments were ubiquitous among immigrant advocates regardless of group affiliation.

Some interviewees shared Patricia's view that the problem involves the greater socioeconomic context that induces transnational migration. One of these was the condition of Mexico, which immigrant advocates tended to describe as economically poor and politically corrupt. Others noted that such troubles are not unique to Mexico but endemic in the global economy. Rhonda (Samaritans) said the biggest cause of migrant traffic is free trade policies that enable US agribusiness to undercut farmers in the southern part of the hemisphere:

> What you're looking at is a primarily agriculture-based, subsistence economy in rural areas all over Mexico and South America. Two things happen. One is the cultural traditions are altered by this influx of available goods or television, and what they've traditionally done but can't do anymore because they can't compete or because they see something else that they need, they sell the farm that's been in the family for eighteen generations and take all the money and pay a *coyote* to go north. That then breaks up the family. It's so wrong on so many levels that people even have to come up here, and then to die.

The real issue, in other words, is not people getting sick or even dying in the desert. Rather, it is the material inequalities that push people to risk sickness and death.

Not surprisingly, given each group's unique founding purpose and regular activities, there are slight differences in the way the members name the problem they are working on. Derechos members are much more likely than other groups to demonstrate a strong regionalist orientation that views the site of conflict as territory that has been defined for generations as biculturally and transnationally interactive. Like Patricia, they note the deaths as necessitating action, but often describe migrant fatalities as only the most egregious among multiple violations of human dignity along the border. Alex, for instance, argues that drawing hard lines between the United States and Mexico hurts "a community that's been a part of this land for hundreds of years. Everyone's together on both sides of the border, and we should do more to not separate us, but to look at us as we're all in the same situation, we're all occupying the same areas and we need to work together to solve the problems that we're having." Carla, similarly, says, "Part of the crisis is the disunity and the chaotic situation of division" resulting from militarization in both rural and urban areas. She decries "the state of siege the border has become, with law enforcement directed to migrants and therefore the generalized community." Derechos' argument that a crackdown aimed at foreigners will inevitably boomerang with damaging repercussions for US citizens is rooted in the perception of a borderlands culture where people, practices, and sympathies sometimes circulate in ways that governments do not dictate.

## Identities in Relation to Migrants

In naming these problems, the speakers implicitly or explicitly claim identities for themselves, assign identities to migrants, and propose relationships between the two. Across the board, they express this relationship in terms of interdependence or underlying similarity. In religious or secular universal frameworks, immigrant advocates characterize migrants as good because they are human beings, and all human lives are, as Annie said, "valuable," with inherent worth. Some metaphorize the connection by referring to migrants as siblings. Charli (Humane Borders), discussing people who are critical of work on behalf of migrants, lamented that "they've lost compassion. They've lost the sense of brotherhood with fellow mankind, you know? It's like, 'Oh, they're not of us.'" Mary (Humane Borders) described how spending extended periods in Latin America gave her such a sense of kinship with the people there that transnational migrants are "like my own relatives coming up. To me they [are] brothers and sisters."

Immigrant advocates also envision themselves and the migrants in terms of more proximal relations, moving from the rarified ethos of "we're all human" to more concrete, social-structural bonds. One basis of proximal relations derives from being part of the United States, though they use the term variously to reference the economy, the government, cherished ideals, and codified laws. Like Annie and Allen in the case studies, other immigrant advocates frequently express a strong association of personal well-being with the functioning of the US economy, saying things like "economically we depend on these people" (Mel, Samaritans) and "our standard of living and cost of living is lower in certain sectors, like food. Our food prices are much lower than many other countries because it's on the back of these people. So I mean we're all benefiting" (Sparkle, Samaritans). Barry (Samaritans) said it is evident that migrants are helpful for the United States, because employers hire them. "I've actually talked to people in Phoenix that are air-conditioning, you know, construction people. Buildings are going up there like crazy, and they said the only reason there's so much construction is because of the illegals. They have so much of a labor pool that they're sort of keeping the economy going. It's almost like an underground. . . . I wouldn't say an underground economy. . . . It's like an underground source of bodies to use for, you know, to keep America going, whatever they're doing—construction or Wal-Mart."

Though the immigrant advocates do not see their personal agency as synonymous with the economy, they understand themselves as part of a social aggregate of buying and selling that assumes a kind of agency through the sum of interactions. They suggest, then, that without ever deciding through formal means such as a vote, "we are inviting people to come to work and we want the workers" (Mary, Humane Borders).

Immigrant advocates also claimed a form of nation-state affiliation in which subjects are responsible for their government's actions. Cynthia (Humane Borders) and Laura (Samaritans and Humane Borders) placed themselves as part of the United States in this sense when they spoke, respectively, of "our immigration policies" and "the policies that we've constructed to keep people out." Rhonda (Samaritans) made the point by relating her experiences on a delegation to Nicaragua at a time when the United States was sponsoring an insurgency against the country's revolutionary leadership:

One of the eye-opening things was that people were so sweet and so kind to us as people. Implicit and sometimes explicit was, "we know it's not you; it's your government." And my only response was, "Dammit, I *am* my government. That's what the United States is. I was ignorant, I had no idea, I wasn't paying attention or this never would have happened. I would have stood in the way of it somehow." [Laughs] And that's kind of where I am with the migrant thing. I can't just let it happen. I have to do what I can, because I am my government. I'm part of it.

Recognizing migrants as people with whom one is interconnected, in turn, seems to stimulate empathic responses. That is, once people perceive a similarity between themselves and migrants, the welfare of the migrant relative to oneself becomes a vital issue. As exemplified in Patricia's and Annie's case studies, immigrant advocates often describe themselves as people with a comparative abundance of something—health, money, opportunity—and claim identities in which it is incumbent on one to alleviate the condition of the afflicted.

Within the universal frame, advocates simply view themselves as human beings helping other human beings access needs fundamental to survival. Barry (Samaritans) says it's important to view the migrant as yourself: "I see it as putting yourself in the other person's shoes. I don't care how they got there. How would you feel if you were totally desperate and out of water? I would feel pretty bad." Moreover, says Rhonda (Samaritans), encountering someone in the midst of such a plight *requires* a lifesaving response: "We can prevent people from dying. It's okay. It's a moral obligation as a human being to do that."

Many immigrant advocates attribute the compulsion to relieve suffering to their identities as Christians. In a portion of an interview quoted at the start of this chapter, Fenton relates:

> I was sort of unchurched most of my life. But once I started going [to church in Tucson] regularly and started learning and paying attention, it became clear that one of the things I really believe is that we're all one. People crossing the border are just like me and you and everyone else. They're like my neighbors down the street, as far as I'm concerned. So that part led me to realize that the situation that's happening in the desert is just insane. There's no reason for it.

Fenton brings together several acts of identification and relation here. One involves a personal transformation where involvement in a church deepened his perception of a common, undifferentiated humanity. From that perspective, he conceptualizes migrants as people on his block—a neighborhood metaphor similar to Annie's comment that if her friends from Mexico died trying to cross the desert, "[i]t would be like they died on my front porch." Fenton combines the familiar and domestic by describing migrants trying to meet the basic needs of their households.

Mel, a Samaritan and Presbyterian Church member, serves as an example of how some movement members link their involvement to Christianity and the example of Jesus: "Certainly some of the teachings of Jesus are concerned with people who are having a rough time—the prostitutes and those who are rejected by society and so forth. I basically feel that this is what the Christian church should be doing, to try to stand up for these people." Christianity is also the driving force for Cynthia (Humane Borders), who says she became involved because of "my faith convictions that have to do with justice and mercy. I happen to belong to the Disciples of Christ, but most of the major denominations at least give lip service to justice and mercy. That's what the life of Jesus was about." Laura, a Methodist who has worked with Samaritans and Humane Borders, attributes her involvement to Christian teachings that she summarized through the migrants-as-siblings metaphor: "To me it's just real simple. We're brothers and sisters, we are on this Earth to help each other, and when one of us suffers, we all suffer, and when one of us is hurting, we all hurt, and it's our responsibility to help each other alleviate that suffering."

Some immigrant advocates express similar views in secular terms. Bruce, for instance, has some antipathy to organized religion and chalks up his involvement in Humane Borders and Samaritans to testimony he heard from family members who lived through the Great Depression: "I developed from these stories a sympathy for the underdog, for the kind of people that don't have the advantages that a lot of us have for one reason or another." Monte, a Derechos Humanos member, says he's not religious and frames his involvement in immigrant advocacy partly in terms of self-defense: "An injury to one is an injury to all. If they go after—and I say 'they' meaning the right-wing or the corporate powers—they go after the minorities first because they figure the white people aren't going to care," next, he says, they'll come after unions, of which he is a supporter. In Monte's view, all social groups are connected, and halting attacks on other people is actually within one's self-interest.

People who have church affiliations also cite nonreligious reasons for their involvement. Sparkle (Samaritans), a Presbyterian Church member who is also a nurse, locates her motivation in the ethos of being a medical professional, as did others working in that field:

> One of the things I made a commitment to when I became a nurse was that I wanted to help [the] disadvantaged. When I went to the first organizational meeting [for Samaritans] I just knew right then that the migrants were individuals who really were desperate and didn't have many advocates for them, especially health advocates. I really think the noblest part of health care is to assist those people who don't have access otherwise. I don't question when someone needs medical help. I believe that one has to help them and professionally that's how I act. I would always use my professional ethic; it's an ethic that I go by, and it transcends the politics of the border.

Interviewees also discussed relative advantage and responsibility in terms of national affiliation. When Allen talked about "inviting" undocumented migration as a source of labor—a concept Mary echoed—he noted that being embedded in economic relationships makes one complicit and responsible for their ethical dimension. Samaritans and Humane Borders volunteer Raleigh concurred: "If you are luring people to come here, then it's your responsibility to make it so it's not deadly." Like Annie and Patricia in the case studies, many understand their membership in the United States as putting them in a position of greater wealth and opportunity than those crossing the border. They expressed a sense that the United States' wealth and power are uniquely great, and that having access to such perks requires them to be accountable to people who do not. Mary (Humane Borders) says,

We have plenty to eat, we have a place to stay, we have all that we physically need to live. And then I look at the ones who are walking across the desert—they do not have all the physical things they need even to live or to support their family. And with such a discrepancy just in the right to live, the right to live as a human person, I feel we in the United States need to balance that somewhat, or to equalize it a bit.

Evelyn, who works with Derechos Humanos, asserted,

It doesn't mean that we have to become martyrs. I believe that we have to live our lives and enjoy our lives and provide for our family, but I think especially the more blessed we are with material goods and good physical health and mental health, then I think we have a responsibility to try to make this world a better place.

Likewise, Mel (Samaritans) said,

I think that our country is a rich country, and the best traditions of our country are those in which people can recognize that we're lucky, that we're really very blessed in many ways. And I feel that as a country we should try to help people in other countries.

He related his work on migrant issues to this greater vision of the world:

We're in a very affluent situation, and the large part of the world is in a Third World country. You see the classified ads in Sunday's paper where Long Realty is trying to sell off several million-dollar homes, and they're pushing affluence, affluence, affluence. I think Americans are forgetting the fact that the world is not that way. My feeling is that we need to realize this, not only practically, but also spiritually, that we have an obligation to change things so that people who are suffering are not going to be suffering. That's just one small thing, the Samaritans.

Many immigrant advocates, in other words, think of migration from Mexico as a manifestation of global economic disparities that pose a moral challenge to the comparatively wealthy.

By relativizing the well-being of migrants to the well-being of people in the United States, advocates downplay the restrictionist portrait of migrants as lawbreakers. Restrictionists see undocumented entrants as forces of chaos and adamantly argue that the most important aspect of entering the United States unlawfully is the unlawfulness. Those who commit such an act should be understood first and foremost as "illegals," "criminals," and "invaders," and undocumented entrants are therefore essentially deviant and antisocial. Immigrant advocates see things differently. Allen, a Humane Borders member, said that among humanitarian groups "the word 'illegal alien' is kind of taboo, because a person can't be illegal. They can *do* something illegal, but they can't *be* illegal. And 'alien' kind of sets them apart from the human race." Patricia from Derechos Humanos argued that "if I'm just 'illegal,' I'm not a woman, I'm not a daughter, I'm not a wife, I'm not a child. I'm 'illegal.' It's an easy way to strip someone of their humanity and it's easier to mistreat something you don't recognize as human." Instead, advocates commonly describe the migrants as conscientious family members seeking a livable wage in exchange for their labor, and express approval of this ambition. Cynthia of Humane Borders says, "Immigrants come here almost entirely because they need a job and they need to have money for their families. They're willing to do most anything to do that—as most responsible Americans would be if they had families to take care of and didn't have a job." Ofelia, who has worked with both Humane Borders and Samaritans, seconds the point: "Like every other race, every other nationality, there's good and bad. And the majority of the people coming here are not coming to rape somebody or destroy somebody's property. They're coming here to better their life or their children's lives. And it's too bad that they cannot do it legally." Sean, a Samaritans volunteer, says "it's the argument of stealing a loaf of bread to feed your family. The law becomes a little bit irrelevant at a certain point."

## Prioritizing Identities

Interviewees unanimously affirm their status as subjects of the United States and sometimes locate their actions, like Mel does, in the country's "best traditions." From the identification of self with government—articulated earlier by Rhonda as "I am my state"—it follows that several immigrant advocates say their work exemplifies and fortifies democratic ideals. They described democracy as a polity in which the government's great technical, legislative power must be checked and energized by the subject population.

Dennis (Humane Borders) said that Congress is the place where the rules can be changed, but the ideas for how to do that come from the population at large. He shared his memory of a radio interview he had heard several years ago: "A congressman was saying that 'Congress takes the lead in formulating laws,' and my thought is that Congress is the last person [*sic*] to know. It's the *people* who have to make their representative realize that changes need to be made."

Other advocates shared Dennis's view that although a government enacts laws, common people are something like the conscience of the state and a democracy is only as good as its subjects are active. Some immigrant advocates call this kind of activity "citizenship" and others do not, but the model of the polity remains the same: the government will do the right thing only if people compel it to do so.

Raleigh, in a similar vein, shared his feeling that the value of Samaritans rests in part on the organization's ability to play a watchdog role:

> I think there are Border Patrol agents who would like to be more militaristic, and we're out there watching them and I think that causes tension, also. I think that's a big part of what Samaritans and Humane Borders does. We're watching everything they do. They can't just do whatever they want. We're right there, and we speak Spanish in our groups, we have actual medical expertise, so when they tell us something it has to be true. Because we can find out straight from the migrants. I think that's really an important role. Witnessing is as good and important a role as anything.

> *You were saying [in a previous conversation] that you see this as a peace issue.*

> It is a peace issue. I think I was talking about seeing *Hotel Rwanda* and seeing what can happen if there's no checks. If there's no balances things can go awry. I guess I see us as being a balance in that witness role. Being a balance in terms of our public relations.

They also stressed the dynamic aspects of democracy as a system based on open, ongoing debate, where different ideas ascend or descend in credibility over time. Carla (Derechos Humanos) commented on this at length:

> I consider myself, and I think most of us would consider ourselves, to be patriots in the sense that we recognize who we are: we are citizens of the United States. Now, some people may call us disloyal because we are not favoring whatever position the government takes.

And it's not that there are not positions the government has taken that we would not favor. But if there is a big position that we need to confront, we will. And that makes us equal patriots with those who support [the government], because that's what a democracy's all about. There has always been a sense of a free press being, like they say, the fourth arm of the government. I believe social movement is the fifth arm. Because it is through social movement that social change truly comes about. It's not coming from the top down. I mean, we can look at *Brown vs. Board [of Education]* and look at what happened. It was pronounced by the United States Supreme Court that segregation was illegal. But that didn't mean that all the schools opened and everybody walked in. There was a long, hard-fought thing to assure that that law became a viable law and not just a law on the books.

*There's a gap, too, between what's on the books and what the actual practice is.*

Exactly. And social movement is the fifth arm of trying to get the ideal and the practice to be closer together. What I see right now[2] is that we're in a very corrupt period, because the ideal is here [holds up one hand to the side] and the practice is way over here [holds up other hand to demonstrate a gap]. And the further away it gets, the more manipulative and corrupt it becomes. Maybe someday we will live in a utopia where it actually matches, but in the meantime the task of this other arm, of social movement, is to push and push for that to be. Now, you may ask, how do you see all those Americans who don't see it this way? Well, that's fine. Our task is to try and bring our information so that Americans become better Americans—better practitioners of what it means to live in a democracy, not to be manipulated by government, to be affronted by violations against other peoples and what we practice outside of our borders as well, not just internally.

Other immigrant advocates were more pessimistic about using the state to achieve justice. Annie's refusal to prescribe a grand ideological model for society parallels Patricia's remark that "no government is perfect. It's ever changing and it has to change with the world." Congressional legislation can approximate "good," but that good is a moving target. Some argued that desirable social conditions can be achieved only through personal, attitudinal change. Mary (Humane Borders) says, "I don't think that creating laws and policies is the perfect way to create equality among nations. . . . I'm not sure that laws or policies will control someone with a lot of power and money. So I think in the United States that motivation has to come from each person's wanting to find an ideal to work toward. Although I'm not totally against laws and policies, either."

Sparkle (Samaritans) specifically cites the Samaritans' work in what some consider a gray area of the law as exemplifying the ability—and necessity—of citizenship to transcend strict legalism: "It's part of the way I interpret being a good citizen. Sometimes as a good citizen you have to . . . it isn't like defy the laws or break the laws, but you have to try to widen the interpretation of them, and that's what we talk about, that civil initiative. . . . That whole idea that the hospitality in the desert and helping your fellow man is part of that, that you broaden what your duties are as a citizen."

Alex (Derechos Humanos) likewise described his belief in human equality as an inviolable principle that requires no legislation:

> The rules could change tomorrow and people could throw the Constitution away. I'm not going to say, "Well, they changed the rule, I'm not going to agree with that anymore because now we must live in a fascist state and that's the way it goes." I think that's the right thing, the way it should be, is the way of the Bill of Rights, the way of treating people on, you know, that level playing field that you shouldn't discriminate against other people. All people are created equal. That's not just an American thing to me; that's a human thing to me. I grew up in a very religious family that was Catholic. I'm not very involved in the church anymore, but some of those teachings kind of stuck with me, that you do treat other people the way you'd want yourself to be treated. You see them as an equal brother or a sister or whatever. So no matter what rules change in the government, that's not going to leave me. That's always going to stay, and I'm never going to change my mind about that whatsoever.

Despite their commitment to principles of freedom and democratic action, immigrant advocates relate to citizenship and patriotism in complex ways and only rarely volunteer those concepts as lamps that guide their decision making. Like Patricia, some see them as consistent with immigrant advocacy. Others, like Annie, reject them as unhelpful. Still others, such as Allen, see them as irrelevant to but compatible with advocacy work.

Most don't see their actions as in any way contrary or antagonistic to their citizenship or patriotism.

Interviewees often spoke gingerly about patriotism and expressed reservations about using the word in reference to themselves. Some said the term had changed, not just during their lifetime, but fairly recently. Laura (Samaritans and Humane Borders) felt patriotism had been "co-opted" and said it is "a pretty ugly term nowadays." Raleigh (Samaritans and Humane Borders) said, "Patriotism has been so misused. It's become more like nationalism than patriotism, the sense that 'we're the best, we're better than anybody else.'"

Many immigrant advocates relativize the concomitants of membership in the United States to larger concerns. Emilia, of Derechos Humanos, for instance, says,

> We're all part of the human race. I know this Mexican woman who's here legally and she doesn't identify at all with these people that come illegally. She thinks it's terrible the way they keep coming. "They know it's dangerous and it's their fault. It's their fault that they're dying." This is a real religious woman. I know her through church. See, that to me is very un-Christian, if you call yourself Christian. Or un-Godlike. To think that way to me is very much more a violation than being unpatriotic.

Emilia's Christian ethics maintain that one is responsible to other human beings first and foremost, and that these responsibilities take precedence over an ethical code based on patriotism. Others concur. Rhonda (Samaritans) says, "I can't imagine a circumstance where my loyalty to the United States would be greater than my loyalty to humanity. I just can't. And to the extent that there's a conflict, I will take on the United States." Charli (Humane Borders) flatly states, "My allegiance is to people." Yet some make the same point using the language of citizenship. Monte, who argues that "an injury to one is an injury to all," says "I look at [immigrant advocacy] as patriotic. It's a duty of citizens if you see some injustice or a wrong to try to stop that."

Others explicitly dilate the concept of citizenship beyond the confines of the nation-state. Fenton (Humane Borders) suggests that the current moment reflects a transformation in which people "are moving more toward [being] citizens of the planet," not just of one bounded territory. Evelyn (Derechos Humanos) sums up the views of a handful of other immigrant advocates when she says, "I believe [I am] a citizen of the United

States and I'm a citizen of the world. Because I feel responsibility for what goes on outside of this country as well. Especially—especially—when the policies enacted by my representatives are impacting the rest of the world. Then we even have more responsibility for that."

Thus, most immigrant advocates suggest that a correspondence between ultimate values and the social order can be approached through the nation-state, but only with appropriate guidance from the nation-state's subjects. The key to that guidance should be a sense of responsibility that understands "society" as larger than any one nationality—living as "a citizen of the world" or having an "allegiance to human beings." Either they see patriotism and citizenship as so separate from advocacy that the latter cannot contradict the former, or they see what they do as a reflection of being patriotic and good citizens, because patriotism and citizenship have value only insofar as they are vehicles for conforming to ultimacy.

## Conclusion

As discussed in chapters 1 and 2, social movements may be seen as "laboratories" that hypothesize and experiment with new forms of society that exist within the present one. But a movement requires participants—people who have decided that something in the world is not as it should be, and that they must act to change it. In the work of Derechos Humanos, Samaritans, and Humane Borders, participants are on some level communicating how they think of themselves, how they think about undocumented migrants, and how they think of themselves and undocumented migrants in relation to each other. The biographical anecdotes they relate to explain their views, like epiphanies in Nicaragua and family stories dating to the Great Depression, are more idiosyncratic than organizational mission statements, but they stake out political perspectives just as surely. These "convictions of the soul" advance the proposition that over and against divides such as language, nationality, and class, the lives of advocates and the lives of migrants are fundamentally similar and even interdependent. Group members sometimes express the bond between migrants and themselves in universal terms, so that they and migrants are connected simply on the basis of being human. Other times, they use more proximal relations, connecting themselves to migrants through the principles of circumscribed memberships that include religious faiths and professions.

These various understandings all in some way seek alternatives to US border policy, yet they do not oppose the United States as such. Instead of disavowing the United States, immigrant advocates claim membership in it. They do not see what they do as contrary to the national interest, nor do they intend it to be. They believe it is legitimate for the United States to create and enforce an immigration policy, and that good can come from doing so. Clearly, by these criteria, immigrant advocates are not operating on the assumption that the nation-state is incapable of bringing social life and ultimate concerns into right relations.

As a concise recapitulation of nation-based ethics among immigrant advocates, consider the words of "Edgar," a No More Deaths volunteer who offered the following message on the group's listserv as a reflection on efforts to fix immigration policy:

> [T]o me it's pretty clear that one solution that doesn't work is to pretend that nothing is going on, to hope that high walls and a treacherous desert will be enough to keep these cold and hungry people away from us. If we don't see them, then we can't feel bad and if we ignore them, then maybe they'll go away. I think it would be better to ask why these people need to leave their homes and make the journey in the first place. Then we would see how interconnected our luxury is to their poverty. . . . In the meantime we have to deal with the situation in a way that does justice to our own humanity and to the principles that we hold most dear in this country.

Edgar's reconciliation of collective identities that include both "humanity" and "this country" shapes and is shaped by the attitude that immigration is an "intermestic" phenomenon—that is, "simultaneously, profoundly and inseparably both domestic and international" (Manning 309). When Edgar argues that instead of building physical barriers, "it would be better to ask why these people need to leave their homes and make the journey in the first place," he shares the frustration of other immigrant advocates that although the economic impact of undocumented laborers is massive enough to implicate everyone in the United States in a web of commercial connections by which day-to-day life is sustained, there is at the same time a refusal to recognize the laborers as even implicit, de facto members in a national community. The refusal mirrors the reasoning behind US immigration policy since Johnson-Reed in 1924, when the decision was made to address fluctuations in the labor market by admitting Mexicans who were good enough to be workers but not good enough to be citizens. Historian David Gutierrez is particularly incisive on this point:

[T]he long history . . . of the ad hoc implementation of arbitrary immigration laws, the selective enforcement of those laws, and the periodic
expulsions of ethnic Mexican workers and their US-born children—in
short, the endlessly sliding mechanisms Americans have used to exclude Mexican aliens from becoming vested members of the American
community—stands as stark testimony of the extent to which business,
government, and the general public have colluded in exploiting and
profiting from the fruits of Mexican labor while they simultaneously
lamented and decried the cultural transformations of American society
caused by those practices. (211)

In the doublethink Gutierrez describes, the United States stands as a
self-contained and self-sufficient entity "innocent" of foreign influences.
Intermesticity, though, insists that the composition of the United States,
like all nation-states, is protean, not permanent, and interactive, not impervious. The United States is bound to other countries by ongoing ex-
changes, borrowings, and abrasions. If, as Edgar suggests, we "ask why
these people need to leave their homes and make the journey in the first
place," we will be unable to think of immigration as wholly "foreign," with
origins unrelated to everyday life in the United States. If we do ask these
questions, he says, we will be drawn into the deeper problems of colonial history and globalization, and "we [will] see how interconnected our
luxury is to their poverty."

Understanding the United States as partially defined by its relations
with a larger world, immigrant advocates insist that they have to look beyond the nation for suitable guides to statecraft. Judging from the comments of my informants, it appears that many advocates hold vernacular
conceptualizations of "patriotism" and "citizenship" as prosocial behavior
toward a population that can be larger than one's national cohorts. To
put it another way, it is as if patriotism and citizenship are Platonic shadows of essential (and perhaps unnamable) identities for doing right.[3] Paradoxically, from this standpoint, crafting an immigration policy congruent
with ultimate concern can only happen through citizen participation, and
that participation cannot be adequately guided by nation-exclusive logics. There must be something higher. John Lancaster Spalding, bishop of
Peoria at the turn of the nineteenth century, said that "he alone is a patriot
who is willing to suffer obloquy and the loss of money and friends, rather
than betray the cause of truth, justice, and righteousness, for only by being
faithful to this can he rightly serve his country" (qtd. in Curti 206). Most

immigrant advocates would agree. They suggest that patriotism and citizenship are simply means to see what is common between ourselves and others, to recognize a social body larger than individual bodies, and that when the given versions of those standpoints fail to do what they are supposed to do, they must be superseded.

# CHAPTER SIX

# Collective Expression

## Dramatizing the Crisis

Social movement organizations form with the intent of converting scattered, individual discontent into unified action. But their initiatives are accompanied by seemingly decorative and even superfluous flourishes that are sometimes denigrated as "merely symbolic" or "merely expressive," since they do not in themselves achieve group objectives. Certainly, any group perceived as limited to logos and slogans acquires a reputation for being "all talk." Yet if "talk"—and, by extension, communication in any form—is not a sufficient condition for effecting social change, it is nonetheless necessary. The struggle to define and mobilize human sympathies is waged through symbol and imagination, for without a compelling narrative that depicts ideals worth preserving, people will not act.

At the same time, creating a coherent, galvanizing narrative can prove difficult, since, as shown in chapter 5, people may be drawn to the same social movement by somewhat different worldviews and analyses. So even as collective expression serves to influence the opinions of outsiders, it also serves the self-reflexive purpose of harmonizing different perspectives among insiders and communicating crucial information about them to themselves (Rappaport 104–106). Successful rituals build solidarity among constituents and also satisfy the constituents' desires to unify identity and behavior so as to live out their "convictions of the soul." Far from being "merely" anything, symbolic action is indispensable for group coherence and perpetuation (Jasper; Nepstad).

The collective's rhetorical representations perform, on a larger scale, the same acts of identification and relation that individual members do.

Immigrant advocacy organizations, therefore, endeavor to develop images, words, objects, and kinetics that name the problems to be solved, characterize migrants and themselves in terms of identities and ethical obligations, and in doing so accommodate the different attitudes of their members toward religion, citizenship, and patriotism.

The first section of this chapter discusses each group's rhetorical representations in two categories. The first is *continuous* representation, which consists of more or less permanent signs that are fixed and generally accessible, such as group names, logos, and mission statements, which appear in numerous venues at any given time. The second is *contained* representation, which is scheduled, ephemeral (with a start and a finish), and, if done on a recurring basis, malleable.

The second section of the chapter examines two characteristic features of the rhetorical representations in each group. One concerns the ways in which the groups reconcile religious and secular perspectives. The other focuses on the groups' efforts to raise the visibility of migrant issues, particularly through acts of mourning for migrants who have died in the course of their journey.

## Rhetorical Representations in Humane Borders

### Continuous Messaging

In its mission statement (reprinted in chapter 4), Humane Borders says it is "motivated by faith" and that it "welcome[s] all persons of good faith." Participants in the group understand the word in more than one way. Allen notes that the term "good faith" is "kind of vague." He says,

> The way I see it is that we're not going to say this is just a Christian group, because obviously other religions find life valuable. I address the issue as a Christian moral issue, definitely, but I think the underlying theme for everybody is that it's more a fundamental moral issue that they find life valuable. And that's not rooted just in Christianity or just in religion.

He adds, "I see it as instead of saying 'all people of religion' or 'all Christians.' 'All people of good faith' means those who are volunteering for good reasons, as opposed to volunteering, maybe, just to find out where the water stations are and go hunting migrants. That would be bad faith [laughs]." Allen's cohorts share his understanding that the term covered religious and secular beliefs alike. Cynthia says people might have "faith in a higher power" or "faith in doing justice," and Laura talks about "a faith in the goodness of all people, a faith in knowing that we walk together."

Humane Borders also represents itself through its logo, which depicts the Big Dipper constellation with a white-on-blue rendition of stars connected by lines. A solid triangle in the "cup" and a series of wavy lines emerging from it suggest water flowing over its side. The logo appears on official vehicles, generally accompanies any in-group publications, and adorns merchandise like bumper stickers, caps, and jackets. In almost all instances, the name Humane Borders is accompanied by a somewhat different Spanish version: Fronteras Compasivas (Compassionate Borders). Allen says the Big Dipper icon on the Humane Borders logo "obviously, first and foremost, is a drinking gourd. That's what the Big Dipper represents. A gourd to ladle up a glass of water and drink it."

Some members, however, find additional meaning in that the Underground Railroad used part of the Big Dipper, the North Star, as a guidepost to help slaves escape to freedom. They explain the reference in different but approving ways. Raleigh says that in the times of the Underground Railroad, the constellation "didn't have anything to do with water. The drinking gourd was really to follow the northern star. But it's a nice symbol. It has a traditionally positive background, a positive movement for change." Cynthia points out a more specific link between assisting runaway slaves and the work of Humane Borders: "when you really start thinking about the group, it does have a connection to the saving of lives that was going on through the abolitionists. Different kinds of migrants, different circumstances, but still, migrants." She acknowledges the self-reflexivity of rhetorical representations in remarking that "the migrants coming across the desert don't know what that symbol means. But to us that's what it means."

At yet another level, the logo implies continuity between Humane Borders and Sanctuary, since the latter was sometimes referred to as a new Underground Railroad. Since Christians played prominent roles in these earlier movements, the logo may have additional resonance for Humane Borders backers who are Christian themselves, though this would not diminish affinity for the logo among other members.

Informants found the name Humane Borders fairly self-explanatory and not so multivalent. In Laura's words, "It basically says that our borders at this time are not humane, and that the goal is to humanize the border, humanize the policy, by doing simple things like offering a cup of water."

The group also depicts its work through a small ramada in the First Christian parking lot, just a few yards away from the organization's vehicles. The ramada, painted blue and white and accompanied by one of the group's blue water station flags, includes benches, a picnic table, and a single wall that is dominated by a display case. The displays include photos of members carrying out group actions, a map of southern Arizona that indicates the sites of water stations and migrant deaths, and a list of the bodies recovered each year since 1999. Above the case is a white sign emblazoned with scriptural verse from Isaiah 49:10: "They will neither hunger nor thirst, nor will the desert heat or the sun beat upon them. He who has compassion on them will guide them and lead them beside springs of water."

## Contained Messaging

Humane Borders sponsors two annual gatherings for volunteers and supporters: an anniversary in the summer, and a memorial service and march in the fall. The format of the anniversary varies somewhat, but usually begins with several activities happening simultaneously in different parts of the church. People can fill a plate of food and talk with friends, bid on silent auction items, watch one or more videos about immigration issues, and so forth. Every anniversary also features a guest speaker who focuses attendees on the group's purpose, but the mood is generally celebratory. The fall event, the Memorial March for Migrants, comes at the end of September to coincide with the release of the Border Patrol's count of migrant bodies recovered over the federal fiscal year. Volunteers and other supporters meet at First Christian on a Sunday afternoon for a program in the sanctuary, followed by a procession and a second, shorter service at their destination. (The Memorial March is discussed in greater detail in chapter 8.)

A similar expression of the group's concerns, "Lost and Found: Remnants of A Desert Passage," may be the most visually striking self-representation among Tucson immigrant advocacy groups. "Lost and Found" is a touring exhibit of items discarded or lost by migrants that members have collected during water runs and trash pickups. The centerpiece of "Lost and Found" is a glass case that contains, among other things, the largest artifacts in the exhibit: a baby stroller and a bicycle. Other items in the case and its smaller, auxiliary versions, are mostly personal effects such as backpacks, toothbrushes, photographs, books, and water bottles that provide a mute but material testament to the migrant journey. "Lost and Found" makes part of the migrant experience portable, so that instead of taking people to the desert, Humane Borders can, in a limited way, take the desert to them—whether in Tucson or more faraway places.[1]

For Humane Borders members, at least, the exhibit summons reflection on the universal and proximal identities that motivate their work, and they hope it will do the same for others. Mary and Cynthia both said that the objective of "Lost and Found" is to educate observers about migrant journeys. Cynthia suggested that the flip-flops, tank tops, and other items reveal "how naïve the people are that are coming. Those aren't terrorists that are trying to cross the desert. They're young people that aren't prepared." Laura described the exhibit as a reflection of the common humanity that some immigrant advocates articulated in chapter 5: "It's another visual of the human suffering. The person is gone; this is what they've left behind for various reasons. And the photographs and the letters and the bus tickets and the baby clothes are another stark reminder for us who see it that these are people just like us. These are families. I think it's a powerful way of creating that message, that everyone must rise up and say 'No!' to this and do something about it."

Bruce locates the source of the exhibit's power in its ability to produce something more ineffable: "You see these artifacts left behind—children's clothing, Bibles, backpacks, bicycles, toys—and they're not just trash in somebody's backyard. This is something that people were carrying. It's a part of their life, part of their spirit. And when they're left in a migrant camp, it's like the ghosts of these people that were left behind." I interviewed Bruce at his house, and as we talked about the exhibit he gestured across the room at a collection of items he had found in the desert over the years. He noted in particular a Bible he had picked up the week before:

It's in perfect condition and it couldn't have been there for very long. In this kind of climate it would have disintegrated really quick. People's garments disintegrate. They've been left behind and bugs get in them and start chewing them up. It's ashes to ashes, dust to dust. So there's a mystery there of who were they? Where were they going? What are their dreams? What did they leave behind? What were they thinking when they were there, and why did they leave this? What were the circumstances of them leaving something like a Bible behind? Did their ride arrive and suddenly, "Just leave everything, we've got to go"? That appears to be the case in some situations. Or they spot Border Patrol coming, they take off, and they can't come back and they leave these things behind. So you have the feeling that these people, when they left [their homes], they only had so much space, and they took these things. Maybe it belonged to their mother or someone. Who knows? So there's all this mystery surrounding migrant artifacts. What do they mean? You're never going to be able to answer that.

The display serves the greater purpose of humanizing the viewer's impression of migrants. It allays fears about their intentions, for one, and encourages the viewer to recognize the migrants on a universalist plane as "people just like us." Bruce, elaborating on this concept, indicates that the power of the artifacts is their capacity to spur speculation about how the artifacts got left behind, which pulls viewers into imagining themselves as migrants, facing the vicissitudes of a desert journey that could result in life or death and make the difference between life and death for others. The concept of mortality, in fact, pervades his explanation, where he names the items as "ghosts" of their former owners and refers to their decay as "ashes to ashes, dust to dust." To preserve the objects, then, is in some sense to preserve lives.

## Rhetorical Representations in Samaritans

### Continuous Messaging

Like Humane Borders, the Samaritans prominently feature "faith" in their mission statement, which identifies them as "people of faith and conscience who want to respond directly, practically and intimately to the crisis at the U.S.–Mexico border." It further notes that the group includes "diverse faiths . . . united in our desire to relieve suffering among our brothers and sisters and to honor human dignity." Samaritans present for the group's early days describe great controversy in discussions over whether they would identify themselves as "faith based." (Obviously, those who favored the "faith-based" designation prevailed.) Polly says, "I think there were a couple of reasons [for the dispute]. At that time George Bush started talking about 'faith-based' groups taking over social services, so we didn't want it to be a Republican thing. And some people have no church identification, like myself, and it's like, I didn't come here because of a church." Despite being unaffiliated with any organized religion, Polly says she "was not one who got up on a soapbox" to oppose the proposed language and has come to see possibilities for being faith based without being tied to a religious institution. "We have faith that what we're doing is the right thing. I can't believe otherwise, that it's not a good thing to help people in need, whatever your ideas are about border policy. It is not bad to be out there helping these people. But you have faith that you're going to come home at night without being arrested by the Border Patrol [or] shot by a vigilante group."

Polly's description, like the one offered by Humane Borders member Allen, makes faith something akin to optimism or holding a conviction. But Rhonda, a Samaritans participant and Presbyterian churchgoer, understands the concept as somewhat more demanding:

> Here's why it's faith based: when we started out, we saw no one. We went out every day for two months and never saw a migrant.[2] All the people who were in it for the action and the drama dropped out, and the people who stayed were the people who had faith they were doing the right thing anyway. We kept saying, "If you don't have faith, you're not going to make it in this business." That's what it amounted to — saying "this is important." People have to have faith. Wherever it comes from, wherever they draw it from. You don't even have to say you're a Christian, but you have to have faith. You have to be doing this for the right reasons and you have to be coming from a faith place or it's not going to work. And they didn't and they fell away. It wasn't very exciting to go out and spend six hours in the desert and not see a soul. They wanted to save a life.

"Faith," then, involves doing or believing without any guarantee of results. "An awful lot of lives were saved that we'll never know we saved," she said. "[And] a lot of the lives we save today may be lost tomorrow." When I commented that she seemed to think of "faith based" as encompassing faith in things besides God, she replied, "All faith is faith in God. All faith in the future, all hope. You look at some of the wonderful things that have been done in the Bible and outside the Bible. Many are led by unchurched people who just were touched. See, my faith is that it's God doing all of that stuff."

The group's promotional pamphlet outlines the group's activities but also casts the group as extending several ethical worldviews. First, the group claims to be "[c]ontinuing the ancient Southwest tradition of hospitality," which connects members to a region bigger than themselves and practices older than memory. Second, the members associate themselves with a heritage of social change by describing their work as "an ongoing exploration of what Sanctuary co-founder Jim Corbett called 'civil initiative.'"

Third, they note that "[f]or some, the work also explores the provocative question asked Jesus: 'Who is my neighbor?'" which acknowledges that Christianity is present but not unanimously held among members. Religious references also appear on the final page of the pamphlet, which lays claim to Jewish and Christian traditions by offering two passages from the Pentateuch: "You shall not oppress a stranger; you know the heart of a stranger, for you were strangers in the land of Egypt" (Exod. 23:9) and "[o]ne law and one ordinance shall be for you and for the stranger who sojourns with you" (Num. 15:16).[3]

As a means of identifying themselves to the Border Patrol and others, the Samaritans apply a magnetized logo to either side of the vehicle's front doors. The logo has white lettering on a red field and says "SAMARITANS" in an arc across the top. Four droplet shapes of increasing size fall from the middle of the arc to the bottom of the magnet, where the Spanish translation "Los Samaritanos" is flanked by circles that bear green medical crosses.

Samaritans members were fairly consistent in their interpretations of the logo. The most concise came from Rhonda, who said, "We wanted a cross and a drop of water, because what we were really trying to do was create something that would impart to a migrant that we had water and it's safe to approach us." And, in fact, the logo only appears on the magnets members affix to vehicles when going out on patrol.

Like the Humane Borders logo, the name Samaritans permits dual religious and secular usage. At one level, it refers to the parable told by Jesus in Luke 10:25–37, which Mel connects to the work of the organization:

> The story in the Bible is that there's this fellow that was set upon on a highway by robbers and was left for dead, lying by the side of the road. Several people came by, I think a priest or a rabbi came by and saw this guy and he went on. And finally a Samaritan came by, and he saw this guy and saw he was really badly injured and put him on his donkey, and took him to the town and set him up for the night and gave the innkeeper money and so forth to take care of this guy. I think the concern has been about so many people dying in the desert, especially in the hot summer months, and if there's some way that we as a group or a people can go out and help these people individually. Trying to help them is, in a way, doing what the Good Samaritan did.

Members relate the story with varying degrees of emphasis and detail, and those who are not Christian accept the name because "Samaritan" has acquired meaning outside of a biblical context.[4] "I didn't even know what the Samaritan story was," said Annie, "but I liked the word and I knew it had something to do with helping people." Even if members differ in their basis for appreciating the name, their acceptance of it as a rhetorical representation lies in its multiple meanings, which bridge Christian "people of faith" with non-Christian "people of conscience."

### Contained Messaging

Unlike Humane Borders and Derechos Humanos, Samaritans does not typically sponsor large public events. But the moment of silence that begins their meetings exemplifies self-reflexive rituals in which the actors themselves are the primary audience.[5] Mel suggests the moment is intended to offer a chance for spiritual reflection that is inclusive of different backgrounds: "It's like a minute of silent prayer or contact with—well, they don't bring up a particular faith or God. This moment of silence could be effective for a Jewish person doing the same thing, or a Muslim person, or a Quaker or a Unitarian." Sparkle described it as "a time to kind of draw in and to, again, touch base in your own heart with why you're there and what the main purpose is." But Polly, who, unlike Mel and Sparkle, is not religious, hypothesized a more mundane rationale: "It may be that it's simply a way to get everybody quiet before we start."[6]

## Rhetorical Representations in Derechos Humanos

### Continuous Messaging

Derechos Humanos, unlike Samaritans and Humane Borders, does not describe itself as "faith based," and its continuous messaging is devoid of religious references. At community events members usually display banners featuring the group's name in Spanish and English, along with the bilingual slogan "Ningun Ser Humano es Ilegal / No Human Being Is Illegal." The group's most commonly used logo, which also appears on the banner, shows a jagged, black form recognizable as Mexico and portions of the greater southwestern United States in silhouette. The upper portion of the map, roughly corresponding to the location of Arizona and New Mexico, is inset with a hole that reveals an eye staring straight ahead at the viewer. Just to the right, in a white space that would ordinarily show eastern Texas, is another eye, and farther down the landmass, half a mouth protrudes out of the eastern coastline into the Gulf of Mexico. A stretch of barbed wire runs horizontally across the bottom of the map, and an open hand reaches over the top of it.

Monte, like several other Derechos members, explained that the logo depicts "somebody looking over" the border from Mexico, "getting ready to cross." Some gave extra attention to the map motif. Alex suggested that the graphic represents the fence "disrupting the continent" and the combination of the continent with the eyes and mouth show that "it's not just land, it's people that are being separated by this piece of wire." Emilia, likewise, said, "It's not just land; it's people and land together." These perspectives are consistent with the propensity (noted in chapter 4) for Derechos Humanos members to stress that militarization has damaged the practice of binational and bicultural community in the borderlands. Emilia also noted that the region depicted appears to be "all kind of one territory" because the map is solid black and does not feature national or international boundaries. Grisele took a somewhat different view by suggesting that the hand represents a border crosser, but "[the] eyes are us, as Derechos. We're like their eyes," watching for potential human rights violations.

Derechos Humanos decorates its news conferences and potlucks with banners and two displays called remembrance boards, which commemorate US citizens killed by border law enforcement. The first of these is devoted to Esequiel Hernandez, Jr., eighteen, who died on May 20, 1997, when he was shot by Marines in Texas doing an antidrug patrol as part of a Joint Task Force Six operation. The second honors Bennett Patricio, Jr., also eighteen, a Tohono O'odham who was hit and dragged by a Border Patrol vehicle on reservation land on April 9, 2002.[7] Each remembrance board stands up in a trifold about four feet wide and a yard tall and bears a photo of the deceased along with accounts of his life and death. The object of the remembrance boards, says Patricia, is to "remind people that the victims are us too. It's not just some immigrant you've never heard of from a country or a state that you've never been to. These are people in our communities that are our sons and daughters and our brothers and sisters, and they don't need to have their lives cut short because of militarization of the border."

## Contained Messaging

Among the most important points on the Derechos yearly calendar is the Corazón de Justicia/Heart of Justice. An awards dinner that is also a fund-raiser for the group, the Corazón de Justicia recognizes the work of "organizers within our communities who have shown exemplary strength in the struggle for peace, dignity, and human rights" (Coalición, *"Corazón"*). The event is held in a large banquet hall, and features a catered meal, followed by the awards ceremony and a keynote speaker. Notably, the award categories include African American issues, labor organizing, and environmentalism, unifying disparate causes under a rubric of "justice" that also includes immigrant advocacy.

Derechos members and supporters also often assemble in public for events, including memorials. Their candlelight vigil in 2000 was the first ceremony convened in Tucson to mourn migrant deaths in the desert, and since that summer they have held a vigil for the same purpose every Thursday night at a local shrine known as El Tiradito. Though Derechos meetings do not feature anything like moments of silence that offer so much as a hint of religion, the vigil functions as a kind of supplement to the meetings, since it happens on the same day of the week and members pace the agenda so that people have time to get there. (The vigil is discussed in greater detail in chapter 7.) Another memorial event Derechos Humanos sponsors is a pilgrimage connected to Día de los Muertos, the Mexican Day of the Dead. The pilgrimage, which has been held every year since 2000, begins at St. John's Catholic Church in Tucson and concludes with a program at San Xavier Mission del Bac, a Spanish mission completed in 1797 and located just a few miles away on Tohono O'odham reservation land. The original impetus for the event seems to have been the rise in fatalities among migrants crossing the desert, but the occasion has also been used to mark the deaths of Patricio and Hernandez, as well as the mysterious killings of women workers in the Mexican border town Ciudad Juárez. (The pilgrimage is discussed in greater detail in chapter 8.) Derechos backers periodically march on other occasions as well, sometimes within Tucson and sometimes in border towns where the march begins on one side and ends on the other.

## Rhetorical Representations: Analysis

Not surprisingly, the rhetorical representations of immigrant advocacy groups often seem to correspond part for part with the perspectives of individual members (as discussed in chapter 5). Despite many differences in their form (word, image, bodily movement, etc.), the joint tendency among them is to characterize migrants as dignified people whose suffering warrants sympathy. They also issue their moral appeals in extranational terms; that is, through frameworks of right and wrong that are not tied to particular nation-states.

Yet many other individual perspectives never appear in collective expression at all, and it must seem that the collective's rhetoric consists of whatever is left over after some perspectives, for whatever reason, have been subtracted. But it is also true that through collaboration, groups may find points of overlap in their various worldviews and end up defining themselves in novel ways as a result. That is to say, instead of an absolute reduction of meaning, collective expressions may bring about an enhancement of meaning, because they mark a creative synthesis of what people believed before they began working together, and the ways in which they have accommodated their differences. As a result, the group's identity is shaped by cumulative interactions that isolated individuals would not have engaged in.

Two standout examples among immigrant advocate groups are the ways in which the groups reconcile religious and secular viewpoints and their mobilizations of public mourning for migrant deaths. A return to individual immigrant advocate comments will illustrate why and how the groups have shaped their collective expressions as such.

## Reconciling the Religious and the Secular

Derechos Humanos, Humane Borders, and Samaritans all maintain pluralistic memberships because they facilitate religious forms of expression without seeming to coerce nonbelievers into insincere pantomimes of piety. One factor contributing to the coexistence of religious and secular members in the organizations is that both tend toward what may be called a humanistic ethos which holds, in the words of one scholar, that "the individual person is a primary source of human value" and "a truly human personality requires cultivation by society" (Reichley 41). The ethos therefore promotes the sanctity of the individual and the validity of individual reason, but rejects any conception of privatized paradise by asserting that the self must exercise its potential collaboratively, through interaction with others. There may be "theist humanists," who believe in the divine, and "civil humanists," who do not (Reichley 41–52), but the difference between them lies in the means of reasoning, not the conclusions.

Though immigrant advocates embrace and deploy religious signs that resonate with members who are Christian, they also attempt to use symbols with enough latitude of meaning to include those who are not, so that all members can feel that their views are compatible with the group mission. One example among Samaritans and Humane Borders is the word "faith," which, as the interviews suggest, is somewhat slippery and may well be used for that very reason. Group informants reveal that "faith" may serve as a kind of code word indicating religious believers who are open both to people who hold religious beliefs but dislike religion in organized forms and also people who do not self-identify as religious believers in any way. For those put off by the word "religion," "faith" may have a softer connotation, yet it is also compatible with the identities of those who view religion favorably.

The potential discomfort of self-identified secularists may also be palliated by something the groups don't do—namely, evangelizing. Humane Borders and Samaritans dub themselves "faith based" and publicly use Christian symbols, but internal procedures tend toward minimization of doctrine. No one is required to attend the Migrant March, for instance, or believe in the Trinity to put the Samaritans logo on their vehicle. Allen (Humane Borders) explains, "Humane Borders focuses less on the religious reasons for action and more on the actions themselves," and Sean (Samaritans) says "singleness of purpose is a focusing element" for Samaritans. Christian and ecumenical religious symbols are used in ways that permit members to interpret the signs for themselves and opt out of certain meanings if they are not comfortable with them. Members do not actively work to convert their cohorts, nor the migrants they assist. In fact, the individual beliefs motivating participants come up so rarely in the course of group activity that Polly, a longtime Samaritan, recalled an instance where she was asked if there were any Methodists in the group and was unable to remember. Later she remembered several, but the fact that she did not immediately associate members with religious institutions spoke well of the group to her because she professes no religious beliefs of her own. "It really very infrequently comes through. To me, that's not an issue. I think if it were, I wouldn't be involved. It would bother me." Charli (Humane Borders), who is also without religious affiliation, said the same thing:

> I was worried that Humane Borders would be, you know, we're doing our water run and we come upon a migrant and suddenly we say, "Okay, give me a moment" and spout some God thing. I'm all, "I'm not going to do that." So when I found out that that's not what they do and it's really just about scrambling and helping people, then I thought, "Okay, this is excellent." And actually, on the water runs and out on the trash run there is nobody going, "Oh, praise God, this is all because of God's work," or anything like that. I don't hear any of that.

Even without actively seeking converts, religious believers may affect the timbre of social interactions by bearing the moral authority of their institutions, and immigrant advocates were well aware of this. On a Samaritans trip I made with Annie, I noticed that during the off-road foot patrols she would call out, "Somos de la iglesia"—"We're from the church"— even though she herself is not religiously affiliated. She later explained to me that

It makes us look, if nothing else, dowdy and harmless, you know? Really. "We're from the church!" and they all go, "Oh, fine. Okay."

*So there's somebody out there; maybe they can see you, maybe they can't, maybe they can hear you. But you can't see them.*

And I want them to know that we're not in any way harmful to them.

*So even though you are not from the church, you are sort of. Southside is a church, and so forth, it's a way of making yourself more approachable.*

It's a way of making contact and letting them know that we're not there to harm them or report them or turn them in. Which doesn't mean that's how all church people are. I'm trying to make contact with invisible beings that are hiding out there, so I'm always trying to figure out what are the things to say and, other than thirst, why would they approach us.

The religious identification may be important for other audiences as well. Polly (Samaritans) noted, "I think it serves a purpose in our presentation to bigger authorities. It distinguishes us from groups on the border like the vigilante groups." Raleigh (Humane Borders and Samaritans) said

There's something about a middle-aged woman—whether it be sexism or whatever it is—a middle-aged woman from a church, you just trust her. [Laughs] That just seems to be. The Border Patrol just trusts that. . . . Maybe "trust" isn't the right word. They're not nervous, they're not intimidated, they're not worried that they're somehow going to overpower them or make them do something they don't want to do or something. I know that I stand back if I'm with a quote-unquote church lady. I feel like they're a much better diplomat in those situations. They present a better front than me, who looks just like another Border Patrol person walking up to them.

Laura (Humane Borders and Samaritans) noted that the church associations help in presentation to the larger public as well. "I think that the religious symbolism in some ways—and I don't mean this in a negative way—I think it in some ways legitimizes the work. I think it makes it easier for people to understand. It touches a place that wouldn't normally be touched if you didn't use religious rhetoric."

No less than Humane Borders and Samaritans, people in Derechos Humanos have found religious signs a way to express the acts of identification and relation that are integral to their work. Ironically, Derechos Humanos convenes a public event based on a religious model—the weekly vigil at El Tiradito—more frequently than either Humane Borders or Samaritans. Despite the absence of religious language in Derechos Humanos' name and mission statement, members acknowledge that faith is a huge part of what motivates some of them, and, like members of Humane Borders and Samaritans, understand "faith" in multiple ways. Emilia says, "I think we all have the same kind of faith-based sort of thing in a way, whether it comes out of a belief in a higher power, force, God, whatever you want to call it. Spiritual being. Or humanistic thinking. I don't think there's any discrepancy." Grisele says her religious convictions and her human rights work are "two separate things," but sees a dimension of faith in both of them. Like the Humane Borders and Samaritans members who described faith as something similar to optimism, Grisele underscored the importance of believing

> that by what you are doing today, or tomorrow or yesterday . . . something will change. And without faith, you're not going to do that. Most of [the members in the CopWatch program] are like, "Why are we going to document just this one abuse?" You have to have faith. If you don't have faith, whether it be in God or reason or whatever, if you don't have faith that you're going to achieve it or you're going to overcome this obstacle, and you're going to have equal, human rights for everybody no matter what, then it's never going to happen.

As with the members of other groups, most people in Derechos Humanos see religious and secular orientations as equally valid. What matters is someone's commitment to principle, not what the principle is founded on, and agreement on the principle is taken to show that religious and secular perspectives are similar or identical beneath the surface. Emilia says, "Wherever your motivation comes from, the idea is that justice is something that is needed. Ours isn't faith based as such. A lot of the people have a certain amount of that. But there's atheists, too, and we work together." Gabrielle, who is not religiously affiliated but grew up Jewish, says she has "a spiritual base" that doesn't correspond to any established, named tradition. Because she has "a really high level of trust, politically and spiritually, in the core people" in the organization, she accepts the presence of Christian elements that might otherwise make her uncomfortable. Speaking of another Derechos Humanos member, she said,

> I experience her as really spiritually grounded. At the level of whatever that is, she's very grounded. So if she identifies as Catholic and that's how she does that, that's cool, as far as I'm concerned. Below the words or below whatever the symbols are, there's something that seems very solid to me and something that resonates with how I feel the world, so it's okay.

A contributing factor to the successful inclusion of some secularists and non-Christians in the groups may be that unlike versions of theism that produce rigid in-group/out-group distinctions, theist humanism corresponds to what Linda Woodhead and Paul Heelas have called "religions of humanity," which "tend to view the only true boundaries of community as coterminous with the human race itself" and "thus hope to transform human society as a whole" (71). They "are characterized by a strong sense of the importance of the collective dimension of human existence and by active ethical and political concern, . . . [arguing] that doctrine and dogma are secondary to action" (71). Hence, theist humanists may consider themselves highly orthodox in their interpretation of sacred teachings, but because they downplay the importance of ideological orthodoxy—"I mumble the creeds," admitted one interviewee—they readily form working alliances with people who have the same objectives, even if those people are motivated by other religions or secular philosophies. These "religiopolitical coalitions" (Cunningham, *God and Caesar* xiii) are inflected by faith but inclusive of people whose religious practices are variously devout, nominal, or nonexistent.

Theist humanists and civil humanists alike hold that every individual has unique, inalienable worth, idealizing a society where people have more similarities than differences and those similarities compel the comfortable to aid the aggrieved. By avoiding any necessary equivalence between the group as a whole and a specific religion, immigrant advocacy groups fuse religious teachings with the rhetoric of human rights and humanitarianism so that individual members can be moved by whichever perspectives seem to make the most sense to them. From two extremes of possibility—only secular or only religious—all three organizations strike a balance so that concrete expressions of sacredness and authority may illustrate group identity without invalidating individual beliefs.

## Migrant Visibility and Mourning

As shown in chapter 5, immigrant advocates typically describe themselves in relation to migrants in terms of interdependence and relative advantage. Though dismayed that many of their cocitizens do not share these perceptions, many advocates hope that publicity about the issue will eventually push levels of concern to the tipping point for change. Fenton (Humane Borders) described the group's work by saying, "We just try to put a face on the migrants, you know? Keep [the issue] out there. Tell their stories so people understand they're just people, and that they have families and they're like everyone else." Fenton's comment suggests that hostility or indifference toward undocumented people is facilitated by thinking of them as an alien, anonymous mass.

By way of remedy, immigrant advocates promote more sympathetic accounts of migrants and their reasons for migrating, a task they often describe with optical metaphors (as seen in two remarks discussed in chapter 5). Charli, for one, told of her own move from ignorance to action by saying, "I was one of the blind people in this city." Similarly, Edgar proposed that "If we don't see [migrants], then we can't feel bad," because by acknowledging their presence "we would see how interconnected our luxury is to their poverty."

Public discourse about undocumented migrants, in fact, frequently features words related to visibility, with figurative language about "shadows" being a particular favorite. A newspaper reports that through congressional action, "illegal immigrants may have a chance to come out of the shadows" (LoMonoco, "Getting Immigrants"); the title of a scholarly study refers to undocumented immigrants leading "shadowed lives" (L. Chavez); and an article in an eminent review of hemispheric politics describes undocumented people inhabiting "a shadowy world where they live in fear of apprehension and deportation and remain vulnerable to every conceivable form of exploitation" (Hellman). These metaphors allude to the problem of crypto-residence, in which migrants cannot assume a fully public life because doing so would be dangerous.

Immigrant advocates also use optical metaphors to talk about crypto-residence, but in an altogether different way, arguing that while undocumented people inhabit a precarious limbo out of necessity, citizens and other documented people condemn them to remain there by refusing to acknowledge their social worth. Robin Hoover of Humane Borders has glossed some brands of anti-immigrant sentiment as indignation over migrants openly pursuing equality: "It's okay for you to come and work here, but it is not okay for you to expect rights. You're becoming too visible" ("Message" 1), and a Samaritans member who frequently sends out group e-mails includes, at the bottom of her messages, the quote "Beware the brutality of the averted gaze." For immigrant advocates, there is an ethical imperative to observe proactively, making sure they "see" and trying to make others "see" as well—not in order to mobilize a deportation dragnet, but to understand the migrant as a social entity. People who do not see migrants, either out of ignorance or conscious avoidance, never have to confront migrant suffering or its root causes. Seeing migrants is also a precondition for stimulating any kind of intermestic analysis, because if migrants do not exist as social phenomena, then neither do the larger processes of migration—push factors like infant mortality and agricultural collapses in the home countries, the separation from loved ones and familiar places, and the humiliations and injuries of the journey north, including, for some, death.

At a Samaritans meeting, group member Sparkle related an incident pertinent to this point that occurred when she and a botanical association were returning to Tucson after a trip to Organ Pipe National Monument. I asked her to retell the anecdote when I interviewed her shortly thereafter, and she obliged:

> On the way back, there had been a horrendous storm that we had missed, and we were coming through the desert area near, between Sells and Three Points, a huge stretch. And the desert looked like a swamp and the water was flowing over the road. Everywhere there were ridges, but the water was just—I'd never seen it like that. And I saw ten migrants stumbling out of the desert toward the road. And I mean it was still pouring rain. And the people in the bus didn't know they were migrants and I knew right away and I just turned to the few that were around me and said, "Well, they're migrants and they're in

desperate shape." And these people on the bus who are educated, educated people—

*Tucsonans.*

Yeah, Tucsonans. And a lot of them were very educated people. I don't know why, but in that society they know the Latin names of everything. That's disgusting—I don't!

*(Laughs)*

But it was very eye-opening to them. I said, "They're in desperate shape, which makes me think that people further up in the mountains are in terrible shape," because the water was flowing so hard people couldn't cross with that water, and in the desert you couldn't walk, because it was like a swamp. It was really sad.

*You said at the meeting that you felt the need to point that out to them.*

I did. I did because I think each time something becomes more concrete for people and they can see these people so desperate that they're willing to—really, this was risking their life—it touches you in a different way when it personalizes it. And this man turned to me and said, "How do you know?" and "Really?" And I thought, "Each time it just helps."

The most complicated optical references involve the different meanings of the word "witness," all of which involve a mode of seeing that is somehow more than just a passive intake of information. Laura (Samaritans and Humane Borders) explained her commitment to the groups by saying, "I feel compelled to be a witness. I feel compelled to put myself in the places where this is happening so I personally can . . . how can I say this . . . can be okay with myself that I didn't stand by and do nothing." Her sense of self (and perhaps her self-respect) at stake, Laura decided she had to renounce apathy by putting herself in the thick of the crisis. The words of Raleigh (in chapter 5) show how sometimes observing the conduct of government agents and contractors can in itself fulfill the aims of the group: "We're watching everything they do. They can't just do whatever they want. . . . Witnessing is as good and important a role as anything."

Simply being present in areas where migrants may be apprehended and detained serves to offset the possibilities for abuse of power by the state.

The concept of witness as seeing and doing is most thoroughly integrated in the Christian use of the term, which covers the actions performed as a consequence of one's beliefs. John Fife explained that, for the congregation at Southside, witnessing means "walking our talk. The talk is the words of scripture—the narratives and the texts to which we are to be faithful. The witness is, 'Okay, we need to match that with what it is we do,' and what we do is a witness to what we believe and what the words are that shape and form this community of faith." But Rhonda (Samaritans) explains that witnessing is also about sharing with others the experiences that result from "walking the talk":

[At] the majority of the [Samaritans] meetings, the format is that we introduce ourselves, we have a moment of silence, and then, probably the most important thing that happens in the meetings, is the testimony. People talk about their experiences.

*Is that really what it's called? Testimony?*

That's not what Samaritans call it. That's what it would be called in Central America with the religious groups down there. They talk about witness.

*So what does that mean? "Witness" usually has a courtroom connotation.*

It's rooted in religion. The whole idea of witness is to witness the Lord's presence in a transaction or a relationship or in your own life. So when you give witness, you're expressing a personal example of faith. In Central America, Witness for Peace—that's where that "witness" comes from. Christian witness is an act where you express your faith that God is with you regardless of what happens, and then we talk about it. That's giving witness. I'm not sure that many Samaritans would call it that, but in terms of Christian peacemaking and Christian humanitarian work, it's witness. It's extremely important, and psychologists will tell you that. Whether it's called witness or "feedback" or whatever it's called, if you have an experience out there, you need to talk about it and you need to talk about it in a group that understands and respects what happened. There are a lot of challenging things that go on out there, among which are finding migrants, having encounters with the Border Patrol, but also, importantly, nothing. When nothing happens, it's important to have an acknowledgment that you did something that was important, that you kept faith. That's probably the most important thing in the meeting, is to give everybody a chance to do their witness. People will come if they have something to talk about.

Immigrant advocates' rhetorical representations, then, depict ongoing efforts to redress the social invisibility of undocumented people by seeing, encouraging others to see, and acting in particular ways because of what one sees. In theory, at least, making the undocumented population "visible" and giving them "a face" will change attitudes in favor of border policy reform.

The most prominent way Tucson immigrant advocates do this is through public mourning rites. To mourn a death asserts that a person's life had value, meaning, and integrity, but even more fundamentally that it was a life at all, and to mark that where there was once a presence there is now an absence. Advocates are determined to inscribe these absences with meaning by insisting that migrants' lives are valuable and that their sudden deaths are tragic.

These rites correspond to a genre of ritual that folklorist Jack Santino has called "performative commemoratives," which differ from other forms of commemorating in their popular origins and political content. First, performative commemoratives emerge through grassroots activity; they are neither decreed by governments nor carried out within the strictures of institutional religion. Second, they are distinguished from private funerals in that they invite the involvement of the population at large and memorialize the dead under improvised circumstances, which is why some are also called "spontaneous shrines" (1).

Although it is possible to publicly mourn in a relatively apolitical conceptual frame, just as charitable humanitarian relief prioritizes aid without interrogating the origins of deprivation, performative commemoratives treat the deaths as unjustified and manifestations of a social problem. Santino argues that performative commemoratives at least imply political content by stressing the uniqueness of each individual decedent and saying, "We . . . will not allow you to write off victims as mere regrettable statistics. We insist . . . on acknowledging the real people, the real lives lost, the devastation to the commonwealth that these politics hold" (15). Further, they do so before a general population who are implicitly invited to join the memorial and work to overcome the forces responsible for the deaths. Personalizing the issue—as Fenton said, "to put a face on the migrants"—makes the commemoratives political issues even if there are no explicit programmatic calls for action by courts, legislators, and other decision makers.

Different ways of understanding and giving meaning to death can infuse memorials with a contentious mood. As an example, consider Diane E. Goldstein and Diane Tye's analysis of the performative commemoratives constructed in a Newfoundland coastal town after three local teenagers drowned. Media coverage of the drownings implied the victims had met their demise through careless daredevilry, but the people of the town resisted "the outside management of memory" (237) that dismissed the teens as unworthy of sympathy. As town residents saw things, the deaths were another chapter in the community's daily battle with a harsh, dangerous landscape that has claimed many of them and their forebears over the years. Through shrines and other forms of commemoration, they "began a re-narration of the tragedy, wrestling the memory of the boys away from the media construction of foolhardy deaths and replacing those images with a very different narrative of heroic bravery" (243) that honored the boys and the town's heritage.

Like the townspeople determined to honor the drowned boys, immigrant advocates' performative commemoratives renarrate controversial deaths. But because these rites mourn undocumented migrants, they are fraught with relevance for the cultural practices by which nation-states justify and perpetuate themselves. Nation-states depend on hierarchies of sentiment in which citizens reserve their greatest sympathies for national "kin." Foreigners, as outsiders to the family, are supposed to be less worthy of one's regard. But in mourning for dead migrants, immigrant advocates perform en masse what they say individually—that their ethical responsibilities apply universally, to an imagined community greater than the United States. The dictum that nationalism is "the shared memory of blood sacrifice, periodically renewed" (Marvin and Ingle 4) applies equally well to other imagined communities. Immigrant advocate mourning implies a moral community bigger than nations and a sentiment unbound by borders. The memorial described in chapter 1 for Prudencia Martin Gomez, for example, may be seen as a rhetorical representation in which the participants re-up their shared commitment to care for foreign nationals in need. Against narratives that elevate the nation to ultimate concern and deem migrants fundamentally alien, mourning rites contribute to a collective identity that emplots migrants and citizens as interdependent, not adversarial, sharing a conflicted past but also a common future.

## Conclusion

Collective expressions sometimes appear wholly extraneous to the technical achievement of a group's tasks, and they do not necessarily fulfill a movement's long-term objectives. In the case of Tucson immigrant advocacy groups, Humane Borders could fill water stations with trucks bearing other symbols on their doors, Samaritans could carry out foot patrols under a different name, Derechos Humanos could conduct abuse documentation without a weekly vigil, and so forth. Collective expressions do, however, address the vital work of attracting and retaining members, without which there would be no organization at all. Immigrant advocates undoubtedly hope their representations will sway the opinions of outsiders. But whatever external audiences the advocates may reach, their primary audience is themselves, for they are attempting to select words, symbols, and actions that will convey, to their own satisfaction, who they are, what they value, and what they want to achieve.

By combining multivalent signs with references to religious and political identities, all three groups harmonize multiple worldviews in the service of common goals. Displaying logos, contributing to performative commemoratives, holding moments of silence, and contemplating a remembrance board or a migrant artifact advance a general goal of humanizing migrants and affirming their fundamental, inalienable dignity. They at once model the world they want to see (the world that ideally results from their labor) and create symbolic repertoires intended to make that world more compelling. Through their rhetorical genres, immigrant advocates reimagine what the border region is supposed to be like—what values should prevail, what traditions should be upheld, what joys and sorrows should be commemorated.

The most public and corporeal collective practices among immigrant advocates commemorate migrant deaths. By mourning migrants, immigrant advocates engage in the complex of memorialization and identity formation by which political communities are innovated and sustained. (Chaps. 7 and 8 consider these rites in greater detail.) Without saying so in as many words, they are exhortations to *see* migrants and think of migrant suffering as a wrong that can and should be undone. Immigrant advocates carry out various material and symbolic interventions toward these goals, arguing that sovereignty is not an inherent good and that rigid mononational identities may not be sufficient for realizing human ethical obligations.

# CHAPTER SEVEN

# The El Tiradito Vigil

On the edge of downtown Tucson, in the historically Mexican American neighborhood Barrio Viejo (the Old Barrio), is a small dirt lot that hosts a shrine known as El Tiradito. The shrine is an arched alcove augmented by a three-sided adobe structure that consists of a main wall some fifteen feet high and thirty feet wide, with two sides that descend in staggered segments. Within the area embraced by the three walls stand a number of wrought-iron racks, which, like the tiers of the shrine and the ground beneath them, invariably bear an assortment of burning, seven-day candles.

Most visitors to El Tiradito come to petition for supernatural intervention in personal crises, and for this reason it has also been called the Wishing Shrine. The candles petitioners use to make their pleas have left a physical mark, for the shrine's back wall is stained with smoke, and the earth at its fore is darkened with deposits of hardened wax. These features, combined with the structure's uneven sides, can give the initial impression of a burned-out building or ruin. But El Tiradito looks the way it does because of use and devotion, not neglect or disaster. It is invested with decades of purpose, desire, and intent, and in that accumulation of private aspirations it has also become a repository of collective dreams.

Every Thursday evening since summer 2000, the shrine has also hosted a vigil sponsored by Derechos Humanos. During the vigil, participants circle in the middle of the lot for a short program of songs, prayers, readings, announcements, and reflections to memorialize migrants who die in their attempts to illegally enter the United States from Mexico.

In some ways, the shrine is an improbable site for the vigil. For one, El Tiradito has traditionally been used for private, personal appeals to divine forces, and the individualism of supernatural petitions is arguably antithetical to the social vision of activism. Furthermore, the shrine has no historical connection to either migrants or mourning rites, and the vigil is not directed to the spirit for which El Tiradito is named.

Despite these incongruities, however, the choice of location is not arbitrary. It contains a logic derived from the shrine's status as a place of folk religion that also became a historic landmark and an emblem of barrio culture. This chapter seeks to explicate that logic by tracing the evolution of El Tiradito's creation and use alongside an analysis of data collected during fieldwork with members of Derechos Humanos. The results suggest how decades of activity have made El Tiradito a cogent venue for the vigil, where secular and religious ideologies are synthesized into universalist concern over migrant fatalities.

## The Ritual of the Vigil

The community vigil is deeply rooted in the history of transnational migrant advocacy in Tucson. The site was used for similar events at least as far back as the Salvadoran Organ Pipe deaths in 1980,[1] and the vigil is facilitated by Father Ricardo Elford, a veteran of Sanctuary and various kinds of barrio issues dating to his arrival in Tucson in 1968. Elford, in fact, had previously convened vigils directed at social concerns, one in 1977 for Jose Sinohui, Jr., a friend who had been shot to death by a South Tucson police officer (Crittenden 25–26; Cunningham, *God and Caesar* 214; Otter and Pine 17, 23), and another that began in 1981 for the wars in Central America (Crittenden 26; Cunningham, *God and Caesar* 16–17; Otter and Pine 17, 23).

At the start of each week's vigil at El Tiradito, participants form a circle around an unlit seven-day candle and a designated facilitator, usually Elford, distributes photocopied sheets that outline the evening's program. The heading of the program, which reads "IN MEMORIAM," notes how many weeks the vigil has been held and indicates the current date. Below that are the words, "Remembering our sisters and brothers who have died crossing the desert in search of work."

To begin the formal order of service, participants sing the chorus of "Envía tu Espiritu," a song that is sometimes used in the Spanish-language Catholic Mass:

Envía tu espiritu
Envía tu espiritu
Envía tu espiritu
Sea renovada la faz de la tierra
Sea renovada la faz de la tierra

Send your spirit
send your spirit
send your spirit
the face of the earth will be renewed
the face of the earth will be renewed.[2]

From there, the program offers an opening prayer for those who have died in the desert and one or more readings, usually from newspaper accounts pertaining to immigration issues. Then there is a bilingual response taken from Proverbs 31:8. "Levanta la voz," says the convener, and the group continues in unison, "por los que no tienen voz; ¡defiende a los indefensos! Levanta la voz, y hazles justicia; ¡Defiende a los pobres y a los humildes!" The verse is repeated in English, beginning with the convener's "Speak out," and continuing with "for those who cannot speak, for the rights of all the destitute. Speak out, judge righteously, defend the rights of the poor and needy." The next part of the program, "Reflections," offers a moment for those present to promote upcoming events or report on various items of interest. These announcements sometimes prompt others to remark on recent social and political developments. Following this period of information sharing and commentary, someone moves to the center of the circle and lights the candle. "We light this candle," declares the convener, and the people continue, "so that all our migrant sisters and brothers who have died in the desert may not be forgotten. Amen." They then observe a period of silence, and read aloud a closing prayer that is addressed to "God of peace" and asks for "blessing upon our torn and tortured borderlands." The event ends with the folk song "Peace Is Flowing":[3]

Peace is flowing like a river
flowing out of you and me
flowing out into the desert
setting all the captives free

In its wider usage, "Peace Is Flowing" facilitates variation in subsequent verses by substituting different words in the place of "peace." The version performed at the vigil conforms to this tradition by adding a second verse that begins with the word "hope." When the song concludes, so too does the program. Someone picks up the candle and leaves it at the shrine with all the others. Meanwhile, the circle dissolves, and those in attendance depart for their next destination.

The vigil contains a greater number of symbols than can be fully explored here, but in pursuing its relationship to the shrine, two aspects of ritual in general are especially pertinent. First is the use of ritual to mark individual and collective changes of state, with the biological changes of birth and death being paramount. The very term "vigil" references such rites in Catholicism, where funerals are preceded by a vigil for the deceased, colloquially known as a wake. What is especially noteworthy about the Derechos Humanos gathering is that with very rare exceptions, the participants are directing their solemnity and attentiveness in remembrance of people they have never met or even heard of. The second aspect of ritual is what is sometimes called ritual's "subjunctive" mode, which describes the world as it could or should be. The vigil's order of service articulates religious principles—peace, righteousness, the affirmation of life—and brings those principles to bear on a very immediate, earthly context. The use of newspaper articles recalls an insight Benedict Anderson (35) attributes to Hegel, that in modernity the morning paper has taken the place of morning prayers—although the vigil actually brings the two into conversation: the insertion of mass media and announcements of upcoming legislation amid prayer and scripture brings out the relevance of each to the other. Having just read a report about the discovery of more bodies in the desert, or of parents and children separated by deportation, there is no doubt that participants are affirming their sympathy for undocumented migrants when they read the injunction from Proverbs to "[s]peak out, judge righteously, defend the rights of the poor and needy." The basis of that sympathy is expressed in the text of the printed program, which refers to migrants as "our sisters and brothers" in its heading and in the statement that accompanies the lighting of the candle.

The most obvious rationale for holding the vigil at El Tiradito is that the shrine's sacredness abets the invocation of a spiritual mood. But beyond this connection is a series of deeper affinities that become intelligible through a formal account of El Tiradito as a site of folk religion.

## El Tiradito as Folk Religion

The most helpful sources for information on El Tiradito's origin and subsequent development come from Southwest folklorist Jim Griffith (*Beliefs and Holy Places*, "El Tiradito"). As Griffith relates, multiple versions of the story behind El Tiradito are told, none of which appears to be definitive. The most that can be said based on what the competing tales share is that the shrine commemorates an event in Barrio Viejo dating to the 1870s or 1880s in which a murder victim was buried at the scene of the crime. Soon, the victim acquired a reputation for being able to mediate human petitions to God, and because the victim was buried in unconsecrated ground, he became known as "El Tiradito"—in Spanish, an affectionate diminutive of "the thrown-away one." El Tiradito's alleged power led to the building of an eponymous shrine that was eventually destroyed by highway construction, but reestablished in 1927 on land donated for the purpose. The shrine's adobe structure was erected in 1940 (T. Turner) and in 1971 the shrine, once again facing demolition for a highway, was put on the National Register of Historic Landmarks ("Wishing Shrine").

At first, this nominal, fragmentary history does not contribute much to understanding how El Tiradito became a compelling site for a vigil in memory of fallen migrants. But the words of Derechos member Carla serve to foreground some salient connotations of the shrine for further analysis. Carla describes El Tiradito as "a place that is very rooted in this community. It isn't a place that is Catholic or Protestant. It is just a religious place that was established by people, you know, who go and light candles there. So it is a place of people, established by the people. Now it's like a city-protected, historical little place. But it's a place that the community has designated as being sacred. And so it just seems very appropriate for us, therefore, to meet there."

Carla emphasizes that the shrine is associated with a "community"—a specific area and its inhabitants—and that it endures because of intrinsic desires among "the people" of that area, not extrinsic appeals from religious authorities. These features point to the importance of seeing El Tiradito as an example of "folk" or "popular" religion. Folk religion emerges when a religious community is stratified by a formally educated caste who occupy an elite position relative to a larger number of adherents. Though the activities of the elite caste may be critical to the institution's coherence and longevity, they may also produce a rarified, intellectual sensibility that does not connect with the plebeian mass. At least as far back as

Max Weber (80–101), religion scholars have noted that among a society's lower economic classes, where day-to-day existence is more precarious and less taken for granted, there is a high demand for a proximal God whose power can be influenced by ritual means. When the official religion fails to explicitly provide such practices, popular classes tend to create them, adapting the official religion in ways that stress the presence and accessibility of supernatural forces in everyday life. The quintessence of popular religious belief, then, is for the faithful to seek "special dispensation and release from personal, familial, or other specific ills" (Sharot 4): healing the sick, melting the cold heart of an unrequited love, or delivering monetary rewards ranging from enough to cover the electric bill to the payoff from a winning lottery ticket.

Folk religion also tends to concretize and particularize the abstract formulations of official cosmology. Popular pleas for intercession are typically not made directly to an omnipotent God, but to an individuated lesser divinity that is believed to have supernatural influence of its own or the power to lobby for dispensation from higher forces. These quasi-divine intercessors take different forms from place to place and person to person. Some may be considered efficacious for solving a particular kind of problem; others may be associated with specific vocations, social roles, or geographic regions. By conceptualizing the supernatural in such discrete varieties, popular cults give the grand generalities of officialdom an intimate and local feel.

Because folk religion distinguishes subordinates from elites, it stands in uneasy relation to the larger social order. Ecclesiastical authorities are routinely pressed to determine whether a deviation from orthodoxy falls within the range of acceptable quirks or imperils essential tenets. Local practice can often be harmonized with the larger institution insofar as it provides parochial constituents with familiar and accessible versions of official doctrine. But when authorities attempt to repress popular religious culture, or when popular religious culture corresponds to one side in a larger social conflict, the maintenance of that culture acquires a defensive, potentially antagonistic character.

The folk religiosity of El Tiradito emerges amid a borderlands region that was dominated for some three hundred years by Catholicism. To situate the shrine within this legacy, consider the role of saints in Catholic praxis. Catholic doctrine contains a canon of saints who have attained their status through an involved and time-consuming process among the uppermost echelons of the church hierarchy. Folk Catholicism appropriates members of the canon for their power to intercede on behalf of a terrestrial agent—a cluster of belief and practice that is usually tolerated but not necessarily promulgated by clergy. Complicating the picture are those instances where cults form around spirits of the dead who have not been canonized. Unlike an appeal to St. Anthony for help in finding a misplaced pair of eyeglasses, which simply adapts officialdom for mundane uses, veneration of these "folk saints" stems from a separate, popular canonization process that supplements that of the Vatican. Some folk saints in the US-Mexico borderlands, like Teresa Urrea, were renowned for their healing powers and wise counsel while living. Others became the subject of devotion only after death, as is true of the spirit commemorated at El Tiradito (Griffith, *Folk Saints*).

Folk religion at El Tiradito is recognizable first in the use of the shrine as a thaumaturgical means toward quotidian ends. But it also demonstrates the propensity for folk religion to thrive among its practitioners as a way "to provide legitimacy and protection for a particular social group" (P. Williams 68)—in this case, the overwhelmingly Catholic, Mexican American barrio residents who established El Tiradito in the late nineteenth century. Despite El Tiradito's popular genesis, there is no evidence that the shrine was intended to express antagonism toward the official Church. But a conflictual dimension in El Tiradito's history may be evident if barrio residents are viewed intersectionally, as not only Catholic but also a marginalized ethnic group.

This point merits a brief digression on social power and ethnicity in Tucson. Anglos were a minority in Tucson for half a century after the Gadsden Purchase in 1853, but they arrived with social and economic capital that gave them an advantage over Mexican Tucsonans in connecting with the greater US economy. The city's balance of political power shifted accordingly. Anglos ruled along nativist lines, raising barriers to the advancement of all people with Mexican heritage regardless of citizenship. The most important of these barriers were inequalities in pay and promotions, which confined most Mexican Americans and Mexican nationals to a lumpen underclass and also resulted in de facto residential segregation. Within these sequestered neighborhoods, native-born Mexican Americans continuously interacted with newer Mexican arrivals, producing a binational population that may be called Tucsonenses (by translating "Tucsonan" into Spanish).[4] Tucsonenses included among their ranks a prominent middle class, but pervasive discrimination ensured there was still a rough correspondence between Mexican ancestry and the lower economic strata (Sheridan 249–55).

The appeal of the shrine should be understood in the context of discrimination that Tucsonenses faced. Griffith puts El Tiradito in a category of folk saints he calls "victim intercessors" who are more famous for having been murdered than for leading virtuous lives. Precisely because they are victims, he suggests, they appeal to people in disadvantaged situations, and their lack of endorsement from Catholic officialdom is unlikely to concern people who feel disempowered by bureaucracies anyway (*Beliefs and Holy Places* 114–15). Furthermore, the Americanist religion scholar Peter W. Williams has argued that among Mexican Americans and other subordinated ethnicities, "the encounter with the hostility of a wealthier and more fully modernized culture has led to a heightened appreciation of religion as a source of pride and identity" (78), and if so, then the El Tiradito shrine was certainly an emblem of dignity for barrio denizens.

Though there is no way of proving this dynamic was at work in El Tiradito's early decades, later events seem to confirm it. In 1971, the shrine, already razed once for being in the path of progress, fell afoul of urban planning yet again when the city announced plans for a new east-west artery called the Butterfield Freeway. The proposed route was poised to inflict serious damage to Barrio Viejo, destroying the shrine and displacing an estimated twelve hundred people (T. Turner). Outraged residents organized in opposition. The ad-hoc community group dubbed itself the El Tiradito Committee ("Butterfield Opposition") and enlisted Tucson Legal Aid to argue on its behalf to the US Department of Transportation (B. Turner).

Meanwhile, a tandem effort to get El Tiradito listed on the National Register of Historic Places met success by the year's end. At a ceremony marking the recognition, University of Arizona professor Arnulfo Trejo, who had led the preservation committee, said that the shrine was a "symbol of 100 years of tradition in this barrio, representing the history of Tucson and the heritage of the Southwest" ("Wishing Shrine"). Simply putting El Tiradito on the register did not preempt freeway construction, but a month after the dedication ceremony the state highway department responded to a formal protest filed by Legal Aid by announcing it would revise the proposal so as to bypass Barrio Viejo.[5] The portion of the neighborhood that had been on the chopping block was saved.

Arguably, in protecting the shrine, the people of Barrio Viejo were protecting themselves. Over the years, El Tiradito had become imbued with countless hopes from petitioners, and these personal stories, in sum, constituted the story of a larger people. As Griffith persuasively argues, the events of 1971 indicate the site's transformation into "a symbol of ethnic

unity and identity" ("El Tiradito" 72). El Tiradito came to symbolize and
even materialize Tucsonense consciousness, and, in that, the perseverance
and value of a regional identity that became binational only after 1854.
But if at one time El Tiradito's ethnic significance stemmed from folk religion among Tucsonenses, inclusion in the National Register denoted how
ethnicity could also be secularized as cultural heritage. To be secularized
in this sense does not mean that the shrine lost its religious import, but that
it took on additional import as well, dilating its original use while retaining
strong associations with the particularities of transnational barrio life.

## Participants on the Weekly Vigil

El Tiradito's history does not predict the vigil, but it enables a greater understanding of Carla's explanation of why meeting at the shrine is "appropriate." If El Tiradito's past explicates Carla's references to "community"
and "the people," comments by Derechos Humanos members indicate
how each of these features finds correspondence in the vigil.

Father Elford connects the idea of the El Tiradito vigil to the broader
meaning and practice of "vigil" in Catholic tradition: "'Vigil' means
'watch'—not just vigilance, but in the sense of waiting. In church liturgy
there's an Easter vigil, which is in the dark, waiting for Easter to come at
midnight. So it's like we're waiting for light. The word means both 'watching' and 'waiting.' So, waiting for change." As for the Thursday vigil in
particular, Elford said,

> We're watching death in the desert. We're also looking at what's going
> on, and therefore in the reflections you get stuff from the newspaper.
> We bring up this stuff so that people can not only watch but get other
> people to look—you know, open their eyes. It's all about awareness.
> It's very much tied in with liberation theology, especially as it was
> and is practiced in Latin America, where you start off by observing a
> situation, but then you talk about it. That's *concientización*—a bad
> word in English in the sense that nobody understands it. It's aware-
> ness and then out of that you act. It's kind of a melding of prayer and
> learning and communicating, making aware—and action is part of
> the vigil also.

Elford's rubric is another case of immigrant advocates describing their
work as a practice of seeing that provokes an informed response. Many

attendees likely agree with his view, but other explanations are evident in the comments of Emilia, Patricia, and Evelyn, each of whom is Mexican American and Catholic. Emilia, a long-time Derechos Humanos member, attends the weekly vigil on a regular basis. She said the aims of the vigil are "to come together remembering, in memory of the people who died in the desert and are dying in the desert—kind of keeping the thought alive. And to share knowledge." Patricia tied the vigil very directly to the work she does for Derechos, which includes interacting with people who are filing claims of abuse by law enforcement agencies:

> This is a personal response, it's not for everyone. But for me, I carry things a lot, emotionally. Traumatic things. So for me the vigil is a way, to, like in Spanish say *desahogar*, to unburden yourself. In the Catholic faith, there's a saying, "offer it up"—you're supposed to offer up your burden to a higher power. You know, "arrogant little human, why do you think you are the only one that can take care of this?" When I think about it, I spend my days documenting abuses, and talking to people and talking about and listening to how horrible people can be to each other, and if it weren't for the vigil, where I can just leave that there and pray for it and acknowledge it, I don't know what I'd do.

Evelyn also explained things differently:

> Going there every week is really important to us on many levels. And I'm sure a lot of people have different takes on what they feel about it. I think for us it's very important that human beings are remembered as individual human beings, not as just statistics. We need to come together weekly because it's so brutal. . . . A third of the people who die are *desconocidos* [not identified]. So even worse than dying, for both of them—the person who died and the person who still lives—is the person dying thinking, "Will my family ever know what happened to me? What will happen to my family?" I mean, what a horrible way to go. And then the family members never knowing that their family members died. So it's important for us really to think about that. If you don't think about that, you just don't have it in you to really change anybody's mind. You have to feel it. The vigil is a place that you can go and tell the world that we are witness to what's going on. Those family members may not even know we're meeting, but we're sending them a message that we're there, mourning their

loved one, that it will not be in vain. There's just so many things. And then of course the vigil also gives us a lot of strength because we're there together and we talk about what's going on.

Evelyn reiterates several key concerns among immigrant advocates, like commemorating the individual worth of each migrant and giving particular attention to those who are not identified. She also uses an optical term to describe the vigil as an act of "witness" in which participants not only see but "tell the world" that they see and thereby connect with the kin of the dead. Carla said that the vigil "gives the faith-based community a place to gather once a week to express their own faith and witness" and elaborated on Evelyn's suggestion that the vigil joins participants in a transnational web of migrants and their families:

What is important about [the vigil] is that it serves the migrant community to know that this is occurring, that their loved ones who have died are remembered in prayer and that becomes very important.

*So part of the intended audience as you see it are migrants themselves.*

Oh, absolutely.

*Even if they don't attend.*

Even if they're not there.

She further explained that in the Catholicism of most of the migrants,

The death ritual is very important in the culture. I mean, essential: the proper burial, the proper wake, the proper prayers, the proper remembrance every year on the Día de Los Muertos. That's why our walk to San Xavier is so essential, because on that day all over Méjico, people are at the cemeteries, cleaning the graves and standing guard over the presence of their family members who have died. And in some indigenous communities they have food out on the graves and music and so forth. The living and the dead in this culture are equally important. For people in the United States sometimes it seems a little overdone, I think, but for those of us from the culture, there's not even a second thought.

I did not really grasp the significance of what Carla said the first time I heard it. I paraphrased her reflections to the effect that people wanted to honor the dead as they would be honored at home, and that she and other Mexican Americans had a bicultural literacy that enabled them to use the vigil, the Day of the Dead pilgrimage, and similar Derechos Humanos events as simulations of what happens in Mexico.

"And here, too," said Carla.

But I still didn't get it. Instead, I rephrased my previous observation, suggesting that the rites at El Tiradito were a sincere but ersatz mimicry of funereal ceremonies carried out by others. Carla patiently steered me back to her original meaning, that mourning the dead is not something done simply out of empathy for other mourners. Rather, she says,

> We have to. Because it isn't just "that's how it is in Mexico." It's the way it is here. This is how *we* feel. Even those of us who are secular. You know, *culturally* it's still important to carry out certain rituals, because it is part of the way we grew up or part of the way we are. So it becomes important even as we are secular, you know, to carry out these rituals.

Evelyn and Carla cannot be assumed to speak for everyone, but their comments reveal that at least some vigil participants conceptualize themselves and migrants from Mexico as part of a common culture. The attitude is not "we care for them as if they were one of us" but "we care for them because they are one of us." As noted earlier, the dynamics of ethnically segregated neighborhoods and routine in-migration from Mexico created Tucsonenses as a binational cultural demographic. But when US nationals appropriate a barrio shrine in order to memorialize Mexican nationals who are utter strangers, it suggests a more subjective facet to Tucsonense life as well—a sense of mutuality that one can rightly call not just a "community," as Carla does, but an "imagined community" in Anderson's sense of people who are "fully aware of sharing a language and a religious faith (to varying degrees), customs and traditions, without any great expectation of ever meeting one's partners" (188). "Tucsonenses" is actually too narrow a term for this imagined community, for the mourning expressed in the vigil is not contingent on whether the deceased intended to reside in Tucson. In fact, the vast majority of those crossing the border from Mexico are going somewhere else. But the term does concisely reference the cultural interfaces among Mexicans and Mexican Americans during more than a century and a half of Tucson history—interfaces that, combined with changes in Mexican American political culture since the 1960s (see chap. 3), have facilitated the perception of a transnational sodality that can be ruptured by the deaths of migrants even if one has never known them.

Monte, like Carla, doesn't identify as a religious believer, but frames his participation differently from her. A longtime political activist, Monte says he attends the event because he sees it as pragmatic from an organizing perspective. "I look at the vigils as being about getting the word out. We attract other people, religious people, and they take it back to their churches and communities and they talk about it. I feel like coalitions are really good. I'll go to events that have a religious overtone. I'll participate in that. We have to reach out to as many people as we can."

Monte's detached pragmatism differs from Patricia and Carla's sense of personal necessity, but the contrast confirms the vigil's success in accommodating a heterogeneity of religious commitment among participants. The vigil has, in Monte's words, "a religious overtone," but the program doesn't hinge on sectarian religious doctrines and is at least intended to be interfaith and welcoming to all.[6] Implicitly, at least, the vigil therefore weakens the divide between religious and nonreligious thought. Evelyn, who says the vigil "is faith based, but it's not just faith based," suggests that there is an underlying compatibility between views that have religious or secular appearances:

> In a lot of ways it's all artificial and semantics. Whether it's faith based or human rights, it still comes down to you wanting to act on behalf of somebody else, to take responsibility to stop the suffering. Language is but an attempt to define who we are and what we think and what we feel. You know, Carla can say she's agnostic or atheist and I'm a Catholic, but we're acting out of the same principle. She may not think it's faith based, but I think it's faith because she's got a faith or a belief in being good. So it's all the same thing. I've met many a communist type that think they don't have faith, but they're faith based, too. Sometimes it's better when we don't try to put a label or limits to it.

What matters, in other words, is someone's commitment to principle, not what the principle is founded on. As Carla puts it, "You'll never see Monte in a church. I mean, he doesn't go to services. I don't know how he believes, but he's a very secular person. I'm a very secular person, too. But we both understand it [the vigil] is not like a political show. It's who we are in the borderlands."

In this succinct equation of identity and action, Carla not only reiterates the concepts of popular agency ("the people") and sense of place ("the community") but joins them. The vigil, she suggests, expresses a distinctive culture among at least some inhabitants of the border region. Within that culture, carrying out traditional funereal rites signifies one's religious affiliation as well as one's regional affiliation. Furthermore, in Carla's experience, it is possible to detach the former while retaining the latter, and from the point of view of such a subjectivity, the vigil capably references particular religious identities outside of their institutional settings. It thereby makes religious and secular meanings simultaneously available and equally legitimate in the same way that El Tiradito denotes both folk Catholicism and Mexican ethnicity. Moreover, because the rites are "who we are in the borderlands," it is apropos to do them at a place that affirms the history of Tucsonenses, who exemplify the region's transnationality.

The vigil acquires additional symbolic resonance in relation to specific aspects of the El Tiradito legend. What makes El Tiradito unique as a shrine and a supernatural patron is that the victim of legend is not a pious martyr, but a sinner. (In the unsavory version adopted as official by the City of Tucson, he is a ranch hand caught in an adulterous liaison with his mother-in-law.) His character and the circumstances of his death explain the ignominy of his burial where he fell, without proper rites—a posthumous ostracization that results in him being dubbed "the throw-away." Part of what makes the legend so compelling, then, is the paradox of an unsympathetic figure who is transformed in death so as to mediate between mortal frailty and benevolent omnipotence. In this, El Tiradito is a kind of trickster figure who is at the same time remote from and near to God, a broken part capable of restoring wholeness, a transgressor whose redemption speaks to some unity of existence that laws, creeds, and social norms cannot implement. It could further be said that his supernatural power indicates a postmortem vindication—that he was falsely accused and punished by his contemporaries, but redeemed by God in the afterlife. Either possibility opens up the shrine to the subtextual moral that even those who are demonized and scorned can prove capable of doing good.

Of course, the most obvious analogue of the condemned El Tiradito in immigrant advocacy is the fallen undocumented migrant—the criminal rule breaker who dies and is in some cases "buried" by windswept earth at the place of death without any formal recognition. The vigil, though, intervenes in the social construction of memory to characterize migrants as people worthy of memory. Elford said that initially he saw no relationship between the legend and border politics, but "as we got going there I thought about it and thought, 'This is really appropriate. The throwaway. Bodies in the desert.'" In Carla's words, migrants "are not just simply thrown-away people"—that is, *tiraditos*—"but each one has dignity, a family, a place, and should be so honored."

Another possibility, in light of the idea that the vigil expresses "who we are in the borderlands," is that any individual migrant may symbolize the dynamics of life along the international boundary. Longtime Derechos member Lupe Castillo frequently relates the incident when she asked a *New York Times* reporter why news from southern Arizona often doesn't get national exposure: "He responded by saying, 'Well, you know, the border area is like a Third World country. And frankly in the United States, nobody gives a shit about Third World countries.'" The connection between the death toll and the territory itself becomes clear when Carla observes, "We are seen as kind of a throwaway region, sort of like neither here nor there, until there is a political reason to bring it into focus." By using a version of *tirado* to refer to both migrants and the borderlands, Carla suggests the broader implications of the vigil in reclaiming and revaluating not just discarded people but a discarded place.

The vigil also resonates with the El Tiradito legend when participants name migrants as their "sisters and brothers." As Sheridan notes, a common (though not uniform) schema in the story's many versions is that the shrine "commemorated a murder, one committed by relatives rather than strangers" (213). In these variants of the tale, El Tiradito can be said to be "about" a dispute among family members that ended in death. This detail acquires exceptional pungence via the insights of Virgil Elizondo and Roberto Goizueta, two prominent theologians of Mexican American popular Catholicism. Elizondo writes that for many Mexican Americans, the concept of family or *familia* "is not the house where people reside; it is the bond that unites persons and allows them to experience that innermost and existential sense of belonging. I am never alone; I am part of the *familia* and the *familia* is part of me" (111). Goizueta amplifies Elizondo's point, arguing that these interdependent relationships must persist even after the corporeal demise of a family member, because "the very existence of the Mexican American people as a people . . . depends upon the people's ability to maintain an intimate connection with one another, their ancestors, and the divine. Without that connection, the individual Mexican American literally does not exist; to 'be' at all is to be-in-relation. Thus, to sever the relationship, and thus the means whereby that relationship is forged and affirmed, is to kill the person" (122–23). Therefore, much as Carla says, "we have to" carry out proper death rites, Goizueta says, "We *must* visit and accompany our deceased relatives and we *must* affirm their ongoing participation in our everyday lives. If not, death has conquered life" (131, emphasis in original). This cosmology elevates El Tiradito's murder and unconsecrated burial from a conflict among relatives to a more profound tragedy in which people are separated from the practices that vouchsafe individual and communal identity.

The theme of a tragedy within the family most literally relates to the biological kin of migrants. Immigrant advocates unstintingly lament that the deaths sever migrants from their families. The unidentified dead are the subject of special attention because there is no closure or certainty for those back home. They are the extreme version of the crisis, the extraproblematic problem. Most immigrant advocates see immigrants as conscientiously providing for their spouses, children, and extended relations. A migrant's death inflicts emotional pain and likely results in greater economic hardship, but the crisis is aggravated in the case of migrants who are never identified or never found at all. Derechos member Kat Rodriguez once remarked during the "Reflections" portion of the vigil that such people were "unknown" and "literally disappearing," which casts a discomfiting pall of ambiguity over their intimates. As Evelyn said earlier, to die alone, far from one's relatives or any other human being, may well be "even worse than dying" for the migrant and his or her family.

Another "family" in vigil discourse is the binational, bicultural borderlands population. Of course, many biological families with members on both sides of the line routinely cross back and forth for vacations, social visits, weddings, and the like. But the concept of a borderlands "family" also extends figuratively to all those who live out a regional identity that is uninterrupted by the international line set down in the nineteenth century. In both cases, the deaths of migrants mark a rupture, a loss that cuts into the relations of a place where people, goods, and ideas have continued to circulate with or without passports.

The evocation of an imagined community in the borderlands doubtless implies solidarity and empathy among US members for their cohorts across the line in Mexico, but comments from Derechos members indicate that the familial metaphors in the vigil go beyond a location-specific ethos. Patricia explains that these references are meant to advance a more peaceful and consensual basis for human interaction: "It's really hard to be mean to a sister or a brother. If you think of them that way, it's hard to exploit them, it's hard to beat them, it's hard to rape them, it's hard to murder them, and if we looked at things that way, there'd be a lot less pain in the world." Emilia says the references mean "we're all part of the same human community. One family." And Carla asserts,

> It's meant in the sense that all humans are humans, right? And if we are a human rights organization, as Derechos Humanos proclaims to be, then we have to understand fundamentally that what we're talking about is the dignity of every individual as a human, and that we respect that. The indigenous always say, "to all our relations," because they, in their sense, believe that we are all interrelated. So it's said on a religious basis, "brothers and sisters," in a sense of preaching. It is also meant from a political, human rights perspective—that we are all in recognition of our basic rights. It can also be interpreted in a very indigenous way "to all our relations."

This figurative meaning proposes that all of humanity is a kind of family, where all people are related and compelled by that bond to relations of reciprocal care. To do so humanizes migrants and asserts that they are tied to the lives of US citizens, represented by vigil participants.

Whether the family is literal or figurative, the vigil epitomizes Goizueta's argument that community always includes people who are not physically present. If the "thrown away one" of legend represents the migrant, and the migrant is part of a family, then the walls and migrant bodies that define current border enforcement repeat the murder and rejection of El Tiradito, because both are about a failure to achieve the familial ideal of reciprocal care. The vigil, in turn, becomes a rite by which the living of the family mourn for their lost one and reaffirm the need to refrain from building barriers that sever relationships and vanquish life.

At first, El Tiradito seems an incongruous place for articulating universalist perspectives. Because folk religion is characteristically local, it cleaves to the particular, stressing personalized divinities, circumscribed populations, and crises that apply to peers instead of distant strangers—all of which seem antithetical to a panhuman ethos. Actually, though, this apparent contradiction simply revisits the means of reconciling folk religious practices with the official canon, wherein the immediate is understood as synecdochic for the general. Just as various Marian apparitions (especially Our Lady of Lourdes and Our Lady of Guadalupe) have acted as accessible gateways for vernacular Catholicisms to affirm the greater church, so does the reality of the borderlands "we" model the kind of compassion for foreigners required by postnational ethics. If, on the one hand, this identity affirms the border (as an ontological point of reference), the sentiments and obligations Carla attributes to it also imply its capacity to overcome the border. But the vigil telescopes this regional epistemology with universalism so that each reinforces the other. In so doing, the border between the United States and Mexico retains its historical and geographical specificities but also becomes one of many interstices that act as primers for developing new forms of spatial and political consciousness. Whether secular, religious, or both, the vision of panhuman unity enunciated in the vigil transcends regional strictures so that the Old Barrio becomes the stage for prophesying a new world.

## Conclusion

The Derechos Humanos community vigil highlights El Tiradito as a dynamic space where old and new meanings continuously interact. Griffith notes the shrine's ongoing transformation when he guesses that "[E]l Tiradito the person may well be losing out to El Tiradito the place as the source of supernatural power" ("El Tiradito" 72)—a thesis the vigil seems to corroborate. Recall that Carla's explanation of El Tiradito alluded to the sociocultural history of the place, not its eponymous intercessor, and that, as noted earlier, the intercessor is never mentioned in the vigil's program. But if the vigil layers new meanings on El Tiradito's origin, that origin is still what gives the vigil a foundation to stand on. Because El Tiradito's Catholicism was that of Tucsonenses, the shrine became an emblem of ethnic identity, which in turn prompted its secular legitimation as a place of cultural heritage. Because its Catholicism was also popular, outside of institutional control, there were no formal barriers to its use by others. The centripetal pressures of a singular tradition were weak and thereby enabled people to use the site according to private reconciliations of individual belief and official doctrine. As a result, the shrine today sustains use as a venue for extrainstitutional religion and a cultural-historic landmark—two modes of signification that are uniquely synergized in the Derechos Humanos weekly vigil.

El Tiradito is a credible, significant place for making a political statement because of its associations with Tucsonenses. Per Clifford Geertz's famous formulation of culture as a story people tell themselves about themselves, the story of the vigil says that the living of the borderlands community must honor their dead, that the living of the borderlands community must honor each other without regard for national boundaries, and that religious traditions provide viable means of doing both. Yet the vigil uses what is familiar and at hand to overwhelm the provincial and proclaim imperatives beyond finite human collectives. In the vigil, the US-Mexico border becomes representative for all instances of collision between racialized social superiors and inferiors and economic haves and have-nots in the world economy. The reference points of a particular folk stand in for the whole, becoming an example, not an exception, as people "act locally" (with "local knowledge") but "think globally" (by imagining a plenary human community).

Juxtaposed, the weekly vigil and El Tiradito are reciprocal commentaries, each revealing something about the other. The vigil illustrates how the shrine has been opened to new uses through secularization. The shrine shows that many immigrant advocates in Tucson have found religious references a means to express what is integral to their principles and purposes. Those acts emerge from a sense of selfhood and place that may be described as "who we are in the borderlands," even as they simultaneously address the moral demands of a geopolitically divided world.

# CHAPTER EIGHT

# Memorial Marches

Cultural geographer Wilbur Zelinksy has observed that "as *the* organizing symbol of [the United States] . . . the flag has preempted the place, visually and otherwise, of the crucifix in older Christian lands" (196, emphasis in original). A casual inspection of most public places would no doubt validate Zelinsky's thesis. But even as the cross no longer occupies the nave, as it were, of a pluralistic society, it has remained a powerful symbol in political discourse. In 2005, when protesters planted two thousand crosses outside President George Bush's Texas ranch to mark the deaths of US troops in Iraq, a local resident took umbrage and knocked them down with his truck (Glionna). Similar displays in Ohio and Georgia met the same fate, indicating that the cross is anything but moribund as a symbolic force, and its formal elegance is capable of plumbing emotional fathoms from serenity to rage.

Crosses are also the most ubiquitous symbol across the events sponsored by immigrant advocacy groups in Tucson. Many times, the cross appears in print form. Samaritans and No More Deaths both use a Greek cross (i.e., with arms of equal length) in their logos, each in the tradition of that symbol as a shorthand for emergency medical assistance; the list of the dead in the Humane Borders ramada includes small crosses between the names; and publicity for the Migrant Trail includes a logo that depicts a cross planted in a desert landscape.

But the most common crosses among immigrant advocates are small, handheld objects that take the "Christian" or "Latin" form, in which the horizontal beam intersects a vertical post just above the midpoint. They measure approximately one foot by one and a half feet and consist of two thin pieces of wood nailed together and painted white. Each is inscribed on the crossbeam with the name of a deceased migrant, along with the date his or her body was discovered. In the many cases where the remains were not identified, the inscription reads "desconocido" (unknown).

These crosses are especially prominent in performative commemoratives among immigrant advocates that may be called memorial marches, which are the most symbologically bountiful of any collective expressions among the groups. Though the marches vary in length and locale, they hold to a fairly consistent itinerary. In the first stage, participants gather for a program that includes the distribution of crosses. In the second, they leave the gathering site and journey to a new location. In the third, they hold a concluding program, similar in content to the opening, and the crosses are either retained by marchers or collected for future use.

This chapter discusses how three memorial marches, the Día de los Muertos Pilgrimage, the Memorial March for Migrants, and the Migrant Trail, serve as acts of identification and relation with migrants. Memorial marches serve immigrant advocates' constant struggle to cultivate sympathy among onlookers and to self-reflexively depict themselves. They draw on extant traditions of mourning and remembrance, particularly crosses, recitations of the names of the dead, and pilgrimages, but imbue these meanings with significance relevant to immigration policy and border enforcement under the Gatekeeper Complex. In doing so, the rhetoric of the events prophesies and rehearses a better world to come, sometimes using Christian terms to compare that future to a resurrection.

## Common Elements of Memorial Marches

Crosses are the most conspicuous example of how immigrant advocates construct memorial marches from the existing cultural archive of mourning traditions. For centuries in the West, the cross has ineluctably been associated with Christianity, and as a burial marker it simultaneously references the resurrection of Jesus and the eternal life of Christian souls. The use of crosses in memorial marches has precedents in other kinds of vernacular mourning, most notably roadside shrines. In the Southwest, the practice dates to Spanish colonists, who employed it when a traveler died in the course of a journey and the body could not be conveyed to consecrated grounds for a proper burial. The cross, then, would hail passersby to say a prayer for the deceased in order to hasten the soul's movement from purgatory to heaven (Griffith, *Beliefs and Holy Places* 100). By the mid-twentieth century, the concept was being applied in the aftermath of fatal automobile accidents on rural roads and in some urban areas as well, marking not the actual body, but the place of death. Roadside shrines are generally made and maintained by the friends and family of the deceased, though some chapters of Mothers against Drunk Driving have used the motif to indicate fatalities from alcohol-related accidents and reiterate their message about automobile safety (Everett). What holds true across these variations is that the crosses have been installed at places where travelers died sudden deaths.

Another common feature of performative commemoratives that appears in memorial marches is speaking the name of each person being mourned. Name recitations appear to be especially important as a way to personalize multiple decedents who may not have been known to the mourners. The most well-known example is "Unto Every Person There Is a Name," a rite on Yom Hashoah, Holocaust Martyrs and Heroes Remembrance Day, in which readers speak the names of Jews killed by Nazi Germany (J. Young 276). Folklorist Jack Santino noted a similar practice at a memorial for women slain in acts of domestic violence. The crowd gathered at a Christian chapel on a university campus to mourn twenty-two specific women, an aim achieved in part by twenty-two women who each assumed the role of one of the victims and related, in first person, her name and the details of her life. There may be many reasons for naming the deceased and providing other information about them at the events, but one appears to be making the tragedy less abstract and the deaths less anonymous. The website for Yad Vashem, the Israeli institution charged with Holocaust memorialization, asserts that through "Unto Every Person There Is a Name," "[e]mphasis is thus put on the millions of individuals — men, women and children who were lost to the Jewish people and not solely on the cold intangibility embodied in the term 'The Six Million.'" As Santino puts it, names call attention to "the personal identity of the victims" (6) so that mourners are better able to emotionally invest in them.

Another conceptual tributary of memorial marches is the pilgrimage. In its broadest sense, a pilgrimage is a journey that confirms or enhances the traveler's connection to an idealized identity. Pilgrimages usually conclude at a sacred place — the tomb of a cultural hero, a site of martyrdom, the home of a revered artifact — and often involve taking items to or from it. Yet in many ways the journey itself is as important as the destination. Because the journey requires the sacrifice of such things as time, money, and comfort, fulfilling it imbues the pilgrim with a degree of sanctity among his or her peers. Furthermore, these sacrifices are frequently accepted as the price of a kind of cosmic reconciliation, whether paying a perceived debt to a supernatural force or atoning for failures to live up to a standard of thought and behavior. In either case, the pilgrimage shows humility before a greater, more perfect power, and demonstrates a desire to merge with that perfection (Everett; V. Turner, "Death and the Dead").

The Día de los Muertos Pilgrimage and the Migrant Trail (which is not billed as a pilgrimage but is sometimes described by its participants as such)[1] owe in part to the prominence of sacred journeys in Mexican Catholic life, most famously the ongoing flow of visitors to the Virgin of Guadalupe's Basilica in Mexico City. But they are even closer in spirit to a series of marches carried out in the 1960s and 1970s by the farmworkers movement, which fused popular Mexican religious piety to grassroots labor organizing. The first and most well known of these marches came in 1966, when César Chávez led a group of Mexican and Filipino grape harvesters on a three-hundred-mile procession from Delano, California, to the state capitol in Sacramento. Chávez explicitly traced the origins of the Delano walk to Mexican pilgrimages, but also to

> Lenten penitential processions, where the *penitentes* would march through the streets, often in sack cloth and ashes, some even carrying crosses, as a sign of penance for their sins, and as a plea for the mercy of God. The penitential procession is also in the blood of the Mexican-American, and the Delano march will therefore be one of penance — public penance for the sins of the strikers, their own personal sins as well as their yielding perhaps to feelings of hatred and revenge in the strike itself. They hope by the march to set themselves at peace with the Lord, so that the justice of their cause will be purified of all lesser motivation. (386)

Against the opposition of secular allies, Chávez insisted that the movement had to express itself in religious terms. Hence, the marchers' public statement, "The Plan of Delano," which described theirs as a quest for "basic, God-given rights as human beings" (198), proclaimed "[w]e seek, and have, the support of the Church" and "we ask the help and prayers of all religions" because "[a]ll men are brothers, son of the same God" (199). In addition, as the pilgrims traversed the bounty and fertility of Imperial Valley, they carried at the fore a banner of the Virgin of Guadalupe and flags of the United States and Mexico.

Crosses, name recitations and marches have all been used in ritual practices elsewhere; all, in fact, appeared during the Central American refugee advocacy movement of the 1980s.[2] But the memorial marches position them alongside other symbols and messages directed at the circumstances of Gatekeeper-style border enforcement, particularly the thousands of migrants who have perished while traveling through the Sonoran Desert.

## The Día de los Muertos Pilgrimage

Since 2000, Derechos Humanos has sponsored an annual Día de los Muertos Pilgrimage from Tucson to San Xavier Mission del Bac, an eighteenth-century Catholic mission on the nearby Tohono O'odham reservation. The pilgrimage comes on the Saturday closest to November 1 and 2—All Saints' Day and All Souls' Day, respectively, in the Catholic calendar—which are celebrated in Mexico as Día de los Muertos or "Day of the Dead." Día de los Muertos syncretizes pre-Columbian rites with Spanish Catholicism in an array of customs that include displaying skeleton imagery, constructing altars in public and domestic space, and maintaining all-night vigils at the burial sites of loved ones. It is a time set aside to honor the dead, especially one's ancestors (Carrasco 142–47; Garcíagodoy). The program that Derechos Humanos distributes to participants every year explains that[3]

> Día de los Muertos, or Day of the Dead, is a celebration of life, a traditional way for the living to affirm their love for those who have passed away. On November 1st and 2nd, the memories and desires of the dearly departed are remembered—it is the one time of the year when our loved ones can return for a visit, and share with the living a little bit of the life that was left behind.
>
> Today, as we make our pilgrimage to the beautiful, historic San Xavier Mission, we walk with the spirits of those who have gone before us. We carry in our hearts the memories and dreams of all who have walked beside us in the journey of life. So long as we remember with love and honor, the dead never really die.

The eight-mile pilgrimage begins in the morning at St. John's Catholic Church, where participants assemble in the parking lot to apply sunscreen and pack provisions like water and fruit for the journey. They also take up the crosses that will be carried along the way, which feature the names of those whose bodies were recovered over the just-completed fiscal year. Prior to departure, the group forms a circle for a series of announcements in English and Spanish. These include safety instructions—"Obey the signals at intersections," "Don't respond to harassment," and so forth—but also focus participants on the purpose of the event. In 2006, for example, a speaker framed the occasion as a remembrance for the dead and urged people to maintain "a solemn mood" as they marched. Isabel Garcia, providing additional remarks, repeated the movement's emphasis on proactive observation by referring to the marchers as "testigos a la injusticia" (witnesses to injustice), who mourn deaths that are not random, but consequences of government policy.

Over the next few hours, the pilgrims travel city streets and highways to San Xavier, carrying, in the tradition of farmworkers' marches, a Virgin of Guadalupe banner at the front. Several other icons follow. One is a large white cross whose horizontal beam reads "Presente," a commemorative interjection that says the spirits of the dead are still "present" among the living (see chapter 3). Marchers also carry flags, usually of the United States, Mexico, and other countries in the hemisphere. They process down major streets, over the interstate, and then to a two-lane highway that enters Tohono O'odham nation land. The pilgrims maintain silence for the final mile, part of which passes along the nation graveyard, then arrive at the vast dirt lot in front of San Xavier. Walkers are met by supporters from the Tucson area and Franciscans from the mission. The entire group gathers around a large circle of stones, which contains dozens of crosses from previous years, arranged earlier in the morning by Derechos members.

Everyone who joins the circle receives a program, which provides crucial information for the service that follows. The covers of the programs change by year, though the ones I saw in 2004, 2006, and 2007 all depicted crosses in some capacity. The first page inside the program offers an explanation of the event (quoted in full earlier), and the opposite page usually excerpts the press release Derechos Humanos issues at the end of every federal fiscal year to report its own count of the dead. Tucked inside the program is a white, double-sided sheet that lists the names and ages of the people whose bodies were recovered. In the case of bodies whose identities have not been determined, the entry reads "Unknown, Unknown Age."

The defining and most consistent feature of the service synchronizes reciting the names of the dead with placing the crosses inside the circle. The list of names is divided among four people, and as the names are read, participants enter the circle to add the crosses they carried on the march to those already on the ground. The basic template can be augmented in minor ways, as in 2004, when each name was followed by four beats of a drum that Derechos speaker Kat Rodriguez explained was done to symbolize "the four directions." On other occasions, participants have been asked to say "Presente" in unison after each name is called. At the close, the group turns to the back of the program for a bilingual reading of the Oración por los Migrantes / Prayer for the Migrant:[4]

> Heart of Jesus, full of love and mercy, I want to ask you for my Migrant brothers and sisters. Have pity on them and protect them, as they suffer mistreatments and humiliations on their journeys, are labeled as dangerous, and marginalized for being foreigners. Make them be respected and valued for their dignity. Touch with Your goodness the many that see them pass. Care for their families until they return to their homes, not with broken hearts but rather with hopes fulfilled. Let it be.

The explicitly Christian nature of this prayer is somewhat anomalous within immigrant advocacy's ecumenical tendencies, but not vis-à-vis the pilgrimage itself. The Día de los Muertos event is the only immigrant advocate mourning rite that ties in with a denominational calendar, and the use of places of worship as start points and end points, along with the presiding role of the Franciscans at San Xavier, gives the event a pronounced Catholic tinge. To end the rite with an appeal to Jesus is not altogether out of place under the circumstances.

## The Memorial March for Migrants

The Humane Borders Memorial March for Migrants is held on the first Sunday after the end of the federal fiscal year. It begins in the First Christian Church sanctuary with a program that undergoes only slight annual revision. Like many of the rites Susan Bibler Coutin observed in her Sanctuary fieldwork (discussed earlier in chapter 3), it is based on a Protestant liturgy, with material pertinent to immigration and Humane Borders inserted into the various "slots."

The centrality of crosses to the proceedings is evident even before the service begins. On arrival, participants find the steps and floor of the chancel covered with dozens of crosses that will later be carried on the march. The printed programs, like those of the Día de los Muertos Pilgrimage, tend to include cross imagery, and an insert in the 2007 edition featured the names of the dead, superimposed on a cross, with small cross icons dividing each name from the next.

The first portion of the event, inside the First Christian sanctuary, establishes the integrity of migrants and cultivates empathy required for compassionate action. The liturgy, for instance, includes declarations like this excerpt from the responsive reading in 2004:

> LEADER: We lift up in prayer and reflection the many families, friends, villages, and whole communities torn apart by deaths that are needless, senseless, and preventable.
>
> PEOPLE: We lift up broken hearts, dashed dreams, lost opportunities. As we can, we feel the pain, the suffering, the exhaustion, the delusions, and the deaths.

Even as the proceedings resemble church services, they adapt the contents to reach an audience beyond denominational confines. For instance, program items are led by Humane Borders members, not just clergy or First Christian parishioners. Also, the rhetoric consistently orients participants to action in a disestablished public sphere, since there is a time set aside for elected representatives and public officials in attendance to speak, and also in that the program serves as a prelude to the second portion of the event, which is outside the church. During a segment in which a group member recites the names of those who died in the last year, participants are invited to come forward to collect one or more of the crosses from the front of the sanctuary. These then are carried out of the church as part of a procession, either on foot or in vehicles. Marchers also carry signs, some in English, some in Spanish, conveying a range of emotional registers: "U.S. Border Policy Kills," "Ningún Ser Humano es Ilegal" (No Human Being is Illegal), "Change U.S. Immigration Law," "Open Hearts." The destination of these processions has varied, but regardless of the site, participants reconvene for a prayer or benediction that reiterates the main themes of the preceding service.

## The Migrant Trail

The Migrant Trail is the longest memorial march, both in terms of distance and duration. The event begins on Memorial Day, which is the capstone of a three-day weekend in the United States that connotes the arrival of summer, the season when migrant casualties are always highest and the need for humanitarian aid greatest. The 75-mile walk spreads out over six days, beginning in the border town of Sasabe, Sonora, and concluding in Tucson. Though the route of the event actually corresponds to hiking trails and highways, not the more obscure paths of undocumented entrants, it nonetheless navigates the corridor where most of those entrants have chosen to journey since the late 1990s. Organizers describe the event as "an act of solidarity with migrants" and a way "to raise awareness about the deaths and terrible plight that migrants face" ("History of the Migrant Trail"). A participant on the 2007 walk said, "We're here to give respect to the people who have died" (Innes, "In Sorrow" B2). Some participants also use the key word "witness" (chap. 6) to explain the meaning of the action. One remarked to a journalist that the Migrant Trail is about "bearing witness to the deaths" (Innes, "In Sorrow" B2), and Reverend Stuart Taylor of St. Mark's Presbyterian Church greeted walkers at the end of the Migrant Trail in 2004 by saying, "Thank you for your witness."

The opening ceremonies for the Migrant Trail are held in a small Catholic church in Sasabe. There, crosses are distributed to marchers, who proceed several blocks to the international port of entry. Following a second ceremony, those able to cross the border continue into the United States and on to the camping grounds where they spend the first night. For the next five days, marchers often carry one or more crosses as they make their way north through the same desert landscape traveled by countless undocumented migrants.

Many supporters unable to commit to the entire event join the group for the final day, swelling the ranks for the final push on to Tucson, where other immigrant advocates greet them for a reception. The reception includes food, music, speeches from community members, and testimony from participants. The most consistent module in the event is a rite in which a small group of walkers have their feet washed by a clergy member. In 2004, Father Robert Carney, who served as a priest for many years in the border town of Douglas, Arizona, presided at the reception and introduced the foot washing by calling it "an ancient tradition of welcoming, of hospitality, of greeting the stranger." Then the walkers chosen for the rite sat in a row of chairs, and as a group of musicians played a soft instrumental, Carney knelt on the ground in front of the walkers to wash their feet in a silver basin. Many pieces of the reception are added or subtracted by year, but the footwashing has been a standard feature from the beginning.

## Strategies of Sympathy and Visibility in
## Memorial Marches

Like other rhetorical activity among immigrant advocates, memorial marches are intended to humanize and raise sympathy for migrants by raising the visibility of migrant issues for audiences that may not be aware of them or would prefer to look the other way. Through the marches, advocates attempt to evoke the volume of deaths while also conveying the individual worth of each decedent, and by bringing the deaths out of the desert and inserting them into public space, the marches are the most confrontational of immigrant advocates' cultural practices.

Some performative commemoratives, like the spontaneous shrine that honored the victims of the Alfred P. Murrah Federal Building bombing in 1995, acquire strength by being situated at or near the place of the death being mourned. But mourning so many migrants in such remote places would be impractical and attract very little attention. Though perhaps not intended to do so, immigrant advocate processions along highways and city streets have the effect of dynamically reinterpreting the tradition of roadside shrines. Like those who make and maintain roadside crosses and other forms of vernacular mourning, immigrant advocates are directing their efforts to the victims of accidents that happened in the course of a journey. And, like roadside crosses, immigrant advocate marches may provide emotional satisfaction for participants but are also intended to influence larger audiences. The crucial distinction is that in the case of migrants, the deaths usually do not happen near the roads that the marchers travel. Rather, they are scattered over a great expanse, far from public view. Migrant memorial processions gather these dispersed sites of loss and reconstitute them in a sequence of motile, kinetic shrines that bring the crisis out of remote areas and into wider visibility.

The marches express an earnest desire to see that no death goes unacknowledged, that every person is accounted for and properly mourned. Reverend Randy Mayer of Green Valley, Arizona, speaking at the conclusion of the Memorial March for Migrants in 2005, lamented that migrants who were as yet unidentified "need a name," and shared his hope that they would be reunited with their families. For some participants, the crosses make a similar statement. As Mary (Humane Borders) put it:

> Putting the name on is putting a face to that person who has died—
> an identity. It's not just a number and not just one of a lot, but these

are all individuals who have died. I think it also shows our belief in an afterlife, that we're concerned about people who have died. But more so it shows that we are also identifying with or have some compassion for the families of those who have died. They're not here. They're not even sure where some of these people are who have died, where they're buried and stuff like that. And I think it's important that we have that feeling for the families.

Likewise, a march with a good turnout, where one or more city blocks are scored by participants holding crosses, individuates the deaths while also conveying their volume. The recitation of names does the same work, dramatizing the magnitude of the problem against the flat statistics of the official count. Furthermore, by moving, kinetic shrines simulate some of the most salient characteristics of migrant deaths en masse—they cover a large area and occur in transit—while simultaneously conveying the distinctive integrity of each decedent.

Immigrant advocates also feel that the appearance of death imagery where it is not the norm may attract interest and jolt observers into sympathy. Laura (Humane Borders and Samaritans) observes that crosses are common enough to send a simple message: "I think that even [for] people who aren't faith-based or religious, the cross is pretty much a universal symbol of respect, perhaps, and remembrance." It is also powerful enough, she thinks, to capture public interest. "That's one symbol that startles people [so] that maybe they 'get it' better. There were a couple of those types of marches where coffins were carried. I think that kind of stops people and reminds them. I think any time you put a person's name on something, or put a photograph on something, that brings it home a little better for them rather than a bunch of people marching down the street." In this case, funereal imagery specifically appeals to onlookers to join a commission of sentiment for the dead, activating a conditioned attitude of respect that implicitly recognizes the value of migrant lives.

## Collective Identity in Memorial Marches

Aside from attracting interest from the population at large, the marches also provide opportunities for participants to profess and strengthen their universalist ethics. As acts of identification, they affiliate marchers with each other and the larger immigrant advocacy movement. As acts of relation, they depict migrants as valuable people. And as rituals, they suspend the everyday world so that the marchers can imagine migrants and themselves in a community across nations.

Sentiments of universality appear most explicitly in the liturgies before and after the march. Prepared oratory and impromptu remarks frequently assert that immigrant advocates and their audiences—both overwhelmingly US citizens—are members of a common humanity that also includes migrants. They often do so by proclaiming a shared ancestry, which, despite a genealogy that outranges anyone's memory, can be metaphorized through sibling terminology (see also chaps. 5, 6, and 7). Father Carney prayed at the 2004 Migrant Trail closing ceremony, "You gave all people one common origin and your will is to gather them into one. Fill the hearts of all women and men with the fire of your love and the desire to secure justice for all of our brothers and sisters." A responsive reading from the 2004 Memorial March for Migrants referred to migrants as "[o]ur neighbors, people who are our brothers and sisters." In a more extended application of the trope from the closing of the Migrant Trail in 2004, participant Wes Cosgrove declared, "We are gathered here today to mourn our dead, and we are also gathered here today to honor them. Because we know that we live in a world of premature and unjust death, where our brothers and sisters from Latin America are forced to leave everything behind and join a northward migration. And here, *en el norte*,[5] in spite of their enormous contributions to our society, they are not made welcome. They are not treated as human beings, they are not treated as our brothers and our sisters." Cosgrove's remark provocatively assumes an intimate enough connection to migrants to describe them as "*our* dead." The mutual construction of mourning obligations and group identity could not be more apparent. Claiming the dead as such postulates a supranational community and in so doing compels members of the community to fulfill the requirements of memorialization, without which there can be no continuity between past and present. Specifically, it compels members in the United States to engage in funereal rites that characterize as social familiars any number of foreign nationals whom they have never met.

Crosses provide another way for immigrant advocates to cultivate and express a bond with migrants. At the Migrant Trail reception in 2004, just before the foot washing, Father Carney drew people's attention to the crosses in their hands and said, "I ask you to take them and look at the name or what is written on your cross. Take that person or that phrase into your heart." The heart, of course, is an organ rich in literal and figurative significance. Its functioning means the owner is alive, but it is also reputed to be the organ most affected by love, where compassion is held and whence it emanates. Catholic theologian Dan Groody proposes, further, that in Mexican Spanish, the heart—*el corazón*—is "the innermost mystery of a person . . . the biological-symbolic site of wisdom and knowledge and a metaphor for the whole of one's conscious, intelligent, and free personality" (47). Connotatively, then, the heart means the center or essence of something (as in "the heart of the matter"), so by asking people to enfold the name there, Carney was requesting that participants incarnate the spirit of that person into the very core of their being and even, in light of the heart's role in circulation, to regard the decedent's blood as that of their own.

Memorial march participants have described the potency of the crosses in similar ways. A Migrant Trail walker related at one point during the week that "[t]he name on my cross belongs to a 23-year-old young man— Gregorio. As I walk, I feel his footsteps and I feel the sorrow of his family" (Innes, "In Sorrow" B2). Mary (Humane Borders) shared a hypothetical scenario in which a marcher carried a cross and later somehow met a relative of the person whose name appeared on it:

> Just to even once have contact with a family and let them know there was someone here who also felt the same as they feel, then you start becoming a real brother or sister to them. I come back to "brother and sister" because it's an easier way to explain that. You start feeling that they're not from Mexico and we're not from the United States, but we're from this global family.

All of these remarks indicate that the crosses serve as conduits between the living and the dead, as devices that facilitate a figurative merger of the bearer and the decedent. But the comments of Mary and the Migrant Trail walker suggest that the crosses do more than this. Contemplating the cross enables the marcher to "feel" or at least "start feeling" a link with the decedent's family and "[become] a real brother or sister to them." The crosses, in this way, are technologies of imagined community, compressing time and space like jet travel or telecommunications, fostering a sense of kinship where no such sense may have existed before.

At times, the crosses even seem to become the transubstantiated body of fallen migrants. Carolyn Marvin and David Ingle find a similar process in the ritual systems of nationalism, where the flag stands in for the nation's fallen soldiers. In nationalist symbolism, they say, "[t]he sacrificed body is resurrected in the flag" (44)—as evidenced by official and popular discourse that says as much.[6] An organizer at the 2007 Migrant Trail made the equation straightforwardly, telling marchers that if they accepted the invitation to carry crosses, they needed to be respectful with them. "Those are people," she said, and warned that if she saw marchers treating them carelessly by leaving them on the ground, she would take them away. On a break during the final day of the event that year, I saw a woman stoop to retrieve one from the ground. "I'm just going to pick this up so no one steps on it," she said, and balanced it in the crook of a stroller's handle-bars. A similar incident happened during a cross-border march Derechos Humanos cosponsored in 2004, where participants received small strips of paper with the names of the dead and affixed the names to crosses that had been hung on the Mexican side of the border wall. The person who cut the strips mentioned offhandedly to me that the names on the page had such symbolic importance for her that she felt "weird" doing the job and obliged herself to take care that she did not accidentally slice through any of the letters.

The transubstantiation of migrants into crosses is also implicitly recognized in the conclusion of the Día de los Muertos march. As the names are read and attendees step into the circle to set their crosses on the ground, they tread gingerly so as to avoid touching any that have already been deposited. They also show a reluctance to have the crosses come into contact with each other, perhaps because overlapping them violates the goal of depicting each death as individual and tragic in itself. Moreover, upon conclusion of the name recitation in 2004, a Franciscan from the mission walked around the circle and dashed the crosses with holy water, consistent with the treatment of the casket following a Catholic Funeral Mass.

## Constructing the Sacrificial Migrant

Arguing that migrant deaths are tragic, preventable, and unjust; that sympathy with the dead requires support for actions that would prevent similar deaths in the future; and that therefore mourning for migrants should be accompanied by vocal opposition to current strategies of border enforcement—all of this can be adequately done without referencing Christianity. Even the cross may be used on the basis of cultural tradition, indexing death without intending any metaphysical significance. (In fact, a speaker at the Migrant Trail in 2007 disavowed any religious purpose behind the use of the symbol.)[7]

Still, a funereal cross is never far away from drawing associations between the decedent and the messianic martyrdom of Jesus. The move is well established as a feature of mourning in modern nationalism, especially in military cemeteries and battlefield memorials, where crosses suggest that the defining features of Jesus's death are recapitulated in fallen warriors. The comparison is based on two premises: that the death is a voluntary sacrifice (Jesus willingly submitted himself to suffering and death) and that it is redemptive (Jesus's death enables the salvation of others). Soldiers are likewise remembered as voluntary sacrifices, putting themselves in harm's way and thereby "giving" their lives for the community. So too are these deaths redemptive, occurring in the service of national preservation (Davies, "Martial" 155), and mythic, for they uphold the sacrificial tradition of the ancestors who made order out of chaos. The soldiers therefore repeat both the sacrifice of the Christian culture hero and the national culture heroes.

Likewise, the crosses in memorial marches do at times take on more explicit Christian significance in their resemblance to crucifixes, that is, depictions of Jesus crucified. Speakers at the Migrant Trail, for example, have raised the Christian significance of the cross by drawing comparisons between the migrants' ordeals and the Passion story. In 2004, the closing ceremony of the Migrant Trail included among its invited speakers Reverend Stuart Taylor of St. Mark's Presbyterian Church. Taylor began with a passage from liberation theologian Leonardo Boff in which Boff argues that "Jesus continues to be crucified in all those who are crucified in history"—naming, specifically, the hungry, the exploited, those wounded in war, the marginalized, and the discriminated against.[8] Using Boff's remarks as a departure point, Taylor led the group in prayer:

O God, in Christ crucified you have revealed yourself to us as a God of compassion and solidarity with those who suffer. In Christ risen, you have unleashed a power in human history that brings life out of death, good out of evil, a way forward where there is no way. You are crucified again in the hunger and poverty of the people of southern Mexico and Central America. You arise in the people's determination to seek a better life. You are crucified again in the suffering and death of migrants crossing this desert. You arise in the courage and faith of the people to continue on. You are crucified in death-dealing immigration policies and by indifference and abuse that immigrants face in this nation. You arise in the efforts of people of faith and goodwill, who strive for a vision of this nation of immigrants as a place of welcome and hospitality. Be with us in this summer ahead. Be with your people as we journey faithfully. Amen.

Similar words were offered at the same event the following year by another Presbyterian minister, John Fife. Echoing Taylor, Fife declared, "The way of the migrant is the way of the cross.[9] It is a social crucifixion [that] the migrant must leave their own culture. It is a psychological crucifixion [that] the migrant must leave home. It is a legal crucifixion because the migrant must become illegal. And it is a human crucifixion because the migrant becomes a suffering one who risks death upon the trail."

Taylor and Fife equate migrants with Jesus by portraying them as people who not only suffer but who suffer for seeking truth. Neither Taylor nor Fife is content to cordon off the fact of migrant casualites from the larger economic and political context of the hemisphere, suggesting that the root causes of migration are as reprehensible as the actual deaths. The goals of migrants are just; their deaths are unjust. And, like Jesus, migrants are persecuted and die for righteousness through policies enacted by the state. In describing the deracination and diaspora of the Americas as an ongoing crucifixion, Taylor and Fife make the Sonoran Desert itself a moral imperative, a landscape scattered not with statistics, but contemporary Golgothas, where deaths of the meek and humble indict the state for its crimes and urge observers to work toward the emancipation of those who suffer.

Moreover, immigrant advocates frame the deaths of migrants, like those of soldiers in the rhetoric of nationalist mourning, as sacrificial and redemptive. That is, they argue that although people are dying, those deaths will result in a new and better world. Evelyn, in the discussion of El Tiradito in chapter 7, remarked that migrants' "family members may not even know we're meeting, but we're sending them a message that we're there, mourning their loved one, that it will not be in vain." At the blessing just before marchers crossed the border on the 2006 Migrant Trail, a speaker said that walking and other actions should be done "so that [migrants'] deaths will not be in vain." The litany offered at the Memorial March for Migrants that same year sounded a similar note: "We resolve to work for changes that show moral courage, achieve hospitality, and strengthen all the nations of God's world. Our brothers and sisters need not have died in vain." These remarks exemplify how the memorials commonly seek to redeem migrant deaths by charging the living—and migrant advocates, in particular—with transforming their sadness into a movement for policy reform. Taylor, for instance, alludes to immigrant advocacy in his reference to "the efforts of people of faith and goodwill" as a Christic resurrection. Cosgrove, in the same address quoted earlier, declared that "the best way to honor our dead, to honor the lives and deaths of the nearly three thousand migrants, is to commit ourselves, each one of us, to transform this desert." Redemption, by this measure, is a task that falls to immigrant advocates as people who enjoy membership in the US polity.

Verbally and materially amplified in immigrant advocacy observances, the cross may be said to represent the injustice of migrant deaths, draw comparisons between migrants and Jesus, and even serve as a corporeal presence by incarnating the martyred "kin." Hence, the cross most overtly signifies migrants, but also signifies the commitment of (some) US subjects to envisioning themselves and migrants in terms of common ancestry and destiny. The cross draws lines of connection and relationship where compassion is untrammeled by nationality. Furthermore, it redeems the dead from the abyss of irrelevance, prophesying that they are part of a larger process that will bring a better world into being.

But at times, immigrant advocates have also promoted a second hermeneutic of redemption that positions migrants themselves as agents of change who are creating the new world here and now. The program for the 2004 Día de los Muertos Pilgrimage featured a photo dominated by a shrine, a pile of crosses like those typically used in the march, and a stenciled placard that reads, "In honor of those souls who have died in the desert in pursuit of life, liberty and happiness, paving the way for those who follow in their footsteps." Applying the most famous phrase from the Declaration of Independence, a sacred text of the nation, to the ambitions of people who have died attempting to enter the country illegally is surely an audacious act of literary appropriation. Synonyms could have been used, of course, but they were not—a choice that seems calculated to argue that the pilgrimage mourns the failure of border policy to comply with values that are both cherished and integral to the United States. They further propose that the ideals legitimating the rebellion of the Founding Fathers also legitimate the transgressions of undocumented migrants, so to fail to respond to migrants' needs is to fail to live up to the demands of national heritage. The reference also links migrants to the heroic bloodshed of protesters and volunteers slain in the War for Independence, so that even if dying means that some migrants never send a cent back home to their families, their deeds will create a better future "for those who follow in their footsteps." The migrant in this narrative becomes a martyr, a visionary who creates a new world, a progenitor of an "American" dream that applies to the Americas as an entire hemisphere.

The migrant martyr narrative also appeared in 2007, when the Rothko Chapel, an unaffiliated religious institution and space in Houston, gave its Oscar Romero Award for Human Rights to No More Deaths volunteers Shanti Sellz and Daniel Strauss. Sellz and Strauss had been arrested and charged with smuggling in 2005, when they attempted to drive two undocumented migrants to Tucson to receive medical care; the charges were later dismissed (see chapter 4). Though Sellz and Strauss accepted the award, No More Deaths, in turn, used a news conference announcing its summer actions to symbolically reaward the prize to those they argued were more worthy recipients: the migrants themselves. The conference, held in the Southside sanctuary, began with several No More Deaths members describing individual migrants and naming them as heroes. Then Sellz announced the decision to transfer the award, declaring, "Every day, people around the world migrate and risk their lives to ensure the human rights of all people: the right to live in safety, the right to eat, the right to have an education and a future." An implicit critique of the tendency for the United States to stress political rights over economic rights,[10] Sellz's remarks also radically reformulated the notion of migrant deaths as sacrifice and redemption. In the migrants' determination to find living wages, even if it requires illegal entry, the act of transnational migration assumes the qualities of a de facto protest against the nation-state system. Call it, perhaps, a vanguard of necessity.

In the discursive depiction of migrant deaths as sacrificial and salvific, migrants are "heroes" because they act against the unjust system that perpetuates hemispheric poverty. Though likely not theorized as such by migrants, the sojourns effect a transnational civil disobedience movement that unites means and ends and insists on practicing the global order as it ought to be (i.e., without borders) in the face of juridical and security apparatuses determined to enforce the global order as it is. Sellz concluded by noting that No More Deaths would be back in the field over the summer, carrying out humanitarian aid and human rights abuse documentation as "works of solidarity with our migrant brothers and sisters who are truly changing the world." From this standpoint, migration becomes archetypal or paradigmatic of the postnational order and migrants become postnationalists par excellence because they are already doing, albeit at their peril, what will be an unexamined part of everyday life in a better tomorrow.

## Memorial Marches as Cosmogonic Rites

The view that transnational migration inaugurates a new epoch in human society recontextualizes the memorial march as a cosmogonic rite, which is to say "an imitation, often a symbolic imitation, of the primordial sacrifice that gave birth to the world" (Eliade 55). By marching, immigrant advocates reenact the actions of the sacrificial culture hero, "migrating" just like the decedent was at the time of death, and carrying the trajectory of the person onward.

The consummate form of the memorial march as a cosmogonic ritual is the Migrant Trail, when participants physically replicate the migrants' journey by crossing the border and traveling north. Though the event is described as a gesture of solidarity, organizers vigorously deny that marchers are doing what migrants do, asserting, "The walk is not intended to simulate the experience migrants face as they cross the gauntlet of death" ("History of the Migrant Trail"). Certainly, event planners ensure that the week is not a grueling test of endurance. Migrants do not have the benefit of walking on designated and maintained roads, periodically receiving water and food, or having tents and sleeping bags hauled by vehicles. But comparisons between marchers and migrants persist all the same. Most obviously, the walk is called "the Migrant Trail" and the route goes through part of the most popular corridor of travel for undocumented entrants. While minimizing the risks, the Migrant Trail provides a direct experience with the harsh realities of making an overland desert journey on foot.

Consider as well that after crossing into the United States on the first day, the marchers deposit their means of identification in a security box for the duration of the event. On one level, this is another symbolic act of solidarity, for migration can efface migrant selfhood in many ways. As discussed earlier, undocumented migrants are popularly referred to as being "in the shadows," occupying a place where they are known by few people or no one (chap. 6). Migrants also sometimes literally lose their proof of identification in the course of their trip. Then, of course, there are the hundreds of recovered bodies that are never recognized and untold others that have never even been found. But the marchers' surrender of passports, drivers' licenses, and so forth is also consistent with Victor Turner's observation that when ritual subjects enter ritual space, they nullify their everyday status markers in order to be remade (*Forest* 93-111, *Ritual Process*). As I overheard one marcher tell another in 2005, "when we cross the border we don't have any identification; we've been stripped of our identity." The breach, in this case, is geopolitical, and so is the status marker. By assuming traits of the migrant, the marcher suspends his or her nationality and imagines, for the next six days, living in a borderless world.

Furthermore, the words of participants and supporters indicate that they process their experiences during the event in relation to the realities of migrant journeys. In his comments at the 2004 closing ceremony, Cosgrove said that "hopefully we now have some better, some small but significant, understanding of the plight of our migrant sisters and brothers." At the closing ceremony in 2005, Isabel Garcia said the walk was "to bear witness to what migrants go through," and earlier in the same program, John Fife told the marchers, "You have joined the way of the migrant, the way of the cross, in solidarity and holy communion." Fife also joined migrants and immigrant advocates in community by praying, "In the name of the Creator and the Redeemer and the Holy Spirit. Creator God, we pray for blessing upon all these walkers, and on all walkers in the desert. As you led the Hebrew people out of bondage and through the perils of the desert, lead all your people by cloud and fire through this desert place." By asking for "blessing upon all these walkers, and on all walkers in the desert," Fife lumps together migrants and marchers, and then applies the story of the Exodus—perhaps the most venerable biblical metaphor in US history—to them. Migrants and social reformers are as one, and Fife ennobles their acts as a mythic journey toward freedom.

The cosmogonic quality of the march also imbues the foot-washing rite, which is predicated on a similitude between marchers and migrants. Father Carney introduced the footwashing in 2004 by saying, "Our ten people seated here represent all of you walkers, and more importantly they represent all of our brothers and sisters who walk greater distances without the support that we have right here, oftentimes alone and lonely and afraid." Aside from his candor in drawing the analogy, Carney's designation of the marchers as substitutes for transnational migrants is no different from the resemblances already discussed. But doing so at the reception enables a new symbolic interaction between the traveler and the host. If the marchers stand in for migrants, then Carney stands in for citizens of the United States, who must respond to encountering the undocumented "stranger" with an act of identification that will reveal their truest selves and deepest convictions. Because the rite consists of Carney performing an act of welcome, it dramatizes "radical hospitality" performed by a resident of the global economy's core who recognizes someone from the periphery as a "brother," "sister," or "neighbor."

The discourse of migrant martyrdom, which renders crossing the border an act of creation, lends migrants the aura of mythic heroes. The border crosser defies the disorderliness of the world as it should not be (installing sensors, drones, walls) in a struggle to achieve the world as it ought to be (providing basic necessities for one's family). If the primal act of the post-national culture hero is crossing a sovereign border, memorial marches take on enormous significance, for to walk with the cross that represents a migrant's body is to symbolically merge with that person and mimic the person's heroism. The marches therefore pay tribute to the world creators, sacralize the landscape where the creators spilled (and continue to spill) blood, remake the self, and refresh the community.

## Conclusion

Memorial marches, like other acts of immigrant advocate mourning, are acts of identification and relation in which participants express sentimental attachments to migrants. The marches are also performative commemoratives, in that they attribute the deaths to a social problem and call for remedial action at the personal and political level. But memorial marches stand apart from other immigrant advocate rites in two respects. One is their public corporeality. In no other mode of signification among immigrant advocacy groups do so many members perform their convictions through physical presence for a mass audience, along the highways and avenues that are routinely traveled by the general population. The second factor that distinguishes memorial marches is the degree to which they spur marchers to imagine familiarity with migrants. As marchers call and hear the names, proclaim their empathy, offer their prayers, and handle the migrants' "bodies" in the form of crosses, the universality they idealize acquires sensory approximation. To remember the migrants in this way summons and welcomes their spirits back into the world for the procession, so that they and their families circulate among the rememberers. The intimacy also seems, at times, to consist of the advocates achieving a figurative merger with the migrants, as if the spirits of the deceased were actually embodied in the movement of the marchers and the acts of marching and remembrance were indistinguishable.

They also cultivate and perpetuate the globalization of advocates' consciousness, for as advocates imagine themselves in communion with migrants and migrants' families, they blur the geographical distinction between the United States and other countries. This blurring, of course, is limited to the perceptions of the participants and has no empirical effect on the ontology of the international boundary. But the marches often acknowledge as much in their liturgies, which predicate the redemption of migrant deaths on the adoption of better, more just patterns of social interaction after the closing of the ritual frame. The functionality and credibility of the marches, that is, hinge to some extent on their success at deepening the participants' determination to resume their structural roles as parents, professionals, voters, church members, and so on according to the knowledge they have acquired in the ritual. Since that knowledge was gained in part by communing with or even embodying the spirits of those being mourned, the ethos with which the marchers return to structure may be metaphorized, at least, as continuing where the migrants left off. Father Carney, closing the reception for the Migrant Trail in 2004 and sending people forth into the rest of the summer, declared: "We are on the move. We are on the move." The immigrant advocates, like the transnational migrants themselves, must be in motion, advancing toward some destination as yet ambiguous but taken to be there, perhaps, on "faith."

*Death. There are roadside memorials (from accidents) up and down Ajo Rd., to and from O'odham land. You also see vultures pretty frequently out here. Perching, soaring, huddled over roadkill on the dashed yellow line of the highway, scattering in their own weird way— spastic flapping it seems like they won't move in time and then it's as if they levitate.*

*Walking around a greening wash, strewn with migrant trash.*

Samaritans volunteer: *Amazing.*

Me: *The grass or the garbage?*

Samaritans volunteer: *Both. Together. The signs of new life and the signs of struggle for a new life.*

*Minutes later, she says "'There will be streams in the desert.' That's from Isaiah."*

*Scattered ironies: A sign at Buenos Aires that reads, "A Resort for International Travelers"—but it refers to migratory birds. Then there's the "Waterworld" sign on Ajo.*

*Going home, the driver talks about his work with the relatively fundamentalist Prison Fellowship. "There are spiritual obstetricians and spiritual pediatricians," he says. The former "only care about getting people born." The latter are interested in the ones already born. The world needs both, he says.*

—MEMO ON A SAMARITANS TRIP, 2004

# CHAPTER NINE

# Ritual Transformation and Cosmopolitics in Tucson Immigrant Advocacy

If, as William Blake wrote, "you can see the universe in a grain of sand," then there are plenty of opportunities to see the universe in the Sonoran Desert. In fact, there are plenty of opportunities to do so with just a footprint in the Sonoran Desert, or a cast-off backpack, or an empty water bottle. For that matter, return to Rick Ufford-Chase's suggestion, noted in chapter 1, that the best place to ponder the question "Who is my neighbor?" in a globalizing world might be a poor neighborhood in a Mexican border town. There, among the cinder block shantytowns, factory assembly lines, newly urbanized refugees, and fortifications at the international port of entry, one could extrapolate an entire planet of comparable divisions and deprivations, because, as two immigrant advocates argue, "the border is . . . just a symbol" (Grisele) of "a huge misdistribution of wealth and land and power" (Patricia). In other words, if you want to understand what is at stake in globalization, you don't have to visit the whole world. The grain of sand that is the border will do—but only if you look.

Though few immigrant advocates used the word "globalization" in their interviews, they routinely described migration as a consequence and demonstration of social connections greater than national parameters. Whether they gave these connections a name or not, they almost unanimously faulted them for failing to alleviate the endemic poverty of the global South, which has produced throngs of people willing to hazard treacherous journeys to more prosperous regions. If, as it seems, commerce has globalized, ethical imaginations have not kept pace.

Immigrant advocacy in the Arizona-Sonora borderlands extends from a desire to close that ethical gap by changing the behavior of the United States in an international community where it holds disproportionate power and wealth. As much as immigrant advocates consider projects with and on behalf of migrants worthy in and of themselves, their campaigns are also self-reflexive commentaries on the need for changes in individual and collective consciousness. The strongest conceptual thread running throughout their work in all its variety is the need for an ethical orientation greater than modern political geographies. To effect and strengthen this orientation, they seek to redeem the interstitial spaces where conventional boundaries of nationality blur, pushing people (including themselves) to recognize interstices as potential encounters with estranged aspects of the self, the community, and the divine.

## "Dirt" and the Nation-State System

Although satellite communications and capital mobility drape the early twenty-first century with a cloak of novelty, the issues these and other globalization touchstones raise for political identity are ancient. Nothing is very original about the need to define society, understand one's obligations to others, find values higher than one's individual life, and achieve material fulfillment. Human sociability seems to require that collective identities be formed (and re-formed) in tandem with visions (and re-visions) of ultimacy, so that adhering to normative relationships is conceptualized as loyalty to transcendent purposes.

In modernity, nationalism has become the dominant framework in which people resolve these vexations. This is true of particular nationalisms, which are exclusive to finite people and places, but also of a more general nation-statist ideology that characterizes nationalism as a natural, divinely ordained organization of the entire human species. Codified nowhere, even as they are present everywhere, its tenets include that "the world is divided into nations, each with its own character, history and destiny"; "the source of all political power is the nation, and loyalty to the nation overrides all other loyalties"; and "to be free, every individual must belong to a nation" (A. Smith 31). That is, each nation is as God wills it, so loyalty to the nation and prioritizing reciprocal care for one's compatriots is obedience to God.

As a means of sorting people and things into categories, nation-statism fulfills a basic human desire to think systematically about similarities and differences. But for all their convenience, categories are imperfect and vulnerable to falsification by whatever they cannot neatly arrange. In her anthropological classic *Purity and Danger*, Mary Douglas borrows from Henry James to describe these unruly phenomena as "'matter out of place'" or, more bluntly, "dirt" (qtd. in Douglas 165). Because dirt threatens the categories that make life comprehensible, it forces the group using them to formulate a response. In extreme cases, it occasions the kind of self-appraisal colloquially referred to as "soul searching," in which people consider thorough overhauls of the way they think and act. The violation of categories, then, has the potential to subvert the repertoire of basic acts by which people perform their membership in the group, causing confusion among group members as to which courses of action will best perpetuate individual and collective identity.

For nation-statism, which is predicated on each nation being to some degree hermetically sealed, anything that juxtaposes "foreign" and "native" elements tracks "dirt" into the system. Globalization presents a host of ambiguities on this count. Undocumented border crossers, for example, are a kind of "dirt" whose status as "matter out of place" vis-à-vis the elision of state protocols brings the ethics of group loyalty to a head. As Humane Borders cofounder Robin Hoover has written, "At the level of values, [dead migrants] ask us what kind of people we are and what kind of people we want to be" ("Basic Decency" V1). Either transnational migrants *are* "us" and we are obligated to provide them welcome, or the migrants are *not* "us," in which case that obligation does not apply. If the imperatives of conduct toward another human cannot be reconciled with the imperatives of conduct as a national citizen, then belief in the nation-state's congruity with ultimacy is diminished. As it happens, immigrant advocates and their critics agree that undocumented immigration confronts people in the United States with a challenge to their moral identities, but they come to that conclusion for very different reasons and prescribe very different responses.

Douglas notes that when contradictions or anomalies challenge the plausibility of worldview, some responses involve avoiding or repressing them (40–41). Many people familiar with an existing system, for all its flaws, do not want to cast it aside, nor do they want to confront the disorientations, grotesqueries, and profanations that come with remaking it. The deeply ingrained self-conception among many US citizens that theirs is a "chosen nation," for instance, has and will undoubtedly continue to inspire strident resistance to any suggestion that the country should heed external influences. When you are the chosen nation, sovereignty serves as a prophylactic against the corruption of your exceptional genius and special destiny. To accept some kind of interlocking global governmentality would be relinquishing the mantle of God's people and betraying the sacrifice of the ancestors.[1] The same stance applies to regulating human movement across national borders, for as some restrictionists tell it, ongoing undocumented immigration will turn the United States into a Third World country.[2] What they mean by this is not exactly clear, but the general message is that to resemble the Third World would be highly undesirable and even catastrophic for the United States. There should be a separation between the two, and strict regulation of immigration must be a part of that separation. As a representative of the Minutemen Civil Defense Corps said in 2007, "a secure border is a safe border," because as long as no one can enter the United States in the first place, no one will die in the desert. "If [migrants] are going to be breaking laws and coming through the porous borders," he continued, "they are going to suffer the consequences, . . . I don't see where America is to blame" (McCombs, "Efforts to Cut" A4). The proper response to dirt, then, is to put up barriers sufficient to prevent encountering it.[3]

But Douglas also points out an altogether different response to dirt, which is to value its irregularity as a window onto some reality that the standing classificatory system excludes but needs to recognize. Even as it rends the fabric of worldview, ambiguity can have "social and cognitive value" (Babcock 169) because it reveals deeper mysteries of creation that abide and escape perception but nonetheless inform how we are to comport ourselves. The outré therefore sometimes symbolizes the noumenal precisely because it unleashes appreciation of a more holistic reality than observers might otherwise access. For immigrant advocates, the "dirt" of globalization reveals the inadequacy of nation-statist ethics and the need to develop a new grid of perception. As Edgar says (chap. 5), the best response to undocumented migrants is not "to hope that high walls and a treacherous desert will be enough to keep these cold and hungry people away from us" but "to ask why these people need to leave their homes and make the journey in the first place." Immigrant advocates sharply dissent, then, from the Minuteman representative who said that America is not to blame for migrant deaths. "We're holding a mirror up to society," Robin Hoover told a *Washington Post* reporter in 2001. "We're saying that we are all, all of us, responsible for what is happening out here" (Booth A1). Hoover's words are another example of immigrant advocates describing

their work in optical metaphors, only instead of calling on his audience to
see migrants, he is calling on them to see themselves, to recognize their
own participation and culpability in the roots of economic refugee flows.

Advocates express concern, though, that people will not take this tack,
perhaps because the prosperity of the United States produces a self-satisfied
moral lassitude. Mary (Humane Borders) said that material wealth

> has gotten us to think "we have what we need, we have worked hard
> to have it"—and that's true, I believe that—"therefore, I'm comfort-
> able and I don't want to know about the uncomfortableness of other
> people." And that is one of the reasons why I am so concerned about
> educating the ones in the United States who are not aware of what
> is happening on the border, and that is another one of the aims of
> Humane Borders, to educate people throughout the United States,
> in particular, or throughout the world, about what situations are in
> countries who do not have all of this materialness that makes people
> comfortable.

Mary's remarks hearken to Mel's belief (previously quoted in chapter
5) that US citizens do not comprehend their nation's relative opulence:
"We're in a very affluent situation, and . . . I think Americans are forgetting the fact that the world is not that way. My feeling is that we need
to realize this, not only practically, but also spiritually, that we have an
obligation to change things so that people who are suffering are not going
to be suffering." The Samaritans, he felt, were "one small thing" rising to
this demand.

Mary and Mel's comments go a long way toward illuminating why immigrant advocates respond as they do to the "dirt" of undocumented migrants. Narrowly defined, immigrant advocates are responding to migrant
suffering, but Mary and Mel place their efforts in the much larger context
of transforming the consciousness of people in the United States. Both
indicate a desire to elevate their fellow citizens' awareness of living in far
greater luxury than much of their human cohort.

Explicating the intended outcome of cultivating this awareness, Mel
says the nation will "realize" a collective responsibility to lessen the suffering of others. The double meaning of "realize" is serendipitous here. Like
"witness" (discussed in chap. 6), "realize" can refer to both an internal,
perceptive event and some sort of external action. The word thereby indicates synchronization of mind and body, as if a particular concept, once
understood, cannot help but bring about a change in behavior. Mel notes

that the realization has to occur "practically"—meaning, presumably, the quantifiable and logistical details of reallocating wealth. But when he adds that "we need to realize this . . . spiritually," Mel recasts the political strife over undocumented migration from a matter of governance to a sign of collective anomie, and reconfigures immigrant advocacy as a project that simultaneously addresses the lives of migrants and the soul of the nation. "Need" of any sort means a gap between what is and what ought to be, and since the spiritual, by definition, refers to realities that transcend matter, spiritual need involves a disconnect between the methods used to perceive those realities and success in doing so. Warnings about this sort of disconnect are central to many sacred narratives, which depict the propensity for cognitive or cultural systems to become maladaptive under selfish stewards. Within these narratives, "dirt" frequently appears as something that is scorned or incongruous but serves didactic purposes, imparting the knowledge essential for spiritual development. Victor Turner found the motif a frequent feature in the rituals of preliterate societies (*Ritual Process* 94–125), but it also appears in the text-based religions of the West that constitute the religious heritage of most immigrant advocates. Moses, a Hebrew raised in the Egyptian palace, warns the royal oppressors that they are violating God's will and must repent. Jesus emerges from the cultural backwater of Galilee to upbraid the authorities and proclaim a liberatory alternative. In the words of Virgil Elizondo, "God chooses the rejected, the ignorant and the downtrodden of this world to be the agents of the new creation" (53).

Theology along similar lines has sprung up around the undocumented. In 2003, the bishops of Mexico and the United States responded to border militarization and rising hostility to undocumented migrants with a document asserting that the church "is constantly challenged to see the face of Christ, crucified and risen, in the stranger" (United States Conference).[4] Irene Morales Acosta of the Catholic group Missionaries of the Eucharist, based in Nogales, Sonora, speaking to a gathering of southern Arizona immigrant advocacy groups in 2004, declared that migrants, as "refugees of globalization and pilgrims of dignity," are "a sign of God." And Tucson-based theologian Jerry Gill has proposed approaching border issues from the perspective that the Incarnation (God taking human form in Jesus) defies classificatory schemes by revealing "that the character of Divine reality refuses to be confined within human limits or boundaries" (2). These commentaries are not deifying border crossers, nor suggesting that they are individually pure in character, but arguing that they summon people in the United States to a horizon of discomfiting but edifying discovery.

Gill, applying the idea of the Incarnation to the ethical quandaries of the nation-state system, argues, "I believe US Christians can learn a great deal from those who would cross our borders" (3), and Homi Bhabha, in a secular vein, has suggested that the value of postcolonial literature is that the traumas of conquest yield wisdom: "[I]t is from those who have suffered the sentence of history—subjugation, domination, diaspora, displacement—that we learn our most enduring lessons for living and thinking" (172).

This is so precisely because of their abject and "alien" condition. Morales described undocumented migrants as people whose existence is marked at every turn by insecurity and contingency. Their home communities are wracked by the dissolution of immemorial subsistence patterns, their departures remove them for indefinite periods from loved ones and familiar places, they journey northward through a gauntlet of human predation and environmental dangers, and if they manage to find work, the jobs are usually difficult and short-term. The indignity is compounded because they have to live in secret, "sin rostro" (without faces), in fear of revealing their identities. Inasmuch as these tribulations expose the fragility of the human form and the precariousness of personhood, they stand to transform anyone who notices them, relativizing discomforts and invigorating compassion among beholders. Following Daniel Carroll, whose application of biblical teachings to immigration advances that "to be hospitable is to imitate God" (94), encounters with want provide opportunities for a more robust and intrepid spiritual life.

At the same time, the ambiguous status of undocumented migrants exposes deficiencies in the classifications of nation-statism. As noted in chapter 5, immigrant advocates' understanding of undocumented migration can be described as "intermestic," for they consider the standard of living in the United States—a paramount "domestic" issue—as a major contributor to the push and pull factors that encourage people to cross international borders. Simply put, the present nation-state system is defined by a metropolitan "core" of former colonial powers in the global North, and a "periphery" of colonized locales, usually in the global South. Everyday consumption patterns in the North reflect five centuries of Euro-American imperial practice, which by appropriating so much wealth from the global South has simultaneously guaranteed that people will need to leave those countries and that the global North will be their most logical destination. This connection has been clear to many members of postcolonial diasporic populations who relocated to the core after World War II and began to organize against the prejudice that greeted them. A slogan among these movements in Europe, "We are here because you were there," succinctly argues that modern imperialism set into motion a sequence of interactions that brought once-separated populations and cultures into relations of reciprocity.

Immigrant advocates, having come to a similar understanding, in effect propose to their citizen peers that "migrants are here because we are there." Trade deals, loan conditions imposed by US-dominated institutions, and a long history of overt and covert military intervention imbricate Omaha and Oaxaca, San Diego and San Salvador so thoroughly that migrants are part of the core even before they leave the periphery. From this standpoint, deaths in southern Arizona relocate deaths that would otherwise go unnoticed, and the Pima County Medical Examiner's office becomes a morgue for collateral damage in the war for cheap commodities. Hoover's "mirror" of immigrant advocacy says that by seeing migrants, the United States also sees itself more clearly, in relationship with others. This intermestic approach to human movement across the US-Mexican border rises to Bhabha's insistence that "[t]he Western metropole must confront its postcolonial history, told by its influx of postwar migrants and refugees, as an indigenous or native narrative *internal to its national identity*" (6, emphasis in original). Undocumented immigrants are part of the country in deed, if not in name. They are strands in the web of connectivity, in the great flows of energy that nourish bodies and fuel all social activity. There is, over and above the kinship of the nation, some ancestry that we are all a part of, and that ancestry must be affirmed.

Hence, a "secure border" may make "a safe border," but by hiding and denying the problem of global poverty, it blames the messenger for the message. In contradistinction, immigrant advocacy sanctifies the dirt of undocumented migration as an invitation to a divine encounter. To accept that invitation means entering the spaces of migrants' sending communities, routes north, and the proverbial "shadows" of their expatriated lives. Going there may be embarrassing and difficult, but power and wealth engender a moral imperative to practice proactive observation, to put oneself in situations where one learns to perceive what would otherwise go unnoticed. Instead of treating the interstitial spaces between and across nations as threats to be avoided or eliminated, immigrant advocates regard them as catalysts for new ways of thinking. The ambiguity enables being part of one's country and something more than one's country, moving beneficiaries of the core toward "realizing"—understanding and achieving, practically and spiritually—their responsibilities in a global context.

## Rites of Globalization

The whole of rhetorical activity among immigrant advocates exemplifies the use of symbol and ritual to resolve social crisis. When fundamental premises of individual or collective identity fall into doubt, the result is a threshold situation that requires either confirmation of the existing identity or the adoption of a new one. Although small-scale threshold situations may be overcome with little fanfare, large-scale ones often receive ritualized procedures that dramatize and instantiate the resolution. Not for nothing are rituals sometimes called "rites of passage," for the term aptly conveys the capacity of rituals to effect "movement" from one paradigm of thought and behavior to another.

Ritual transformation, if successful, has the twofold outcome of altering individual identities and benefiting a larger community. The first outcome, in which the ritual subject crosses the threshold from the old self to the new self, is sometimes thought of as a figurative ontogeny, as with the Bemba of Zambia, who describe their female puberty rite as "growing a girl." Turner observes that the rite "is felt to change the inmost nature of the neophyte. . . . It is not a mere acquisition of knowledge, but a change in being" (*Forest* 102). The ritual process also keys the individual's metamorphosis to collective purposes by temporarily leveling status hierarchies and fostering an egalitarian spirit that Turner calls communitas. Though short-lived and fanciful, this erasure of social difference reminds social actors of "[t]he ultimate desideratum . . . to act in terms of communitas values even while playing structural roles" (*Ritual Process* 177), and nudges them to minimize egocentric attitudes that violate the sense of interdependence necessary for social reproduction. In other words, the ritual domain provides a forum to critique and even regulate behavior that could imperil the group. Turner makes the point by referring to an annual Swazi rite in which the village chieftain is cast down and made lower than a commoner. He is "divested of all the outward attributes, the 'accidents,' of his kingship" so as to impress an appreciation of "mystical solidarity" upon him and the people (*Forest* 110). The rites therefore humble the socially powerful in order to facilitate the empathy necessary for prioritizing collective over private gain.

When immigrant advocates talk about their power and luxury in the United States as a matter of chance and about having an obligation to share those assets, they are talking about trying to overcome the accident of their kingship in the global economy. Their rituals then become acts of contrition in which advocates acknowledge the spiritual liabilities of their material privilege and "grow" or "make" themselves into new people better able to resist the temptations of power. Immigrant advocates' regard for the power of interstitial spaces to effect this change is nowhere more evident than in their mourning rites, which bring the interstices into view for nonparticipant audiences, and provide participants with acts of identification for becoming a new self. One way this is done is by figuratively merging with migrants in memorial marches. As discussed in chapter 8, the crosses carried in the marches are portals between the living and the dead, and in bearing them, marchers symbolically continue the journeys that the decedents were unable to complete. But "becoming" migrants also provisionally annuls the differences between the marchers and migrants that result from disparities of globalization: superiority and inferiority, advantage and disadvantage, the documented and the undocumented, core and periphery. This temporary dismantling of political boundaries is an appeal to the government and citizens of the United States to welcome the stranger with greater magnanimity. The marches proclaim, as Turner says of ritual's egalitarian dimension, "a model of human society as a homogeneous, unstructured communitas, whose boundaries are ideally coterminous with those of the human species" (*From Ritual to Theater* 47).

At the marches' conclusion, two kinds of transformation or "passage" have been achieved. The deceased migrants have moved from the world of contemporaries to the world of ancestors, and the presence of their spirits during the march has enabled the marchers to overcome their "blind," disconnected self for rebirth to a new life in which they experience humanity as more interrelated and interdependent. By entering the margin and becoming, even if only temporarily, alien to and alienated from their national endowment, they enter a time and space in which they deepen their understanding of society on a global scale.

Rituals are just a pause, however, in the ongoing controversy that provoked them, and their performances are vacuous if the new identity they model never achieves structural expression. Since belief in the oneness of humanity may be difficult for immigrant advocates to sustain outside of the consensus of the group, the cadence and mechanics of ritual serve to internalize universalist rhetoric so that participants may return to the world with stronger convictions. Mary (chap. 8), for example, cited holding the cross in a memorial march as a way to "start feeling" related to the migrants and their families, invigorating what might otherwise be a sincere but depthless metaphor. The rites also consecrate the groups' daily operations as a kind of perpetual pilgrimage to or through the interstice, where exposure to the brute realities of dislocated lives will reveal new and perhaps difficult work still to be done. Morales spoke to the importance of entering the interstice with humility and openness when she asserted that "God calls us in the figure of these pilgrims of dignity. God expects their stories will touch us and we will see a way to create a community. This is a dream we can share together." She joined advocates and pilgrims in a migration metaphor, saying "We are all travelers moving step by step," with geographical and spiritual journeys converging in a cooperative vision of a future society.

All of this means that although water distribution, documentation of rights abuse, and other routine tasks of immigrant advocacy are informed by prior conviction, they are also acts of ongoing revelation, self-discovery, and renewal. In the summer of 2004, for instance, No More Deaths volunteer "Naomi" wrote that through her experiences with the organization, she was "coming close to what it means to be a North American and an American in the early twenty-first century." In this brief remark, Naomi suggests that as a result of her work as an immigrant advocate, she is understanding more deeply who she is and who she must be. Though she does not describe the content of that ideal, her references to being "North American" and "American" offer some clues. Since "American" may rightly refer to a person or thing from anywhere in the Western Hemisphere (i.e., "the Americas"), its designation for a person or thing from the United States alone can seem imprecise and presumptive. At least as early as the 1980s, many US-based activists in Sanctuary and like causes began to call themselves "North Americans,"[5] thereby reserving "American" for hemispherically inclusive matters. "North American," of course, also includes Canada, but the term makes sense insofar as it denotes wealthier nations in contradistinction to their poorer neighbors. By using these terms, Naomi is reimagining where she stands in relation to other people historically and geopolitically, identifying herself as part of the core, but also part of something bigger. The identity she wants to be, and the one she feels she is "coming close" to achieving, requires seeing herself as part of relationships greater than individual nations and nationalities.

## Postnationalism and Cosmopolitics

The nation-state is so taken for granted that it is absurd to speak of it as an idea whose relative merits are subject to debate in popular media. No one is featured on Sunday morning talk shows, for instance, as a "nation-state proponent" (or "opponent"). But nation-statism must continually earn the support it enjoys as a viable and credible utilitarian system. Over time, it will either preserve its legitimacy by providing satisfactory answers to questions like transnational migration, or a system that can provide satisfactory answers will take its place.

Since advocacy on behalf of undocumented migrants challenges the logic of sovereignty by which the nation-state allocates material and political resources according to membership, it raises the question of whether those involved aspire to abolish or simply refashion the nation-state. The norms of performing loyalty to the nation-state require reserving one's greatest concern for the members of the society defined by the nation-state's territorial boundaries. Tucson immigrant advocates, however, give aid to migrants, memorialize foreigners who have violated national sovereignty, refuse to play the role of citizen-based law enforcement, and attribute migrant deaths not to illegal entry but to the US government's border policy. They proclaim a universalism (whether based on human rights or religious compassion) whose law is higher than that of the state, and argue that the United States is part of a world community whose ills cannot be relieved without an ethical imagination that extends beyond the nation.

But while this rhetoric can justifiably be called postnational, it should not be considered antinational. Immigrant advocates are not seditious, however much their flummoxed and infuriated critics claim otherwise. They do not proclaim allegiance to foreign powers, promote secession, or reject the nation-state outright. They readily identify themselves as members of the United States, embrace legislation and other governmental levers of power as viable means to desired ends, and consistently affirm US heritage and law. Immigrant advocates are sometimes vehemently accused of treason, but their relationship with the nation is much less a matter of disloyalty than of ambivalence.

This ambivalence is evident in the three case studies featured in chapter 5. Patricia, who claims her own patriotism is unimpeachable, says one's qualities as a human being are more important than one's qualities as a citizen. Annie says no ideology works out in the end, and "what counts" is a broad allegiance to human beings, not places or systems. Allen touts the importance of citizenship participation, but says his moral compass points to being Christian, not American. The ambivalence can also be inferred by the scarcity of nationalistic identity markers in the organizations' store of symbols. As seen in chapters 6 through 8, the groups' rhetoric usually neglects nationalism and appeals instead to faith-based compassion and humanitarian concern.

Consider as well the handful of immigrant advocates who in the course of explaining their orientations to advocacy work expressed a need for people to adopt the status of "citizens of the world." Although such cosmopolitanism[6] sometimes coincides with the jet-setter or compulsive itinerant's refrain that "wherever I lay my head is my home," immigrant advocates tether it to national and state-sponsored identities. Some do so indifferently, of course, since if, as they argued, public action is the final reserve of political legitimacy, then the actual form of state is fairly irrelevant. However, this indifference runs the other way as well, for not agitating against the nation-state lends it de facto support. By holding their government to universal ideals, immigrant advocates make commitment to the well-being and dignity of all people a civic or patriotic virtue, accepting the nation-state as a means of achieving that ideal without endorsing it as the ultimate actualization of collective identity. This is what Pheng Cheah and Bruce Robbins have dubbed "cosmopolitics"—a field of action in which the social and cultural institutions of the nation are not outright dismissed, but strategically engaged as fulcrums for stimulating the imagination and practice of supranational consciousness.[7] The sentiment concurs with a bumper sticker I read on an unrelated errand at one point during my fieldwork that happened to employ yet another optical metaphor: "I love my country, but I think we should start seeing other people."

Therefore, immigrant advocates are not replacing nationalism, but offering a kind of corrective, dialogical interlocutor to it, so that nationalism can be leavened with the universal value of human life. Further, they typically bring that outlook full circle as something that will contribute to their country's quality of life. Mel warned, "I think the American electorate has got to wake up and start taking notice of what's going on in the world. If we have a bad leader, then I think we can be sucked into things that are going to drag us down, too." Without saying so, Mel is inverting the jingoistic convention that serving one's country means touting its superiority. If a conscientious and civically engaged population can be what Carla called "the fifth arm" of democracy (chap. 5), "national interest" may be well served by citizens capable of empathizing with people in other parts of the world.

That immigrant advocacy does not provide a lived alternative to nationalism can be shown through Carolyn Marvin and David Ingle's exegesis of nationalism as a religion. Marvin and Ingle argue that although nationalism is like other imagined communities in its faux kinship and heroic ancestry, it is religious in its ultimacy. Culture, in general, serves to make life meaningful. But the meaningfulness of the nation has become supreme, for no other imagined community has such a strong hold on the claim that dying on its behalf will benefit the greater good. An imagined community that outranks all others has what Marvin and Ingle call "killing authority," which is to say the power to organize the sacrifice of its own members, as exemplified by subjects mobilized for war. In modern times, the killing authority of nationalism enjoys unparalleled legitimacy. The nation is the imagined community of highest value—the group, we might say, of the final instance.

Marvin and Ingle provide a blunt criterion for evaluating the viability of rivals to the nation-state system in their insight that "the sacrificial system of nationalism can be challenged effectively only by those who embrace with still greater commitment alternative sacrificial systems to replace it" (8). The rhetorical world of immigrant advocacy undoubtedly resembles nationalism by describing migrants as kin and characterizing their deaths as sacrifices worthy of mourning and remembrance. But applying what might be called the Marvin-Ingle test demonstrates that the movement does not in itself elaborate a sacrificial system, nationalist or otherwise. Even though the advocates' mourning rituals present a narrative of sacrifice, they do not commemorate people who are dying in submission to a killing authority invested with ultimate values, as there is no institution commanding migrants to sacrifice their lives for the greater good of an imagined collective. Where sovereignty requires some locus of power authorized to send social members to their deaths, immigrant advocates' performative commemoratives have a vacuum.

Moreover, the imagined community immigrant advocates postulate exhibits a flagrant disequilibrium in that while immigrant advocates envelop undocumented entrants in a panhuman sodality, nothing suggests that their perspective is reciprocated. Transnational migrants elect to make perilous journeys, but unlike soldiers of nation-states or subnational militants who aspire to state power, they do not understand themselves as expendable in pursuit of a collective goal beyond the family. Migrants do not think of their journeys as a boon to human rights activists, Presbyterians, Catholics, nurses, or other participants in the immigrant advocacy movement. Soldiers of nation-states killed in war are not understood as having failed in their purpose, but the same cannot be said for migrants, whose deaths cut off a lifeline of much-needed income back home. The community of immigrant advocates and "migrant brothers and sisters" is not imagined evenly across its members.

To say that immigrant advocates in Tucson are not beholden to a supranational killing authority is not to say that they eventually will be, nor that universalist imaginings are destined to remain, by default, deferential to the jurisdiction of the United States. Postnationalism seems limited to playing gadfly to the nation-state, yet there may be some threshold at which postnational imaginations will attract greater loyalty than that now ceded to nations (i.e., a willingness to die for the collective good). One possibility is that the world will gradually see forms of political imagination that are not global, but regional, along the lines of the European Union. Luis Alberto Urrea conjures a similar prospect in his account of "home" (discussed in chap. 2) as "[a]ll three Americas, from the Arctic circle to Tierra del Fuego," and so does Naomi when she underscores the importance of learning "what it means to be a North American and an American." Even then, however, the result may not spell the end of nationalism. In the EU, "national German or French identity now includes a supranational element of commitment to Europe, but that element is not in opposition to or in conflict with the national attachment. The concrete content of national identity has changed; it has not been superseded or replaced" (Sorensen 98).

Making predictions would be grandiose, for paradigm shifts in the organization of planetary society are not zero-sum ventures. New political formations may take shape gradually, and social movements, like art, often explore questions protostructurally, on a symbolic plane, in lieu of access to the levers of comprehensive structural change. (After all, who in the age of feudal fiefdoms would have anticipated the modern nation-state enshrined by the Treaty of Westphalia?) The imagined community of immigrant advocacy is something like the way Mikhail Bakhtin describes the imagery of medieval and Renaissance folklore, where "[o]ne of the fundamental tendencies . . . is to show two bodies in one: the one giving birth and dying, the other conceived, generated and born. This is the pregnant and begetting body, or at least a body ready for conception and fertilization. . . . From one body a new body always emerges" (26). The Migrant Trail, for instance, opens every year on Memorial Day, a point in the United States' sacred calendar that is specifically set aside to remember the sacrifice of ancestral border makers. On one level, this coincidence is simply a matter of pragmatism, for scheduling the event on a holiday helps boost attendance. Nonetheless, there is an unavoidable temptation to see the conjunction as a case of historical change assuming poetic significance, as one system of defining a political community through mourning is supplemented by another. Immigrant advocacy thereby presents ways for people to extemporize a transcendent orientation to sympathy and responsibility while remaining within the nation-state paradigm.

Organized work on behalf of displaced people is a recent phenomenon, but not an ephemeral need. Wars, political persecution, and poverty continue to deracinate populations around "The Great Ball on Which We Live,"[8] and the prospect in this century of extreme climate change opens the possibility of new cataclysms that may strain the generosity implicit in notions of human interrelatedness. Flooding, drought, crop failures, and armed conflict ignited by the scarcity of essential resources will disproportionately affect the world's poor. Expressing their refusal to die, they will migrate—for higher ground, for better land, for any place that offers greater security and provision of basic needs—and in doing so, test the stability of the receiving political, economic, and cultural systems. They may be seen as threats, met with aggressive rebuffs, described as trespassers, looters, or parasites, and made into criminals. Amid ominous portents of climatological catastrophe, the need for theologies and philosophies that compel reflection on human obligations across political geography is enormous.

The stakes are high, even if reduced to the single criterion of migrant deaths, which in the summer of 2010 were comparable to the worst years on record (McCombs, "July Proved"). Tucson immigrant advocates, for their part, continue to fill water tanks, carry medical supplies down dusty paths, offer legal counsel, pray, light candles, and hope, in the words sung at the El Tiradito vigil, that in the parched landscape where so many sojourners have lately perished, "the face of the Earth will be renewed."

# Notes

## Chapter 1. Migrant Deaths and Immigrant Advocacy in Southern Arizona

1. The term "restrictionist" as applied here is common in academic literature on immigration; "expansionist" comes from Fry. For a comprehensive survey of radical nativist restrictionism in the United States, see Bennett, *Party of Fear*.

2. The term comes from the famous closing lines of the Emma Lazarus poem "New Colossus," which adorns the Statue of Liberty: "Give me your tired, your poor, / Your huddled masses yearning to breathe free, / The wretched refuse of your teeming shore. / Send these, the homeless, tempest-tost to me, / I lift my lamp beside the golden door!"

3. For a brief but suggestive discussion of this point, see Southwest folklorist James Griffith's essay "Meeting la Corúa" in *Beliefs and Holy Places*.

4. In 2000, the US immigration commissioner, Doris Meissner, conceded, "We did believe that geography would be an ally to us. It was our sense that the number of people crossing the border through Arizona would go down to a trickle once people realized what (it's) like" (qtd. in Borden).

5. The government's fiscal year begins October 1. Thus, fiscal year 1998, for instance, runs from October 1, 1997, to September 30, 1998. Indications are that Border Patrol calculations undercount migrant deaths and the actual toll is much higher. The official counting method excludes many deaths because of where or how they occurred, and bodies found by other law enforcement agencies are tabulated only if Border Patrol representatives request such information. In fiscal year 2004, for example, the Border Patrol issued the official count of recovered bodies at 172, whereas county medical examiners in southern Arizona gave the total as 221 (Almond; LoMonaco, "Accuracy"; Turf).

6. Since the word "immigrants" literally means people who intend to live in their new country permanently, most members of the groups in this study prefer to say "migrants," which encompasses both those who stay and those who plan on returning to their homelands. Therefore, "transnational migrant advocacy" would be a more accurate label for the movement of which these groups are a part. However, I have chosen with some reluctance to use "immigrant advocacy," since "immigration" is still

the most widely used term in the mass media and among the general public for the issues the groups address. My tendency throughout the book is to use "immigration" (and "immigrants") to discuss the general phenomenon of human movement across borders and policy debate about it, but "migration" (and "migrants") in the more narrow context of group operations.

7. The language of the law is as follows:

(A) Any person who—

(i) knowing that a person is an alien, brings to or attempts to bring to the United States in any manner whatsoever such person at a place other than a designated port of entry or place other than as designated by the Commissioner, regardless of whether such alien has received prior official authorization to come to, enter, or reside in the United States and regardless of any future official action which may be taken with respect to such alien;

(ii) knowing or in reckless disregard of the fact that an alien has come to, entered or remains in the United States in violation of law, transports, or moves or attempts to transport or move such alien within the United States by means of transportation or otherwise, in furtherance of such violation of law;

(iii) knowing or in reckless disregard of the fact that an alien has come to, entered, or remains in the United States in violation of law, conceals, harbors, or shields from detection, such alien in any place, including any building or any means of transportation;

(iv) encourages or induces an alien to come to, enter, or reside in the United States, knowing or in reckless disregard of the fact that such coming to, entry, or residence is or will be in violation of law; or

(v)

(I) engages in any conspiracy to commit any of the preceding acts, or

(II) aids or abets the commission of any of the preceding acts,

shall be punished as provided in subparagraph (B).

8. Sources identified by first name only are aliases for people interviewed under conditions of anonymity.

## Chapter 2. Political Imagination in the United States

1. For a more extended analysis of this archetype, see Eliade 29–58.

2. The phrase comes from the first charter of the Virginia Company, which was written to establish the Jamestown colony in 1607 ("Three Charters" 2).

## Chapter 3. US-Mexico Border Enforcement and the Emergence of Immigrant Advocacy in Tucson

1. In addition to Texas, whose independence Mexico had always contested, the territory included all of what are now California, Nevada, and Utah, along with most of Colorado, Arizona, and New Mexico and portions of Wyoming, Kansas, and

Oklahoma. In 1853, the United States bought additional Mexican territory through the Gadsden Purchase; this land, added to the 1848 acquisitions, rounds out present-day Arizona and New Mexico. See Griswold del Castillo for a map (9) and a detailed examination of the boundary's precursors, establishment, and ongoing contestation.

2. In 2003, the INS was reorganized into the Department of Homeland Security as three new agencies: US Citizenship and Immigration Services, US Customs and Border Protection, and Immigration and Customs Enforcement.

3. Precursors to immigrant advocacy can be found among abolitionists, civil rights groups, and organizations founded by recent immigrants to help recently arrived compatriots. The first stirrings of immigrant advocacy proper at the turn of the twentieth century were both secular (e.g., Hull House and the Illinois Immigrants' Protective League [Abbott]) and religious (e.g., the Scalabrinian Order [Brown] and the Hebrew Immigrant Aid Society [Wischnitzer]). Their activities often simply focused on helping immigrants adjust to their new country, but this cut against popular convictions that immigrants did not deserve help, should not be made at home, and were not capable of playing constructive roles in society. After Johnson-Reed, though, immigrant advocates like ethnic associations, social workers, and legal professionals took to Congress and the courts to stop the government from deporting foreign nationals who were in the country unlawfully but had families and enjoyed good standing in their communities (Ngai 76–90). Herein lies a seed of subsequent immigrant advocacy, which has argued in multiple contexts that knee-jerk application of immigration law does not necessarily facilitate the good.

4. One of the greatest barriers to admitting European refugees was anti-Semitism: many Americans rejected the idea of an admissions program because they (erroneously) believed that most DPs were Jewish. Although the American Jewish Committee and American Council for Judaism provided the initial spark for the CCDP, they determined that their efforts stood a better chance of success if they were nonsectarian and therefore built alliances with Christian and secular organizations (Genizi 69–70; Loescher and Scanlan 9–10).

5. The phrase "fair share" appears to have been first used by the American Jewish Committee and was subsequently taken up and popularized by the CCDP (Genizi 70).

6. The trend has held through to the present. For later uses of the Leviticus text, see Corbett 131; "Interfaith Statement"; D. Martinez; Nolan 4:169; and Sahagun; . The verses from Matthew appear, for example, in Corbett 122; Elliot; "Interfaith Statement"; United States. Cong. 539, 553; and Nolan 2:230, 4:167.

7. As had happened during the controversy over DPs, refugee advocates in Tucson faced vocal opposition from restrictionists and responded with appeals to both political and religious idealism. Reverend Hayden S. Sears, whose Catalina Methodist Church was among the sponsors, argued that "[o]ur religion has a cross in it, on which Christ died to save others. We should be willing to take up our cross and sacrifice for others," and that "[o]ur nation was founded with the idea of providing home and freedom for people in need. . . . We are simply following out our national purpose" (Rutherford). As DP backers had done before him, Sears marshaled the dual missions of Christianity and the United States and suggested that work with Cubans fulfilled both.

8. As seen in the case of Hungarians after the 1956 Soviet invasion, however, the US government did not hesitate to waive these touchstones of eligibility to suit Cold War priorities (Loescher and Scanlan 50–51).

9. The speaker, Basil E. Malof, was a Latvian exile and president of the Russian Bible Society.

10. Martin Luther King, Jr., and Malcolm X, for instance, both argued incisively that racial equality and anticolonialism were kindred struggles. In 1964, Malcolm X said, "As long as we think . . . that we should get Mississippi straightened out before we worry about the Congo, you'll never get Mississippi straightened out. Not until you start realizing your connection with the Congo" (90). King, writing in 1967, observed, "All over the world like a fever, freedom is spreading in the widest liberation movement in history" (169), and that "with his black brothers of Africa and his brown and yellow brothers in Asia, South America and the Caribbean, the United States Negro is moving with a sense of great urgency toward the promised land of racial justice" (170). King and Malcolm X were preceded, though, by W. E. B. DuBois, who analyzed the 1914 US invasion of Haiti as part and parcel of the white supremacist ideology that also perpetuated domestic racism (Kaplan; Luis-Brown).

11. Precedents for the sympathetic attitude toward Third World cultures could be found in long-standing missionary anxieties that the non-European pagans they had been sent to convert were arguably more admirable than many self-professing Christians back home (Hutchison).

12. Corona and Alatorre left CASA by 1974, but the organization maintained a pan-Mexican perspective that included US-born citizens as well as documented and undocumented Mexican nationals (A. Garcia 73–74). Corona and Alatorre pursued their vision under other auspices. A. Garcia says that Corona and Alatorre began the organization as CASA and took up the HMN designation after resigning; M. Garcia, though, implies that Corona and Alatorre called the organization HMN to start with and renamed it CASA.

13. The number of files appears to be either 260 ("All Manzo Counts") or 360 ("Aid to Aliens").

14. See Hulsether 140–44 for an examination of how the mainline Protestant journal *Christianity and Crisis* sharpened its criticism of US policy toward the Third World in the 1960s and '70s.

15. MacEóin authored several books on religion and politics in Latin America as well as an autobiography, *Memoirs and Memories*. He worked from an office in St. Mark's for several years in the 1970s and 1980s.

16. The precise number of people involved varies by report. For instance, Crittenden says that there were twenty-seven Salvadorans and that thirteen of them died of dehydration (3). Cunningham says the original number in the group was twenty-six, but does not say whether she counts the Mexicans among them (*God and Caesar* 14).

17. The bail money in this case apparently came from MacEóin, who borrowed the money against his house. The practice of using homes as collateral for bonding refugees was soon taken up by others. Although in the case of MacEóin and at least some of those who came later, the refugees jumped bail, the insurance company was unable to collect by foreclosing on homes used as collateral because the agent who wrote the bonds had not kept records of them (John Fife, personal conversation, 1 Mar. 2005; Otter and Pine 13).

18. To get the process underway, volunteers from Tucson decamped to El Centro, where they shuttled back and forth between interviewing Salvadorans in the detention

center and typing asylum claims onto government forms in their motel rooms (Crittenden 43–47).

19. Literature on Sanctuary ranges from popular to academic. The best historical account of Sanctuary through the 1986 trial is Crittenden; Otter and Pine provide an oral history that covers the movement's duration; MacEóin, *Sanctuary* collects commentaries on Sanctuary's philosophical and political dimensions; and Coutin and Cunningham, *God and Caesar* are movement ethnographies.

20. As Fife related to me, "I was just helping out around the edges" because "Dave was, quite frankly, better equipped, from experience with the Chilean refugees and his fluency in Spanish, to be the point person for the Presbyterians on that one. So Dave and Gary and the Diocese of Tucson, the bishop, were the people who were the focus of that effort to help the folks from Organ Pipe."

21. Jim Corbett made the comparison at the news conference when the Tucson Sanctuary movement publicly declared its operations, and it gained widespread currency (Crittenden 73). The parallel was somewhat problematic, however, since it cast Sanctuary participants as outlaws even as they eventually adopted the line that their work was actually legal (Cunningham, *God and Caesar* 49).

22. Partner institutions at this juncture included churches in Berkeley, Los Angeles, Washington, and Long Island (MacEóin, "A Brief History" 22–23).

23. The letter appears in Crittenden 74.

24. The basis for this argument was the UN Protocol of 1967 , but also the Refugee Act of 1980, which was the first piece of legislation to formalize refugee admission procedures as part of US immigration law and sought to standardize the existing ad-hoc admissions system and eliminate its biases. Specifically, it replaced existing preferences for claimants from communist countries in favor of language that stressed humanitarian principles, and its definition of "refugee" conformed with the nondiscriminatory language of the UN Protocol (Loescher and Scanlan 154–55). Carrying out the Refugee Act in spirit and letter meant that admissions criteria would be evenly applied, with no consideration other than evaluating whether the person's fear of persecution in their home country was "well-founded."

25. By the early '90s, the state-sponsored terror campaigns that had spurred Central American emigration were deescalating. The number of refugees coming to the United States gradually tapered off, and due to changes in US asylum law, those seeking asylum through the courts started winning their cases (Cunningham, *God and Caesar* 203–106; Otter and Pine 347–50). This sea change in the courts was attributable to a 1987 ruling by the Supreme Court that said the INS had not been complying with the asylum standards established by the 1980 Refugee Act (Crittenden 346–47).

26. This includes the many people who learned to navigate immigration law in order to pursue asylum cases in court as well as those who lobbied in support of legislation that would legalize the presence of undocumented Central Americans. Undocumented people who had entered the country before 1982 became eligible for citizenship through the Immigration Reform and Control Act (IRCA) of 1986. Salvadorans who came later could win temporary stays through provisions of the Immigration Act of 1990. In addition, resolution of the suit *American Baptist Churches v. Thornburg* in 1991 permitted Guatemalans and Salvadorans whose asylum requests had been denied to reapply (Cordova 31–53).

## Chapter 4. Immigrant Advocacy in Tucson Responds to the Gatekeeper Complex

1. IRCA awarded citizenship to over 3 million people, of whom 2.3 million were Mexican (Massey, Durand, and Malone 90).

2. The post-IRCA milieu has also seen many cases of private citizens aspiring to enforce immigration law on their own. For a review of and argument against vigilante activity in southern Arizona, see the report by Hammer-Tomizuka and Allen.

3. Upon folding, Manzo transferred extant asylum cases to a new program under the wing of the TEC, Tucson Ecumenical Council Legal Assistance.

4. The effort, formally known as the Immigration Law Enforcement Monitoring Project (ILEMP), grew out of a more general border program AFSC began in 1979 (American Friends 1). An ILEMP report on human rights along the border released in 1992 asserted that border law enforcement agencies did not have adequate internal or external review procedures to respond to abuse claims, but also noted that "no amount of regulatory activity will protect the integrity of immigrants and border residents without major changes in immigration policies that define international migration as a law enforcement issue, and the international migrant as an intruder" (American Friends 4). Members of Tucson ILEMP, including Lupe Castillo and Isabel Garcia, are credited as having contributed to the report (American Friends 48). In 1995, the international NGO Human Rights Watch issued similar findings, which concluded that members of the Border Patrol and the Immigration and Naturalization Service "are committing serious human rights violations, including unjustified shootings, rape, and beatings, while enjoying virtual impunity for their actions" (1). The report also documented cases where US citizens had been harassed and noted with chagrin that although previous reports by the group had made several recommendations to improve agency practices, none of those recommendations had been implemented.

5. The Tucson-based organization BorderLinks exemplifies the shift in which people involved in Central American issues became interested in the economic dimensions of US foreign policy. BorderLinks formed in 1987 with the charge to coordinate volunteers from other parts of the country who came to Tucson to work with Sanctuary and to organize trips to Mexico for churches wanting to learn more about Sanctuary. But when the Sanctuary movement came to a close, its trips shifted to emphasize international trade, immigration, and economic development. It continues to offer educational trips, often, though not exclusively, to delegations from religious organizations and schools (Cunningham, "Transnational Social Movements"; Gill; Otter and Pine 309–12).

6. Focused on mitigating US contributions to repressive regimes and armed conflicts in Latin America and southern Africa, social movement organizations in the United States did not turn their attention to neoliberalism until the early 1990s. To the extent that "anti-" or "counterglobalization" consists of opposition to neoliberal doctrines, it was arguably over two decades old in other parts of the world by the time its US versions captured widespread media interest (Walton).

7. This systemic analysis included addressing the difficulties of indigenous communities whose populations are divided by the border. Border militarization made it increasingly difficult for these tribes to bring members from the Mexican side to the

United States for religious ceremonies, so in 1997 Derechos formed an associated project called the Alianza Indigena (Indigenous Alliance). The Alianza became a separate organization in or around 2007.

8. "Unlike Cubans, Haitians were never characterized as voting with their feet against an oppressive regime, nor was there any U.S. effort to portray the Duvalier regime [in Haiti] as one of the most abusive in the world" (79).

9. Nevins and Rubio-Goldsmith et al.

10. These names were not reported at the time, but later became known (e.g., Innes, "Migrants Need Help").

11. From 1989 to 1990, the Lower Rio Grande Valley was the site of an INS detention sweep, the largest since the 1950s, directed at Central American asylum applicants. The operation incarcerated detainees in temporary camps and deported many (Dunn, *Militarization* 91–94).

12. Slang in Mexican Spanish for a person involved in smuggling people across the border, *coyote* has entered the lexicon of some English speakers in the borderlands as well.

13. Luis Alberto Urrea utilizes interviews and government files to reconstruct these events with lyrical intensity in his novel *The Devil's Highway*.

14. After the fact, Fish and Wildlife Service officials agreed to post flags that would alert people to the presence of existing wells that agency staff maintain for use by wildlife.

15. Humane Borders became a 501c4 organization in 2002.

16. Those in Cabeza Prieta are the exception.

17. Here, and at other places in the text, I use present tense to describe conditions as they existed during my fieldwork even though they have subsequently changed. In the case of Humane Borders, the organization relocated in 2010 to the House of Neighborly Service in South Tucson.

18. Charter Samaritans endorsers were St. Francis in the Foothills Methodist Church; St. Mark's Presbyterian Church; the Diocesan Border Ministry Team of the Roman Catholic Diocese of Tucson; Dioceses without Borders: Roman Catholic Dioceses of Hermosillo, Tucson, and Phoenix; Southside Presbyterian Church; Humane Borders; the Community of Christ in the Desert; Reverend Robin Hoover of First Christian Church; and the Pima (Quaker) Friends Meeting.

19. For numerous anecdotes of Samaritans work, see *Crossing with the Virgin*, compiled by group members Kathryn Ferguson, Norma Price, and Ted Parks.

20. South Tucson measures one square mile, and has approximately fifty-five hundred residents (City of Tucson).

21. "Crossing the Line," a report on findings from 2006 to 2008, is available on the No More Deaths website.

22. Samaritans and No More Deaths protocols used to allow for volunteer-conducted evacuations if a medical professional determined that a migrant was in life-threatening condition. Though the Sellz/Strauss case was dismissed, both groups eliminated medical evacuations from their operations.

23. For example, the Mennonite Central Committee (MCC) has participated every year since 2006, with the exception of 2009. Most years, MCC staff, MCC board members, or others associated with MCC have been part of the walking delegation. In some years, MCC has also sponsored the walk.

24. The Minutemen, an organization aspiring to take vigilante border enforcement to the national level, enjoyed a flurry of media attention in 2005. The national organization soon fragmented with infighting, but Minutemen predecessors and splinter organizations have carried on.

25. The sharpest rift between any of the groups occurred in 2002, when the Tohono O'odham Nation refused Humane Borders a request to install water stations on tribal lands. Humane Borders denounced the nation's decision with an op-ed newspaper piece (Holt), which some immigrant advocates objected to as a neocolonial dictation to indigenous peoples. Since 2002, Mike Wilson, a tribal member and Presbyterian minister, has set out one-gallon containers of water in areas where migrant traffic is heavy.

26. Of John Fife's speech at the 2001 candlelight vigil for migrant deaths, Isabel Garcia recalls, "We decided to ask John to become involved with the issue of the deaths of migrants and to speak at the prayer vigil, reminding him that as he demonstrated in the call for Sanctuary for political refugees from El Salvador in the 1980s, he would be able to reach certain non-minority communities that those of us from Derechos Humanos possibly could not."

## Chapter 5. Individual Worldviews: Humanity, Nationality, and Ultimacy

1. The term comes from Nepstad.

2. This interview was conducted in 2005.

3. See Curti 201–22 for a discussion of similar critiques of nationalism in the United States from Emerson, Dewey, Veblen, and others.

## Chapter 6. Collective Expression: Dramatizing the Crisis

1. Several photographs of like items appear in *Migrant Artifacts*, a compilation of work by Tucson photographer Michael Hyatt that also features photographs of migrants, Migrant Trail participants, and members of Humane Borders and Samaritans.

2. Other Samaritans who have been in from the start tell much the same story, though the period of time without contact with migrants depends on the teller.

3. As of at least 2007, these quotes were joined by one translated from the K'iche' Mayan sacred text, the Popol Vuh: "Let us all go forward together; let no one be left behind."

4. Case in point: during the fieldwork in preparation for this book there was an incident in Tucson where a passerby stopped to help a sheriff's deputy who was struggling with a man on the median of a busy street. All three men fell in the path of oncoming traffic and were killed by a motorist. A representative of the Sheriff's Department later said of the passerby, "That good Samaritan put his life on the line" (Huicochea).

5. The same is true of the moments of silence at the end of Humane Borders meetings, but I do not have a sense of how Humane Borders members understand that act because the organization did not begin to do it until I had concluded my interviews.

6. The moments of silence at Samaritans meetings are a constant, but the opening and closing may be supplemented according to the wishes of the facilitator; at a 2008 meeting, facilitator John Fife read Santo Toribino's prayer as it appears in Urrea's *The Devil's Highway* (78), then said, "Let's take a moment of silence to remember why we're here and to remember the folks in the desert." At the end of the meeting, Fife read the passage from Urrea's book that follows the prayer and then called for the closing moment of silence.

7. A grand jury declined to pursue charges against any of the Marines involved in the operation that killed Hernandez, and a federal judge ruled Patricio's death an accident (K. Smith). For more on the Hernandez case, see the documentary *The Ballad of Esequiel Hernandez*, produced by Tommy Lee Jones.

## Chapter 7. The El Tiradito Vigil

1. Derechos member Carla related, "Before any of this, even before Sanctuary . . . we did a walk one time from St. Margaret's over here to El Tiradito that was on behalf of the people who had died from El Salvador out in the desert."

2. The song, written by contemporary liturgical composer Bob Hurd, is bilingual, for it also includes three verses in English. These, however, are not sung at the vigil.

3. The use of this song to end the El Tiradito vigil may have provided a precedent for its use at the conclusion of the memorial for Prudencia Martin Gomez, discussed in chapter 1.

4. One precedent for doing this comes from the Arizona historian Thomas Sheridan, who uses the word this way most prominently in his *Los Tucsonenses*. Another was Tucson's largest Spanish-language newspaper, *El Tucsonense*, which ran from 1915 to 1964.

5. Three new routes were proposed in April 1973 ("Possible Butterfield Routes"), but each one generated so much opposition throughout the city that planning for the project was canceled altogether the following year ("Study of Proposed").

6. Anecdotal evidence suggests participants may overestimate the extent to which their symbology is actually interfaith. One migrant advocate, who is not religiously affiliated but grew up Jewish, has participated in some events where Christian language and symbols were present, but does not attend the Thursday vigil. "That *is* a little too Christian for me," she says. "That's why I don't go."

## Chapter 8. Memorial Marches

1. One participant remarked in 2007: "I walk as a pilgrimage to be with the migrant and with Christ" (Innes, "In Sorrow" B2).

2. Sanctuary pilgrimages (in the form of caravans) and name recitations (with cries of "Presente!") were discussed briefly in chapter 3. Nepstad (131) provides at least one instance of Sanctuary supporters using crosses emblazoned with names.

3. The explication of Día de los Muertos, like the rest of the program, appears in English and Spanish.

4. The authorship of the prayer is unknown.

5. Translated "in the north"—i.e., the portion of the hemisphere that commences on the other side of Mexico's border with the United States.

6. Federal law, for instance, reads, "The flag represents a living country and is itself considered a living thing" (qtd. in Marvin and Ingle 41). See Marvin and Ingle (41–62) for a longer discussion of the flag as body.

7. Even in its allegedly secular uses, the cross still speaks to a specifically Christian cultural inheritance, and for that reason is hardly a neutral, universal sign of commemoration. Christian-centric observers, however, often do not understand this, as illustrated by the 2010 Supreme Court case *Salazar v. Buono*. The case concerned a cross erected as a war memorial in the Mojave National Preserve; at issue was whether use of the cross on public land violated the establishment clause of the First Amendment. By ruling (5–4) that the cross could stay, the court's majority effectively endorsed the paramount sign of Christianity as an appropriate burial marker for soldiers of any religion.

8. The text appears in Boff's *Way of the Cross* (92).

9. The phrase is borrowed from Groody 32–33.

10. Several articles in the United Nations Declaration of Human Rights, adopted by the UN General Assembly in 1948, address issues of material well-being such as access to adequate food and shelter (article 25). A nonbinding agreement, the Universal Declaration lay the groundwork for the UN's International Covenant on Civil and Political Rights and the International Covenant on Economic, Social, and Cultural Rights, both of which were adopted in 1966. The latter includes economic provisions, though its terms specify that governments need only commit to achieving the goal "progressively" (i.e., over an unspecified period) (Texier).

## Chapter 9. Ritual Transformation and Cosmopolitics in Tucson Immigrant Advocacy

1. The ideological continuity between nineteenth-century nativism and contemporary objections to United States membership in the United Nations is outlined in Bennett, *Party of Fear*.

2. A speaker at a restrictionist rally in Tucson declared, "'We have to protect our nation or we'll be another Third World country'" (qtd. in Borowitz). A letter to the editor of the *Arizona Daily Star* on November 3, 2005, criticizes the paper for giving favorable coverage to "people who go into the desert and 'rescue' the violators of our laws." If the trend continues, he says, "we should have a Third-World-type state soon" (Newton). Likewise, Gordon Baum of the Council of Conservative Citizens: "The very heart and soul of [the immigration debate] is, do we want to keep America as it is, more or less, or do we want it to be changed into a Third World country?" ("Supremacist Groups").

3. "Dirt" in Douglas's meaning is not necessarily pejorative, though in conventional usage it often is. Immigrants and other social groups said to debilitate national cultural have historically been associated with uncleanliness, disease, and other biologically polluting behavior. Sundberg and Kaserman find the pattern at work in media accounts that characterize migrants in southern Arizona as "threats to nature"

(730) due to discarded items, cactus carvings and bodily excretions made during treks through the wilderness.

4. The discourse is long-standing among faith-based immigrant advocates and precedes the furor over undocumented migration from Mexico. In 1946, in the early stages of the campaign to resettle European DPs, one publication argued, "It is our Christian duty, our moral obligation, and even our selfish interest to help them. In the deeper sense, we need them almost as much as they need us" (qtd. in United States. Cong.). The US National Conference of Catholic Bishops wrote in 1976 that "Jesus specifically promises His Kingdom to those who recognize Him in the immigrant," and "the Church is called to participate in human affairs and to recognize in the poor, the afflicted, and the oppressed the presence of the Lord summoning the Christian community to action" (Nolan 4:167).

5. See, for instance, the various interviews in Cunningham, *God and Caesar* and Coutin.

6. "Cosmopolitan" derives from the Greek words *kosmos* (the universe) and *polis* (a plenary of citizens) to mean, in effect, something that pertains to all the world.

7. See especially Cheah's and Robbins's introductions to *Cosmopolitics*.

8. This phrase is a section heading in the geography text of a third-grade girl from one of the tenant farmer families Agee discusses in *Let Us Now Praise Famous Men* (lii).

# Bibliography

Abbot, Edith. "Immigrants at Hull-House." *Eighty Years at Hull-House.* Ed. Allen F. Davis and Mary Lynn McCree. Chicago: Quadrangle, 1969. 113–16.

Agee, James (text), and Walker Evans (photographs). *Let Us Now Praise Famous Men.* New York: Houghton, 1988.

Ahlstrom, Sidney. *A Religious History of the American People.* New Haven: Yale UP, 1972.

"Aid to Aliens Not Proper, Judge Says." *Arizona Daily Star* 24 Apr. 1976: B1.

Alaimo, Carol Ann, and Joseph Barrios. "Teen Mom Dies to Save Tot." *Arizona Daily Star* 1 June 2000: A1.

Albanese, Catherine L. *Sons of the Fathers: The Civil Religion of the American Revolution.* Philadelphia: Temple UP, 1976.

"All Manzo Counts Dismissed in Deal." *Arizona Daily Star* 3 Mar. 1977: B1.

Almond, Andrea. "Groups Want Better Migrant Death Tallies." *Newsday.* Newsday, 6 Nov. 2004. Web. 8 Nov. 2004.

Alonso, Ana. "The Politics of Space, Time and Substance: State Formation, Nationalism and Ethnicity." *Annual Reviews in Anthropology* 23 (1994): 379–405.

American Friends Service Committee. "Sealing Our Borders: The Human Toll." Philadelphia: AFSC, 1992.

Anderson, Benedict. *Imagined Communities.* Rev. ed. London: Verso, 1991.

Andreas, Peter. *Border Games: Policing the U.S.-Mexico Divide.* Ithaca: Cornell UP, 2000.

Anzaldúa, Gloria. *Borderlands/La Frontera: The New Mestiza.* San Francisco: Aunt Lute, 1987.

Appadurai, Arjun. *Modernity at Large: Cultural Dimensions of Globalization.* Minneapolis: University of Minnesota Press, 1996.

Babcock, Barbara. "Why Frogs Are Good to Think and Dirt Is Good to Reflect On." *Soundings* 58.2 (1975): 167–81.

Bakhtin, Mikhail. *Rabelais and His World.* Trans. Helene Iswolsky. Bloomington: Indiana UP, 1984.

*The Ballad of Esequiel Hernandez*. Dir. Kieran Fitzgerald. Documentary Educational Resources, 2007. DVD.

Bello, Walden. *Dark Victory: The United States, Structural Adjustment and Global Poverty*. Oakland: Institute for Food and Development Policy, 1994.

Bennett, David H. *The Party of Fear: The American Far Right from Nativism to the Militia Movement*. New York: Vintage, 1995.

Bhabha, Homi K. *The Location of Culture*. London: Routledge, 1994.

Boff, Leonardo. *Way of the Cross—Way of Justice*. Trans. John Drury. Maryknoll: Orbis, 1980.

Booth, William. "In the Desert, A Drink of Mercy, Protest." *Washington Post* 11 June 2001: A1+.

Borden, Tessie. "INS: Border Policy Failed." *Arizona Republic* 10 Aug. 2000: A1.

Borowitz, Adam. "Immigration Backlash." *Tucson Citizen* 19 June 2002: C1.

Bosniak, Linda. "Opposing Prop. 187: Undocumented Immigrants and the National Imagination." *Connecticut Law Review* 28.3 (1996): 555–619.

Bowden, Charles. *Laboratory of Our Future*. New York: Aperture Foundation, 1998.

Bramhall, Wes. "Water Stations Should Come Down." *Tucson Citizen* 15 June 2001.

Brown, Mary Elizabeth. *The Scalabrinians in North America (1887–1934)*. New York: Center for Migration Studies, 1996.

Butler, Jon. *Awash in a Sea of Faith*. Cambridge: Harvard UP, 1992.

"Butterfield Opposition Expressed." *Arizona Daily Star* 2 Oct. 1971: A2.

Calavita, Kitty. "U.S. Immigration and Policy Responses: The Limits of Legislation." *Controlling Immigration: A Global Perspective*. Ed. Wayne A. Cornelius, Philip L. Martin, and James F. Hollifield. Stanford: Stanford UP, 1994. 55–82.

——. *U.S. Immigration Law and the Control of Labor, 1820–1924*. London: Academic, 1984.

Carlson, Lewis H., and George A. Colburn, eds. *In Their Place: White America Defines Her Minorities, 1850–1950*. New York: Wiley,1972.

Carrasco, Davíd. *Religions of Mesoamerica*. New York: Harper, 1990.

Carroll, Susan. "Divine Intervention: Clergy-Run Network Helps Illegal Crossers in U.S." *Tucson Citizen* 1 Feb. 2001: A1+.

Carroll R., Daniel M. *Christians at the Border: Immigration, the Church, and the Bible*. Grand Rapids: Baker, 2008.

Casanova, José. *Public Religion in the Modern World*. Chicago: U of Chicago P, 1994.

Chávez, César. "Peregrinacion, Penitencia, Revolucion." *Aztlan: An Anthology of Mexican American Literature*. Ed. Luis Valdez and Stan Steiner. New York: Knopf, 1972. 385–86.

Chavez, Leo R. *Shadowed Lives: Undocumented Immigrants in American Society*. Fort Worth: Harcourt, 1992.

Cheah, Pheng, and Bruce Robbins, eds. *Cosmopolitics: Thinking and Feeling Beyond the Nation*. Minneapolis: U of Minnesota P, 1998.

City of Tucson. *The City of South Tucson*. City of Tucson. 2001. Web. 21 Sept. 2005.

Coalición de Derechos Humanos "Corazón de Justicia Awards Dinner." Event program. 2003.

Corbett, Jim. *Goatwalking*. New York: Viking, 1991.

Cordova, Carlos. *The Salvadoran Americans*. Westport: Greenwood, 2005.

Coutin, Susan B. *The Culture of Protest: Religious Activism and the U.S. Sanctuary Movement.* San Francisco: Westview, 1993.

Crittenden, Ann. *Sanctuary: A Story of American Conscience and Law in Collision.* New York: Weidenfeld, 1988.

Cunningham, Hilary. *God and Caesar at the Rio Grande: Sanctuary and the Politics of Religion.* Minneapolis: U of Minnesota P, 1995.

———. "Transnational Social Movements and Sovereignties in Transition: Charting New Interfaces of Power at the U.S.-Mexico Border." *Anthropologica* 44 (2002) 185–96.

Curti, Merle. *The Roots of American Loyalty.* New York: Columbia UP, 1946.

Daniels, Roger. *Coming to America: A History of Immigration and Ethnicity in American Life.* 2nd ed. New York: Harper, 2002.

Davies, Jon. "Ancestors—Living and Dead." Introduction. *Ritual and Remembrance: Responses to Death in Human Societies.* Ed. Jon Davies. Sheffield: Sheffield Academic, 1994. 11–22.

———. "The Martial Uses of the Mass: War Remembrance as an Elementary Form of Religious Life." Davies, *Ritual and Remembrance.* 152–64.

Donovan, Judy. "Agents Using Manzo's Files against Aliens." *Arizona Daily Star* 27 Aug. 1976: A1.

———. "Board Cuts Off Manzo's Federal Funds." *Arizona Daily Star* 29 Jan. 1978: A1.

———. "Once Indicted for Aiding Aliens, Manzo Council Now Gets the Job." *Arizona Daily Star* 24 June 1977: B1.

Douglas, Mary. *Purity and Danger.* 1966. New York: Routledge, 1999.

Duchrow, Ulrich. "Capitalism and Human Rights." Trans. Emma Dowling. *The Essentials of Human Rights.* Ed. Rhona K. M. Smith and Christien van den Anker. London: Hodder, 2005. 33–36.

Dunn, Timothy J. *Blockading the Border and Human Rights: The El Paso Operation That Remade Immigration Enforcement.* Austin: U of Texas P, 2009.

———. "Border Enforcement and Human Rights Violations in the Southwest." *Race and Ethnic Relations in the United States: Readings for the Twenty-First Century.* Ed. Christopher G. Ellison and W. Allen Martin. Los Angeles: Roxbury, 1999. 443–51.

———. *The Militarization of the U.S.-Mexico Border, 1978–1992: Low-Intensity Conflict Doctrine Comes Home.* Austin: Center for Mexican American Studies, 1996.

Eck, Diana L. *A New Religious America: How a "Christian Country" Has Become the World's Most Religiously Diverse Nation.* New York: Harper, 2002.

Eliade, Mircea. *The Sacred and the Profane.* Trans. Willard R. Trask. 1957. New York: Harcourt, 1987.

Elizondo, Virgil. *Guadalupe, Mother of the New Creation.* Maryknoll: Orbis, 1997.

Elliot, Roland. "Our Duty toward Displaced Persons." *Christianity and Crisis* 9.8 (1949): 58.

Eschbach, Karl, Jacqueline Hagan, and Nestor Rodriguez. "Deaths during Undocumented Migration: Trends and Policy Implications in the New Era of Homeland Security." *In Defense of the Alien: Proceedings of the 2003 Annual National Conference on Immigration and Refugee Policy.* Ed. Joseph Fugolo. New York: Center for Migration Studies, 2003. 37–52.

Everett, Holly. *Roadside Crosses in Contemporary Memorial Culture.* Denton: U of North Texas P, 2002.

Ferguson, Kathryn, Norma A. Price, and Ted Parks. *Crossing with the Virgin: Stories from the Migrant Trail.* Tucson: U of Arizona P, 2010.

Fox, Ben. "Flags Mark Water for Immigrants." *Denver Post* 26 July 2000: A2.

Fox, Stephen. *Blood and Power: Organized Crime in Twentieth Century America.* New York: Morrow, 1989.

Fry, Brian N. *Responding to Immigration: Perceptions of Promise and Threat* New York: LFB Scholarly, 2001.

Garcia, Arnoldo. "Toward a Left without Borders: The Story of the Center for Autonomous Social Action–General Brotherhood of Workers." *Monthly Review* 54.3 (2002): 69–78.

Garcia, Ignacio M. *Chicanismo: The Forging of a Militant Ethos among Mexican Americans.* Tucson: U of Arizona P, 1997.

Garcia, Juan Ramon. *Operation Wetback: The Mass Deportation of Mexican Undocumented Workers in 1954.* Westport: Greenwood, 1980.

Garcia, Mario T. *Memories of Chicano History: The Life and Narrative of Bert Corona.* Berkeley: U of California P, 1994.

García Canclini, Néstor. *Hybrid Cultures: Strategies for Entering and Leaving Modernity.* Trans. Christopher L. Chiappari and Silvia L. López. Minneapolis: U of Minnesota P, 1995.

Garcíagodoy, Juaníta. *Digging the Days of the Dead: A Reading of Mexico's Días de muertos* Niwot. Boulder: UP of Colorado, 1998.

Garcia y Griego, Manuel. "The Importation of Mexican Contract Laborers to the United States, 1942–1964: Antecedents, Operation and Legacy." *The Border That Joins: Mexican Migrants and U.S. Responsibility.* Ed. Peter Brown and Henry Shue. Totowa: Rowman, 1983.

Genizi, Haim. *America's Fair Share: The Admission and Resettlement of Displaced Persons, 1945–1952.* Detroit: Wayne State UP, 1993.

Gill, Jerry. *Borderland Theology.* Washington: Ecumenical Program on Central America and the Caribbean, 2003.

Glaude, Eddie S., Jr. *Exodus! Religion, Race and Nation in Early-Nineteenth-Century Black America.* Chicago: U of Chicago P, 2000.

Glionna, John M. "A Pointed Symbol Brings Cross Words." *Los Angeles Times* 26 Mar. 2006: B1.

Goizueta, Roberto S. "The Symbolic World of Mexican American Religion." *Horizons of the Sacred: Mexican Traditions in U.S. Catholicism.* Ed. Timothy Matovina and Gary Riebe-Estrella. Ithaca: Cornell UP, 2002. 119–38.

Goldstein, Diane E., and Diane Tye. "'The Call of the Ice': Tragedy and Vernacular Responses of Resistance, Heroic Reconstruction, and Reclamation." *Spontaneous Shrines and the Public Memorialization of Death.* Ed. Jack Santino. New York: Palgrave, 2006. 233–54.

Goodstein, Laurie. "Church Group Provides Oasis for Illegal Migrants to U.S." *New York Times* 10 June 2001: A1.

Gorman, Robert F., and Edward S. Mihalkanin. *Historical Dictionary of Human Rights and Humanitarian Organizations.* Lanham: Scarecrow, 1997.

Griffith, James S. *Beliefs and Holy Places: A Spiritual Geography of the Pimería Alta.* Tucson: U of Arizona P, 1992.

——. "El Tiradito and Juan Soldado: Two Victim Intercessors of the Western Borderlands." *A Shared Space: Folklife in the Arizona-Sonora Borderlands.* Logan: Utah State UP, 1995. 67–81.

——. *Folk Saints of the Borderlands: Victims, Bandits and Healers.* Tucson: Rio Nuevo, 2003.

Griswold del Castillo, Richard. *The Treaty of Guadalupe Hidalgo.* Norman: U of Oklahoma P, 1990.

Groody, Daniel G. *Border of Death, Valley of Life: An Immigrant Journey of Heart and Spirit.* Lanham: Rowman, 2002.

Gutiérrez, David. *Walls and Mirrors: Mexican Americans, Mexican Immigrants, and the Politics of Ethnicity.* Berkeley: U of California P, 1995.

Hammer-Tomizuka, Zoe, and Jennifer Allen. "Hate or Heroism: Vigilantes on the Arizona-Mexico Border." Tucson: Border Action Network, 2002.

Hellman, Judith Adler. "A Bill Only Bush Could Love." *NACLA Report on the Americas* 40:5 (2007): 3.

"Hiker Finds Body, High in Snowy Huachucas." *Arizona Daily Star* 6 Apr. 2004: B2.

"History of the Migrant Trail." Coalición de Derechos Humanos. 8 May 2007. Web. 23 June 2007.

Holt, Tim. "Guest Opinion: O'odham Rescue Cattle but Not Dying Migrants." *Tucson Citizen.* Tucson Citizen, 26 July 2002. Web. 26 July 2002.

Hondagneu-Sotelo, Pierette. *God's Heart Has No Borders: How Religious Activists Are Working for Immigrant Rights.* Berkeley: U of California P, 2008.

Hondagneu-Sotelo, Pierette, Genelle Gaudinez, and Hector Lara. "Religious Reenactment on the Line: A Genealogy of Political Religious Hybridity." *Religion and Social Justice for Immigrants.* Ed. Pierette Hondagneu-Sotelo. New Brunswick: Rutgers UP, 2007.

Hoover, Robin. "Basic Decency Demands That We Help." *Arizona Daily Republic* 14 Sept. 2002: V1+.

——. "A Message from Rev. Robin Hoover, Ph.D." *Desert Fountain* Sept.–Oct. 2007. 1–5.

Huicochea, Alexis. "Deputy, 2 Others Hit by Truck, Die." *Arizona Daily Star* 11 Aug. 2005: A1.

Hulsether, Mark. *Building a Protestant Left: Christianity and Crisis Magazine, 1941–1993.* Knoxville: U of Tennessee P, 1999.

Human Rights Watch. "Brutality Unchecked: Human Rights Abuses along the US Border with Mexico." New York: Human Rights Watch, 1992.

Hutchison, William R. *Errand to the World: American Protestant Thought and Foreign Missions.* Chicago: U of Chicago P, 1987.

Hyatt, Michael. *Migrant Artifacts: Magic and Loss in the Sonoran Desert.* Los Angeles: Great Circle, 2007.

"Illegal-Entrant Death Count Keeps Rising." *Arizona Daily Star* 9 Aug 2004: B2.

Immigration and Nationality Act. 1995. 8 USC Sec. 1324a.

Innes, Stephanie. "In Sorrow, Solidarity." *Arizona Daily Star* 3 June 2007: B1.

——. "Migrants Need Help, Present Risk." *Arizona Daily Star* 18 June 2000: B1.

"Interfaith Statement in Support of Comprehensive Immigration Reform." *United States Conference of Catholic Bishops.* United States Conference of Catholic Bishops. 18 Oct. 2005. Web. 9 Nov. 2007.

Jasper, James. *The Art of Moral Protest: Culture, Biography and Creativity in Social Movements.* Chicago: U of Chicago P, 1997.

Kaplan, Amy. *The Anarchy of Empire in the Making of U.S. Culture.* Cambridge: Harvard UP, 2002.

King, Martin Luther, Jr. *Where Do We Go from Here: Chaos or Community?* New York: Harper, 1967.

Kirby, Lou Anne. "Cuban Families Melt into Routine of Work, Play in Old Pueblo." *Arizona Daily Star* 4 Aug. 1963: B1+.

Lacey, Marc. "Somalis Brave a Sea of Perils for $50-a-Month Jobs Abroad." *New York Times* 29 May 2006: A1.

Loescher, Gil, and John A. Scanlan. *Calculated Kindness: Refugees and America's Half-Open Door, 1945 to the Present.* New York: Free P, 1986.

LoMonaco, Claudine. "Accuracy of Migrant Death List Challenged." *Tucson Citizen.* Tucson Citizen, 26 May 2005. Web. 26 May 2005.

——. "Getting Immigrants Out of the Shadows." *Tucson Citizen* 13 May 2005: A1+.

——. "No Drop in Migrant Flows or Deaths." *Tucson Citizen* 16 Mar. 2005: A1.

Longley, Clifford. *Chosen People: The Big Idea That Shaped England and America.* London: Hodder, 2002.

Luis-Brown, David. *Waves of Decolonization: Discourses of Race and Hemispheric Citizenship in Cuba, Mexico, and the United States.* Durham: Duke UP, 2008.

Lumley, Robert. *States of Emergency: The Cultures of Revolt in Italy from 1968–1978.* London: Verso, 1990.

MacEóin, Gary. "A Brief History of the Sanctuary Movement." MacEóin, *Sanctuary* 14–29.

——. *Memoirs and Memories.* Mystic: Twenty-Third, 1986.

——, ed. *Sanctuary: A Resource Guide for Understanding and Participating in the Central American Refugees' Struggle.* San Francisco: Harper, 1985.

Malcolm X. "At the Audubon." *Malcolm X Speaks.* Ed. George Breitman. New York: Grove, 1965.

Manning, Bayless. "The Congress, the Executive, and Intermestic Affairs: Three Proposals." *Foreign Affairs* 55.2 (1977): 306–24.

Marizco, Michael. "When the Deadly Trek Turns Even Deadlier." *Arizona Daily Star* 31 July 2004: A1.

Martinez, Demetria. "Reviving the Sanctuary Movement." *National Catholic Reporter* 6 July 2007: 20.

Martinez, Oscar. *Border People: Life and Society in the U.S.–Mexico Borderlands.* Tucson: U of Arizona P, 1994.

Marvin, Carolyn, and David W. Ingle. *Blood Sacrifice and the Nation: Totem Rituals and the American Flag.* Cambridge: Cambridge UP, 1999.

Massey, Douglas S., Jorge Durand, and Nolan J. Malone. *Beyond Smoke and Mirrors: Mexican Immigration in an Era of Economic Integration.* New York: Sage, 2002.

McCombs, Brady. "Efforts to Cut Summer Deaths along Border Aren't Working." *Arizona Daily Star* 24 June 2007: A1+.

———. "July Proved Deadly Month for Migrants." *Arizona Daily Star*. Arizona Daily Star, 3 Aug. 2010. Web. 14 Sept. 2010.

McDivitt, Anita. "Troublesome Traffic Light Will Go." *Arizona Daily Star* 22 Jan. 2001: B1.

McRobbie, Angela. "Post-Marxism and Cultural Studies: A Post-script." *Cultural Studies*. Ed. Lawrence Grossberg, Cary Nelson, and Paula A. Treichler. New York: Routledge, 1992. 719–30.

Monroe, Linda Roach. "Struggle for Justice Weds La Margo to Her People." *Arizona Daily Star*. 21 Aug. 1977: D1.

Moore, R. Laurence. *Selling God: American Religion in the Marketplace of Culture*. New York: Oxford UP, 1994.

Napier, Davie. "Hebraic Concepts of Sanctuary and Law." MacEóin, *Sanctuary* 33–38.

Navari, Cornelia. "The Origins of the Nation-State." *The Nation State: The Formation of Modern Politics*. Ed. Leonard Tivey. Oxford: Robertson, 1981. 13–38.

Nepstad, Sharon Erickson. *Convictions of the Soul: Religion, Culture and Agency in the Central America Solidarity Movement*. Oxford: Oxford UP, 2004.

Nevins, Joseph. *Operation Gatekeeper: The Rise of the "Illegal Alien" and the Making of the U.S.-Mexico Boundary*. New York: Routledge, 2002.

Newman, Gemma Mae. "Earl G. Harrison and the Displaced Persons Controversy: A Case Study in Social Action." Diss. Temple University, 1973.

Newton, Bill. "'Red Star'-Type Brainwashing." Letter. *Arizona Daily Star* 3 Nov. 2005: B7.

Ngai, Mae. *Impossible Subjects: Illegal Aliens and the Making of Modern America*. Princeton: Princeton UP, 2004.

Nichols, J. Bruce. *The Uneasy Alliance: Religion, Refugee Work, and U.S. Foreign Policy*. New York: Oxford UP, 1988.

Nolan, Hugh. Ed. *Pastoral Letters of the United States Catholic Bishops*. 4 vols. Washington: National Conference of Catholic Bishops, United States Catholic Conference, 1984.

Otter, Elna, and Dorothy Pine, eds. *The Sanctuary Experience: Voices of the Community*. San Diego: Aventine, 2004.

"Parish News." *Shalom*. Tucson: St. Mark's Presbyterian Church. Jan.–Feb. 1977.

Perea, Juan F. "*Los Olvidados*: On the Making of Invisible People." *New York University Law Review* 70 (1995): 965–91.

Pierard, Richard V., and Robert D. Linder. *Civil Religion and the Presidency*. Grand Rapids: Academie, 1988.

"The Plan of Delano." *Aztlan: An Anthology of Mexican American Literature*. Ed. Luis Valdez and Stan Steiner. New York: Knopf, 1972. 197–201.

"Possible Butterfield Routes." *Arizona Daily Star* 20 Apr. 1973: B1.

Preston, Julia. "As Immigration Plan Folded, Grass Roots Roared." *New York Times* 10 June 2007: A1+.

Raboteau, Albert J. "African Americans, Exodus, and the American Israel." *Religion and American Culture: A Reader*. Ed. David G. Hackett. New York: Routledge, 1995. 75–86.

Rappaport, Roy. *Ritual and Religion in the Making of Humanity*. Cambridge: Cambridge UP, 1999.

Rawlinson, John. "Agents Seize Files of Social Aid Office." *Arizona Daily Star* 10 Apr. 1976: A1.

Reichley, A. James. *Religion in American Public Life.* Washington: Brookings Institution, 1985.

Reimers, David M. *Still the Golden Door: The Third World Comes to America.* 2nd ed. New York: Columbia UP, 1992.

Ross, John. *The Annexation of Mexico: From the Aztecs to the IMF, One Reporter's Journey through History.* Monroe: Common Courage, 1998.

Rubio-Goldsmith, Raquel, M. Melissa McCormick, Daniel Martinez, and Inez Magdalena Duarte. *The "Funnel Effect" and Recovered Bodies of Unauthorized Migrants Processed by the Pima County Office of the Medical Examiner, 1990–2005.* Tucson: Binational Migration Institute, 2006.

Rutherford, E. C. "Sears Defends Refugee Plans." *Arizona Daily Star* 2 Aug. 1962: B1.

Sahagun, Louis. "LA Church in Forefront of Sanctuary Movement." *Los Angeles Times* 23 Mar. 2007: B1.

Santino, Jack. "Performative Commemoratives: Spontaneous Shrines and the Public Memorialization of Death." *Spontaneous Shrines and the Public Memorialization of Death.* Ed. Jack Santino. New York: Palgrave, 2006. 5–15.

Sharot, Stephen. *A Comparative Sociology of World Religions: Virtuosos, Priests and Popular Religion.* New York: New York UP, 2001.

Sheridan, Thomas E. *Los Tucsonenses: The Mexican Community in Tucson, 1854–1941.* Tucson: U of Arizona P, 1986.

Simon, Rita J., and Susan H. Alexander. *The Ambivalent Welcome: Print Media, Public Opinion, and Immigration.* Westport: Praeger, 1993.

Smith, Anthony D. *Chosen Peoples.* Oxford: Oxford UP, 2003.

Smith, Kim. "Border Patrol Agent Cleared of Wrongdoing in Accident That Killed Teen." *Arizona Daily Star.* Arizona Daily Star, 17 Feb. 2006. Web. 31 Jan. 2009.

Sorensen, Georg. *The Transformation of the State: Beyond the Myth of Retreat.* New York: Palgrave, 2004.

"Study of Proposed Butterfield Parkway Halted by Opposition." *Arizona Daily Star* 11 May 1974: B1.

Sundberg, Juanita, and Bonnie Kaserman. "Cactus Carvings and Desert Defecations: Embodying Representations of Border Crossings in Protected Areas on the Mexico-U.S. Border." *Environment and Planning D: Society and Space* 25 (2007): 727–44.

"Supremacist Groups Take Up Immigration." *Morning Edition.* National Public Radio. 6 Mar. 2007.

Swarns, Rachel L. "In Georgia, Newest Immigrants Unsettle an Old Sense of Place." *New York Times* 4 Aug. 2006: A1.

Taylor, Charles. *Sources of the Self: the Making of Modern Identity.* Cambridge: Harvard UP, 1989.

Texier, Philippe. "Economic Rights." Trans. Rhona Smith and Audrey Guichon. *The Essentials of Human Rights.* Ed. Rhona K. M. Smith and Christien van den Anker. London: Hodder, 2005. 100–105.

"The Three Charters of the Virginia Company of London: With Seven Related Documents, 1606–1621." Williamsburg: Virginia 350th Anniversary Celebration Corporation, 1957.

Tipton, Steven. "Globalizing Civil Religion and Public Theology." *Religion in Global Civil Society*. Ed. Mark Juergensmeyer. Oxford: Oxford UP, 2005. 49–68.

Turf, Luke. "County: Many Victims Evade Border Patrol Tally." *Tucson Citizen* 4 Oct. 2004: A1.

Turner, Bill. "Butterfield to Bypass Barrio Libre." *Arizona Daily Star* 12 Jan. 1972: A1.

Turner, Tom. "Tucson Shrine Endangered by Proposed Expressway." *Arizona Daily Star* 15 Mar. 1971: B1.

Turner, Victor. "Death and the Dead in the Pilgrimage Process." *Blazing the Trail: Way Marks in the Exploration of Symbols*. Ed. Edith Turner. Tucson: U of Arizona P, 1992. 29–47.

——. *The Forest of Symbols*. Ithaca: Cornell UP, 1967.

——. *The Ritual Process*. 1969. New York: De Gruyter, 1995.

——. *From Ritual to Theatre: The Human Seriousness of Play*. New York: Performing Arts Journal Publications, 1982.

Ufford-Chase, Rick. "Who Is My Neighbor? Reflections on Our Changing Neighbor-hood in the Global Economy." *Getting On Message: Challenging the Christian Right from the Heart of the Gospel*. Ed. Rev. Peter Laarman. Boston: Beacon, 2006. 84–96.

United States Conference of Catholic Bishops, Inc. and Conferencia del Episcopado Mexicano. "Strangers No Longer: Together on the Journey of Hope." *United States Conference of Catholic Bishops*. United States Conference of Catholic Bishops. 2003. Web. 20 Sept. 2004.

United States. Cong. House. Subcommittee on Immigration and Naturalization of the Committee on the Judiciary. *Permitting the Admission of 400,000 Displaced Persons into the United States*. 80th Cong., 1st sess. Washington: GPO, 1947.

United States. Immigration and Naturalization Service. Office of Policy and Planning. *Retiring to A New Beginning: An Illustrated History of the Immigration and Natu-ralization Service*. Washington: INS.

Urrea, Luis Alberto. *The Devil's Highway*. New York: Little, 2004.

——. *Nobody's Son: Notes from an American Life*. Tucson: U of Arizona P, 1998.

Vanderpool, Tim. "The Activist Question." *Tucson Weekly* 9–15 July 2009: 14–17.

Vogt, Heidi. "Desperate Voyage." *Arizona Daily Star* 21 May 2006: A14.

Walton, John. "Urban Protest and the Global Political Economy: The IMF Riots." *The Capitalist City*. Ed. Michael Peter Smith and Joe R. Feagin. Oxford: Blackwell, 1987. 364–86.

Waterman, Peter. *Globalization, Social Movements and the New Internationalisms*. London: Mansell, 1998.

Weber, Max. *The Sociology of Religion*. Trans. Ephraim Fischoff. 1922. Boston: Beacon, 1964.

Wheaton, Philip. "Response by Philip Wheaton." MacEóin, *Sanctuary* 44–48.

Williams, Peter W. *Popular Religion in America*. Englewood Cliffs: Prentice, 1980.

Wischnitzer, Mark. *Visas to Freedom: The History of HIAS*. Cleveland: World Publish-ing, 1956.

"Wishing Shrine Entered in Register." *Arizona Daily Star* 13 Dec. 1971: B1.

Wood, Forrest G. *The Arrogance of Faith: Christianity and Race in America from the Colonial Era to the Twentieth Century*. New York: Knopf, 1990.

Woodhead, Linda, and Paul Heelas. "Religions of Humanity." *Religion in Modern Times*. Ed. Linda Woodhead and Paul Heelas. Oxford: Blackwell, 2000. 70–74.

World Bank. "Guatemala Poverty Assessment." World Bank. 2003. Web. 27 Apr. 2008.

Yad Vashem. *"Unto Every Person There Is a Name."* Yad Vashem, the Holocaust Heroes' and Martyrs' Remembrance Authority. 2009. Web. 8 Feb. 2009.

Young, James E. *The Texture of Memory: Holocaust Memorials and Meaning*. New Haven: Yale UP, 1993.

Young, Michael P. "Confessional Protest: The Religious Birth of U.S. National Social Movements." *American Sociological Review* 67 (2002): 660–88.

Zelinsky, Wilbur. *The Cultural Geography of United States*. Englewood Cliffs: Prentice, 1992.

# Index

213

# About the Author

Lane Van Ham holds a PhD in comparative cultural and literary studies from the University of Arizona. He is a full-time faculty member in the English department at the Penn Valley campus of Metropolitan Community College in Kansas City, Missouri, and an adjunct faculty member in the University of Arizona's religious studies program.